KALAKAUA
RENAISSANCE KING

D0958025

Other Titles by the Author

KALAKAUA
RENAISSANCE KING

BY

HELENA G. ALLEN

MUTUAL PUBLISHING
HONOLULU, HAWAII

Design
Mark Abramson, Zen Jam

First Printing February, 1995
1 2 3 4 5 6 7 8 9

ISBN 1-56647-059-5

Mutual Publishing
1127 11th Avenue, Mezz. B
Honolulu, Hawaii 96816
Telephone (808) 732-1709
Fax (808) 734-4094

Printed in Australia

Dedicated to Dr. Paul F. Allen, my late husband, who encouraged me throughout my writing career and who also was a Renaissance man.

They loved him; they honored him
and they called him their king.
They hated him; they maligned him,
but they called him, "Your Majesty."

Helena G. Allen

Table of Contents

Acknowledgements

No acknowledgment for this book would be correct if I did not mention foremost Dr. Richard Kekuni Blaisdell of Honolulu, Hawaii, who not only gave me invaluable help in writing *The Betrayal of Liliuokalani, the Last Queen of Hawaii, 1838-1917,* but also first awakened my recognition of King Kalakaua's greatness.

Special acknowledgments also go to Professor Richard L. Wilkerson for research, proofreading, and constant encouragement.

It is impossible for me to mention all the dedicated workers in the repositories of Hawaii and the mainland whose help has made this book possible, but I wish to thank Barbara Dunn of the Hawaiian Historical Society and Library; Mary Jane Knight of the Hawaiian Mission Children's Library, as well as Victoria Nalani Knuebuhl; Richard Thompson of the Hawaiian State Archives; Henry James Bartels of the Iolani Palace for his unfailing support; Marguerite Ashford of the Bernice Pauahi Bishop Museum and Lynn Davis for photographs; Charles Nakoa, director of the Liliuokalani Children's Center; and staff members of the Hamilton Library, University of Hawaii, and Hawaii State Library. On the mainland my thanks and appreciation go to the staffs of the University of Redlands Library, San Bernardino Valley College Library, Crafton Hills College Library, San Francisco Public Library, and Mills College Library; and to Tom Nichols of the Library of Congress, Washington, D.C.

Appreciation goes also to the staffs of the British Public Records Office, London, England; Bibliotheque historique of service de travaux historique de la Villa de Paris, Paris, France; and the Tourist Information Center, Beijing, China.

Special thanks and appreciation are given to the estate of the late David M. Bray, Kailua-Kona, Hawaii, and Floyd J. McDonald, San Bernardino, California, for use of private collections of pictures, manuscripts, and books; to the late Dr. Herbert B. Wilson, professor emeritus of the University of Arizona, for discussions of intercultural relationships; to Professor Niklaus R. Schweizer, University of Hawaii, for guidance in research; and to Phillip J. Livoni, for general criticism.

Of course, there are three special people to whom go my deepest thanks: my typist, Lois L. Headley, who reads my handwriting; my son Randall Kauhimokakaukalani Allen, who helps keep me Hawaiian-oriented; and last but, as they say, certainly not least, Dr. Paul F. Allen, my late husband, who survived my writing hours with patience and encouragement and to whom this book is dedicated.

Special thanks and acknowledgment go to Glen Grant for research and for turning my one-sided king into a more three-dimensional one, and to Bennett Hymer for critical analysis.

Permissions

Special acknowledgments are given for reprint rights to the following: Mana Press, Hawaii, *Kalakaua, Hawaii's Last King*, by Kristin Zambucka, pp. 90, 140; A. Grove Day, author of *Hawaii and Its People*, p. 202, published by Appleton, Century, Crofts, New York; Niklaus Schweizer, author of the unpublished manuscript, *Kalakaua Revisited*; University of Hawaii Press: unpublished master's thesis "Primacy of Pacific," by Jason Horn, pp. 9, 90; *Victorian Visitors*, by Alfons Korn, pp. 88-89, 170; *Hawaiian Kingdom*, Vol. III, by Ralph S. Kuykendall, pp. 180, 466; *Fantastic Life of Walter Murray Gibson, Hawaii's Minister of Everything*, by Jacob Adler and Robert Kamins, p. 145; *Hawaiian Music and Musicians, an Illustrated History*, by George S. Kanahele, pp. 200-201; *A Tree in Bud: The Hawaiian Kingdom, 1889-1893*, translation by Alfons Korn, pp. 68-69; and Samuel H. Elbert and Noelani Nahoe, authors of *Na Mele O Hawaii Nei*; Friends of Iolani Palace, *Looking Back a Thousand Years*; Queen Liliuokalani Children's Center, *By Royal Command*, by Curtis P. Iaukea and Lorna Kahilipuaokalani Watson (Iaukea), pp. 28, 61, 66; Hawaiian Historical Society, *Hawaiian Journal of History*, Vol. 22, Agnes Quigg, p. 171; Julius Scammon Rodman, author, *Kahuna Sorcerers of Hawaii, Past and Present*; Yale University Press, *Hawaiian Americans*, Edwin Grant Burrows, p. 223; Tuttle Publishers, *Legends and Myths of Hawaii*, by Terence Barrows, (Introduction); Arthur Stephenson, Scottish Rite Library, Hawaii, J. M. Kapena speech; Georges Borchardt, Inc. Literary Agency, *Hawaii: The Sugar Coated Fortress* by Francine du Plessix Gray, published by Random House, pp. 32, 51-52, copyright 1972 by Francine du Plessix Gray; *Honolulu Advertiser* for *Memoirs of*

Hawaiian Revolution by Sanford Ballard Dole, pp. 42-50, and *Memoirs of Hawaiian Revolution* by Lorrin A. Thurston, edited by Andrew Farrell, pp. 21-22, 34-40; Pacific Basin Enterprises, *Rise and Fall of the Hawaiian Kingdom* by Richard A. Wisnieawski, p. 75; Glen Grant, author of unpublished manuscript; and Huna Press, *Recovering the Ancient Magic* by Max Freedom Long, p. 288.

Glossary

A glossary of frequently appearing names of persons, places, and things follows. It is hoped that this listing will aid the reader in identification.

The Hawaiian plural is the same as the singular and is so written throughout the book.

Terms
Ali'i: chief
'Aumakua: household god
Awa: an alcoholic drink
Hanai: "foster" child and parent
Haole: foreigner
Hapa-haole: part-Hawaiian/part-haole
Heiau: temple
Kahili: feather standard
Kahu: servant
Kahuna: priest
Kane: man (also a god)
Kapu: forbidden
Konohiki: land manager
Kuhina nui: premier (co-ruler)
Lanai: porch or balcony
Lei: garland worn around the neck
Mahalo: thank you
Makahiki: harvest season
Mana: special power
Mele: chants

Moʻi: king
Moʻi wahine: queen

Places

Hawaiʻi: the island chain; the largest island
High Chiefs' School: later called the Royal School
ʻIolani: Palace
Kailua-Kona: west coast, the Big Island of Hawaiʻi
Kawaiahaʻo Church: Missionary Church
Nuʻuanu: Valley to east of Honolulu

Principal Characters

ʻAikanaka: Kalakaua's grandfather (mother's side)
Prince Albert: "Prince of Hawaii," son of Kamehameha IV
Auhea: Premier after Kinau, mother of Lunalilo
Henry Berger: German band-master
Prince Bill: see Lunalilo
Charles Reed Bishop: husband of Bernice Pauahi
Boki: husband of Liliha
Archibald Cleghorn: husband of Likelike
Juliette and Amos Starr Cooke: teachers at High Chiefs' School
Sanford Ballard Dole: opposition leader
Walter Murray Gibson: Prime Minister for King Kalakaua
Haʻaheo: Kalakaua's hanai mother
Curtis P. Iaukea: Emissary for Kalakaua
John Iʻi: Hawaiʻian teacher
Kaʻahumanu: favorite wife of Kamehameha I
Princess Kaʻiulani: child of Likelike and Cleghorn
Kalakaua: king
Queen Kalama: wife of Kamehameha III
Jonah Kuhio Kalanianaʻole: nephew of Kapiʻolani
(Liliʻu) Kamakaʻeha: Liliʻuokalani's name given at birth
Kameʻeiamoku: Kalakaua's grandfather (father's side)
Kamehameha I: unifier of Hawaiian islands
Kamehameha II: son of first Kamehameha and successor

Kamehameha III: second son of first Kamehameha and king at time of Kalakaua's birth

Kamehameha IV: see Liholiho

Kamehameha V: see Lot

Kana'ina: father of Lunalilo

Kapa'akea: Kalakaua's blood father

Queen Kapi'olani: wife of Kalakaua

Prince David Kawananakoa: nephew of Kapi'olani

Keawe-a-Heulu: ancestor of Kalakaua (mother's side)

Kekaulike: sister-in-law of Kalakaua

Keohokalole: blood mother of Kalakaua

Ke'opuolani: sacred wife of Kamehameha I

Kina'u: Premier at time of Kalakaua's birth

Liliha: Kalakaua's early mentor

Leleiohoku: brother of Kalakaua

Liholiho: successor to Kamehameha III as Kamehameha IV

Likelike: sister of Kalakaua

Lili'uokalani: sister of Kalakaua

Prince Lot: successor to and brother of Liholiho as Kamehameha V

Lunalilo (Prince Bill): successor as king to Kamehameha V

Prince Moses: student at High Chiefs' School, brother of Lot and Liholiho

Bernice Pauahi (Bishop): sister-in-law of Kalakaua through hanai

Princess Po'omaikelani: sister-in-law of Kalakaua

Emma Rooke: student at High Chiefs' School, later Queen Emma

Princess Ruth: half-sister of Kamehameha IV and V

Lorrin Thurston: adversary of Kalakaua

Princess Victoria: sister of Lot and Liholiho

Introduction

This book, *Kalakaua, Renaissance King*, is the third in a trilogy extending in time over ninety years (1836-1926) and spotlights some crucial years of the Hawaiian monarchy—the period of Kalakaua's reign (1873-1891) preceding the overthrow of the monarchy.

Because this book is the last in a trilogy, I have made a concerted effort not to be repetitive. More expanded explanations of Hawaiian life are found in *Betrayal of Liliuokalani, Last Queen of Hawaii, 1838-1917*, (Arthur H. Clark Co., Glendale, California, 1983; reprint [paperback], Mutual Publishing, Honolulu, Hawaii, 1991), and certainly more detailed and documented information of the political reign of King Kalakaua can be found in *Sanford Ballard Dole, Hawaii's Only President, 1844-1926* (Arthur H. Clark Co., Spokane, Washington, 1988).

While writing *Betrayal of Liliuokalani, Last Queen of Hawaii, 1838-1917*, I became intrigued with her brother, David Kalakaua. But the story was hers, and I could not deviate into sidelines. My sympathies were with her, yet her sympathies were not always with her brother. As sister and brother they sometimes disagreed, but her deep love and admiration for him never faltered. I wanted to pursue the story focussed on Kalakaua. I wanted to do so all the more because I too had fallen into the cliche trap at times of disparaging him for his lavish spending of moneys and what appeared to many as his ego and vanity: hence the label the "Merry Monarch."

However, before turning my attention solely to Kalakaua, I felt I should prepare a book that showed the other side of the coin—a story of Sanford Ballard Dole, who succeeded Queen Liliuokalani after she was deposed and the government overthrown, as president of the Provisional Government, president of the Republic, first governor of the territory, and later federal judge—*Sanford Ballard Dole, Hawaii's Only President, 1844-1926.*

While researching that book and finding heavy antagonism toward King Kalakaua, I became more interested in him. Nearly everything written in Hawaii about King Kalakaua by his *haole* (foreigner) contemporaries, except for a brief nod toward his charisma, had been negative. The question *why* continually disturbed me. Kalakaua was intelligent beyond his peers; he was perceptive, intuitive, socially acute, deeply dedicated to his people. Why then did he make so many mistakes? Or did he? What lay behind his decisions?

In 1930, in "Some Recollections of Kalakaua," *haole* businessman William R. Castle wrote: "LAST FALL [1930] A GOOD DEAL WAS SAID about making Kalakaua's birthday a national holiday. There seemed to be a disposition to glorify his name and place him on high as an illustrious benefactor of Hawaii. It is a long time since his death, and the whole move appeared to come from friends who were afraid that he and his name were in danger of fading from the memories of the nation.

"I believe the Catholic Church does not canonize a person, no matter how good, till a hundred years have passed since his death. Probably this is to avoid mistakes in too hasty actions–to prevent placing a halo on the head of one, whose good acts may not appear so noble and saintly after years of scrutiny of his life. It may be that Kalakaua after a hundred years will have grown so illustrious as to be worthy of canonization, or at least entitled to a high niche in the temple of fame . . ."

My first reaction was to defend Kalakaua as a defense attorney might, seeking such defense in all aspects. I found that much recent research had been complimentary and, as Castle said, of "a disposition to glorify his name." But a dual man emerged: the political man and the Renaissance man. While Kalakaua seemed to fail politically, he excelled brilliantly as a Renaissance man. To be brilliant in one area is not necessarily to be brilliant in all areas. Bright and talented men make mistakes, and so it was with Kalakaua. He was a man whose interests in life were in the arts—music, literature, philosophy. He neither understood nor cared about the world of the *haole* businessman. The new political world into which the Hawaiian people were being forced with little preparation was sometimes incompatible and distasteful to them. Hence, Kalakaua preferred advisors who promoted the Renaissance part of his life.

On the other hand, the business and anti-royalist-oriented political men had little or no understanding or respect for this Polynesian dreamer who loved his own culture and traditions. A clash was inevitable.

A child of two cultures—Hawaiian and missionary-school—Kalakaua entered his young manhood as a cross-cultured person, trained in *haole* politics, the law, and the military, but Hawaiian in newspaper ventures and a search for his roots. With both success and failure he engaged in work as a postmaster, fireman, inventor, writer, editor, lawyer, government official, historian, musician, and philosopher.

He began his reign as king in the latter part of the nineteenth century, an era of invading imperialists and buccaneering business barons, a time of luxurious living among some and poverty among others and a collision of ideas. A Protestant missionary religion developing in a world of sharp business practices was set against a growing awareness of the loss the Hawaiians had suffered not only in life (the population had dropped from 500,000 to 70,000) but in culture and tradition.

My deepest regret in writing this book has been the paucity of personal papers, diaries, and journals of the king. Members of the Provisional Government wantonly destroyed Kalakaua's personal papers at the time of the overthrow (1893), according to his sister Liliuokalani. A few bits and pieces remain in Hawaiian archival repositories, a few in private collections.

It has been difficult to surmise Kalakaua's thoughts and feelings about the upheaval that was going around about him. Certainly my research in foreign archives (e.g. Europe, Asia, the Orient, and the

South Seas) showed a man held in much higher esteem by those abroad than by the *haole* in his own country.

A careful review of the papers and notes I made from Miss Lydia Aholo, Queen Liliuokalani's *hanai* (foster) daughter, when researching *Liliuokalani*, produced secondary shadows of Kalakaua's thoughts and beliefs, as did the few writings of his that have come to view in recent research—from 1930 to 1994—over 100 years after his death in 1891.

While some have said he ploughed the soil for the overthrow, can it now also be said that he planted the seeds of the new Hawaiian sovereignty movement—a part of the nationalism so conspicuous all over the world in this late twentieth century?

* * *

Personal note: Like Max Freedom Long in his apology to the *kahuna* in *Recovering The Ancient Magic*, I also wish to offer my apologia to Hawaiians for any unintentional misinterpretation of their cultural, traditional, or social-psychological-economic beliefs.

This book is as complete a biography of a man I admired—King Kalakaua as the Renaissance man—as I could find documented by his opponents and supporters. It is in no way a social-psychological in-depth study of the Polynesian. Such a book should—and I hope will—be written by a Polynesian.

Helena G. Allen
Redlands, California

---

* Notice to all Kahunas: Aloha. I apologize for any mistakes I may have made in telling of you or your long-preserved wisdom. If I have hurt any of you, I ask that I be allowed to make amends rather than that punishment be sent. I have violated no confidence. I have written under permission. I have only love and gratitude for you in my heart. Aloha nui oe. M.F.L. (Huna Press)

1 Formative Years

Even at birth Kalakaua was controversial.

On November 16, 1836, the hot sun blazed on the compound of High Chief Aikanaka at the base of Punch Bowl Hill in Honolulu, Hawaii. It was an inauspicious day for an *alii* (high chief) to be born. The day should have been filled with nature's fury of torrential rain, lightning, and angry winds as when Kamehameha I, Hawaii's first king (1758-1812), was born. *They* were portents for royalty. But this child who was about to be born was not a Kamehameha royal—yet he was prophesied to be Hawaii's last king. How could this be?

* * *

In High Chief Aikanaka's compound of many grass structures for cooking, eating, gathering, and retainers' quarters was one larger hut in which lay Keohokalole, the child's mother, awaiting the birth of her second born[1]—the first had died at birth. Would this one live? Keohokalole wondered. The great prophetess and High Chiefess Liliha had said it would be a man-child, and he would live. She had cast his horoscope for this day and had prophesied: "From this child, the bones of our ancestors will have life." It was a curious prophesy, but Hawaiians were used to enigmatic prophesies.

She had also said that he would see the demise of the Kamehamehas, the then-ruling line, but Liliha hated the Kamehamehas, and this might have been wishful thinking, for there were three throne-aligned young princes *hanai* to Kamehameha III, the ruling king. (*Hanai* was a Hawaiian custom in which a child was given at birth from one high chief to another to cement relationships between the families and to elevate the child's status. It was practiced among commoners as well.) Surely the Kamehamehas and their offspring would rule Hawaii forever. The three young heirs to the throne were the children of the king's half-sister, the Prime Minister Kinau.

The child about to be born was promised in *hanai* to Liliha, waiting now in her frame house in Honolulu. She was particularly pleased with this *hanai*. She and her husband, Boki, had no sons. Liliha had two daughters: Abigail and Jane Louea. But she had seen great things in her prophesies for the child who was soon to be her *hanai*.

However, Liliha was controversial among both the new missionary *haole* (foreigners) and the Kamehamehas. Liliha had been a close friend of Kamehameha II and his wife Kamamalu, and had accompanied them on their trip to England in 1824, where, unfortunately, they had both died. But before their deaths, she had been entertained as royalty, having been fêted and taken to the Royal Theater. She had seen the outside world. She and Boki had brought back the bodies of the king and queen and the story that Kamehameha II had gone to England to ask for British missionaries to be sent to Hawaii and for a set of political laws for governing Hawaii.

Lord Byron, cousin of the poet, had brought the royal entourage back in the *Blonde* and had replied to Kaahumanu, ruling regent for the new king, Kamehameha II's twelve-year-old brother (Kamehameha III), that the King of England did not wish to interfere in the islands nor give any rules, but advised that those "that best fit the Islands" should be retained.

Liliha had formed an attempted revolt against missionary-oriented Kaahumanu's authority and rule, which was put down almost before it began. Nevertheless, because of it Liliha had lost popularity among many of the Kamehameha supporters.

She was thoroughly ostracized by the missionary *haole* because she and Boki owned and operated a house of prostitution in Honolulu, to the amusement of many Hawaiians. She beat the *haole* at their own game. The sailors now paid more than a scarf or a silver coin to the young Hawaiian girls who in the past had swum naked to the anchored ships.

Aikanaka, the child's grandfather, thought Liliha was the perfect *hanai* for his daughter's child. Liliha was glamorous: she wore the latest European styles brought to her by seamen and whalers. She entertained lavishly, having rich lands of her own, and she was enormously popular among many Hawaiians and non-missionary *haole*.

❋ ❋ ❋

In the compound Aikanaka and Kapaakea, the child's father, waited for the birth of the baby. The pregnancy had been difficult, and Keohokalole had lain long and laboriously on the *pandanus* mats that were piled high in the windowless grass hut. With her were a number of high chiefesses, bosoms bared, for it was a hot day, playing cards, chewing grass, and accurately using gourd spittoons.

Keohokalole's cries became louder, and many retainers walking among the huts and sparse trees stopped to listen. If she should die there would be great wailing and keening as expressions of grief. The kind that sent chills of horror through the missionary women. But there would also be feasting and riotous living—if allowed—especially if the child lived. This was a period between the pre-Christian (only sixteen years previously the first missionaries had come) and the new ways; and no one knew what to expect—the unemotional missionary way or the loose Hawaiian custom.

One of the women moved out of the doorway of the hut and called for a *kahuna* (priest) to come quickly. The *kahuna* rose quickly from his cross-legged position on the ground. He glanced anxiously around for fear of being caught by missionary converts. He saw none. The household of

Aikanaka and Kapaakea had not been totally swayed by the missionary doctrine, and certainly were not at such a crucial moment.

The child was being born. The chanters began their *mele* (chants). The child's ancestry was extolled: His mother was descended from Keawe-a-Heulu and his father was the grandson of Kameeiamoku. The two had been trusted warriors and close advisers to Kamehameha I. It was a worthy line.

The child was born—a head of curly black hair and a perfect body with a large penis. Now a glorious *mai mele* to the high chief's genitals could be composed, as was customary.

The chiefesses were overjoyed. It was a wonderful sign: he was to be the father of many. He would increase the rapidly dying race now being destroyed by the foreigners' diseases. And he would be a great lover. The Hawaiian women admired this.

News traveled quickly, and suddenly the compound was crowded with people, rejoicing, singing, dancing. There was stout Kinau, the prime minister, clad in European fashion, followed by her retinue. The highest *alii* in the land had come to name the child. It was her privilege. Without a Gregorian calendar, children were named by notable historical events, which would date their birth. Kinau decreed: Kalakaua , "Battle Day." History gives the complete name as Laamea Kamanakapuu Mahinulani Nalolaekalani Lumia-Lani Kalakaua. November 16, 1836, was the day that the treaty with Lord Edward Russell was signed, giving the British subjects the right to come to the Sandwich Islands[2] (Hawaii), to reside as long as they conformed to the laws of the island, to build houses for themselves and their merchandise "with the consent of the king."

Liliha, wearing a fashionable *holoku* and many flower *lei*, came to collect her *hanai* child. Preceding her entourage, arms open, she moved barefoot toward the tapa-wrapped infant. Then the large Kinau stepped between her and the child.

"The child is to go to Haaheo," she decreed. Kinau was a Christian, and Haaheo was not only a new convert, she lived on the Honolulu royal grounds as a Kamehameha lineal heir. In the early decades of the monarchy the "palace" and court moved to wherever the king resided. At this time the king had his court primarily in Lahaina. But when the twenty-three year old king visited Honolulu, he lived at the compound of Kinau. It became the official palace in 1845.

Liliha protested bitterly but knew she could not win, for Kinau's word was law in this matter. She swept her way out of the compound, followed by her entourage. Once in the privacy of her home, she began to wail and keen, mourning the child that should have been hers. She continued, it was reported, long after the sun, a red ball of fire, had dipped into the ocean. It had not rained.

"His," Liliha declared, having already studied the Keawe-a-Heulu line carefully, "shall carry the flaming torch as his symbol into his reign. For reign, he shall. Kamehamehas shall be gone, and from him shall our ancestors' bones have life. Our traditions, our heritage shall live because of him." She looked toward the ever-misty Nuuanu Valley, and there shimmered a pale rainbow as fleeting as a memory. But Liliha smiled. The gods had sent their blessing.

* * *

The tiny Kalakaua was wrapped in a felted mulberry tapa and taken by his *hanai* mother, Haaheo, to the royal grounds, followed by the entourage of Kinau.

Kalakaua was given to a *kahu* (a wet nurse) to be fed and nurtured. His warm infancy was, however, short-lived, for Haaheo died a year later and Kinimaka, her husband, took the baby to live in Lahaina, Maui. However, he lived only a short time on the palace grounds there—as Kinimaka's high chief lineage was less than his late wife's. Kinimaka moved to a frame house on the outskirts of Lahaina. Within the year he married a Tahitian woman, Pai, who welcomed Kalakaua with love and tenderness, but he no longer had a *kahu* (servant) of his own. Pai shortly gave birth to another child, and Kalakaua became second in her affections. Before he was three, he had a fragmented life.

The old *ohana* (family) system was disappearing. *Ohana* was a family system in which the older members reached out loving and welcoming arms to all–no matter how distantly related–or sometimes not related at all. *Hanai* was also disappearing under the missionaries' stern edict that one did not give children away "like puppies." Two customs that had served the Hawaiians well were soon to be lost.

❊ ❊ ❊

When Kalakaua was nearly four, his biological mother, who served on the king's privy council with one of the most powerful women in Hawaii, Konia, the granddaughter of Kamehameha I, appealed to her to have Kalakaua sent to the High Chiefs' Children's School in Honolulu. Kinau, the premier, had died the year previously, and the young twenty-six-year-old king had taken things into his own hands. He had at first rebelled against Kinau and spent years in drunkenness and debauchery, but he had finally acceded to her wishes of a stable government. He approved of the High Chiefs' Children's School and had sent his three *hanai* sons there–Moses, Lot, and Liholiho.

Thus Kalakaua was admitted to the school, but not before he was baptized and given the name "David."

Amos Starr and Juliette Montague Cooke had taken charge of the High Chiefs' Children's School in 1838. They were both missionaries of the Eighth Company. In their thirties, with young children of their own, they were not overly pleased with the growing number of children in the school, but a Kamehameha descendant such as Konia could not be refused.

The High Chiefs' Children's School (often shortened to "High Chiefs' School"), the boarding school for the royal children and those of the highest chiefs, was a long, two-story frame building with a large dining room and separate sleeping quarters for the children and for the Cooke family. There was also the New England parlor, furnished with handmade and treasured furniture sent from home, and with much brought from China. It resembled nothing Hawaiian in its appearance nor its atmosphere.

It stood near the palace, near Beretania Street, on ground that Kamehameha III had given the Cookes for the school.

In 1839, when Kalakaua entered the school, the three throne-aligned princes were also attending: Moses, twelve; Lot, ten; and Liholiho, nine. Other Kamehameha-related children were also at the school: Pauahi, the great-grand-daughter of Kamehameha I, also nine; and Lunalilo, the child of the new premier (Auhea), only six. The two youngest were Kalakaua and Emma Rooke (a Kamehameha descendant through John Young's wife[3] and *hanai* to Dr. T.C.B. Rooke).

Despite their youth, the children were well aware that they were Kamehameha while Kalakaua (now called by his Christian name, David) was not a direct descendant.

The Cookes, in general, had a shaky understanding of the high chiefs. They had little real knowledge of the royal children except that Kamehameha III, their father, was the king and had power to give or withhold lands, supplies, or moneys from the school. They were puzzled about where other high chiefs' children belonged on the scale of importance. The bottom line was that they were heathens who must be saved from themselves by education and religion.

＊ ＊ ＊

Two childhood events were to stay in Kalakaua's memory that pointed out to him his inferior status and fueled his resentment against the missionaries.

Dr. Gerrit Judd, a missionary, years later was to write that Liholiho was not so much anti-*haole* as anti-missionary ". . . his heart hardened to a degree unknown to the heathen."[4]

The stern discipline of the Cookes had made him rebellious. The same could have been said about Kalakaua, but in even stronger terms.

When Kalakaua was six years old, the Cookes sent him to see his grandfather hanged. Had the Cookes not been indifferent as to who the boy was, this would never have happened. But Juliette wrote almost casually in her journal, "A man is to be hanged and he wants to see David."[5] Had David been a Kamehameha there is no doubt the "man" would have been checked out more thoroughly. As it was, David was sent to the gallows on the plain of Honolulu to witness the hanging of his grandfather, Kamanawa. It was said that he had poisoned his wife to circumvent punishment for adultery. Strong punishment was imposed for adultery—banishment to the barren island of Kahoolawe. Kamanawa now was to hang for both adultery and murder. There is no evidence of why Kamanawa wished to see his grandson, but one can certainly surmise that it was not to praise the missionaries for their strict laws against adultery that had been incorporated into Hawaiian justice system.

Seeing a man hanged was a traumatic experience for a six-year-old child, and to know it was his grandfather did not lessen the experience. Kalakaua, coming from the tradition of *ohana*—close family relationships—had known his grandfather.

Rumor later had it that he saved a piece of the rope to remind him of the atrocity. But it seems unlikely that a six year old would have been given a piece of hanging rope no matter how indifferent the executioners were.

At the school, Kalakaua was not known for his scholarship so much as for inattentiveness, singing, and fighting. He frequently fought the older Kamehameha boys, especially Moses, when they teased him or others who were not Kamehamehas. He frequently suffered illnesses and bruises and even broken bones, sometimes inflicted by the stern disciplinarian, Amos Starr Cooke.[6]

It was an incident involving Cooke that caused him to miss out on a historical celebration. Kalakaua, who loved celebrations, remembered his disappointment long enough to write his sister Lydia about it in later years.[7]

* * *

In 1843, Alexander Simpson, a Canadian citizen and visitor to Hawaii, linked himself with Richard Charlton, British consul, regarding some land disputes and lodged complaints against the Hawaiian government. Charlton, hoping to bring his complaint to England, then met on his way in Mexico, Rear Admiral Richard Thomas. He succeeded in convincing Thomas to send the frigate *Carysfort* under Lord George Paulet's command to Honolulu to investigate. Paulet, an ambitious man, decided the islands should be under British rule. He was aware that a few years before LaPlace, a Frenchman, had forced Kamehameha III to yield to his demands that the Catholic religion be brought safely to the islands, that French imports and French residents be given preferential treatment, and that a sum of $20,000 be paid to LaPlace as a guarantee that the terms be carried out. Paulet threatened the king with "coercive action" unless "complete restoration" for Simpson and Charlton was given, plus land, an indemnity of over $200,000 for "unfair treatment of British subjects." Guns from the *Carysfort* were aimed at Honolulu.

As the king could get no help from the French consul or his good friend and adviser, Gerrit P. Judd, who had left the missionary field to enter the government at the king's request, Kamehameha III said, "Let them take the country."

Kalakaua and the older children of the High Chiefs' School were indignant. Nevertheless they marched, two by two, to Honolulu's crumbling fort to see the Hawaiian flag lowered and the British Standard raised. It was a subdued but resentful crowd that watched in silence.

Kalakaua heard Kamehameha speak the historic words: "Hear ye! I make known to you that I am in perplexity by reason of difficulties into which I have been brought without cause; therefore, I have given away the life of the land, hear ye! But my rule over you, my people, and your privileges will continue, for I have hope that the life of the land will be restored when my conduct is justified."

Kalakaua and the children caught the spirit of revolt and played at retaliation. They held "indignation meetings;" Lot, to the delight of the other children, called the British officers "lobster backs," and they glared at them with scorn whenever they met on the street.

Further, Moses put up the American flag, but Mr. Cooke took it down. Kalakaua and Lot were angry that it was the American flag and not the Hawaiian. A quarrel broke out between them and Moses, ending in a fist fight and a black eye for Kalakaua.

It became immediately evident that Paulet had no intention of allowing Kamehameha to have any rule over his people nor allow their privileges to continue. He recruited a native regiment, calling it the Queen's Own (in reference to Queen Victoria), and began a heavy taxation system. It was then that Dr. Judd moved into action by joining the king in withholding records of lands, which resulted in endless legal upsets; refusing to grant moneys for payment to the regiments and others; and lastly working secretly at night in the Royal Mausoleum, using Kaahumanu's coffin as a desk, to send envoys to England.

The envoys reached Great Britain and notified the queen. Admiral Sir Richard Thomas also received word of Paulet's action. Thomas sailed for Honolulu from the west coast of South America. He arrived on July 26, 1843, six months after Paulet's "takeover."

Thomas made short order of Paulet; he conferred with Judd and the king, drew up articles of parity for British subjects, similar to those of the French, and "restored" the islands.[8]

On July 31, 1843, a wildly cheering crowd gathered on the plains east of Honolulu, waving and shouting as the king appeared with his royal guards. The children of the High Chiefs' School stood at attention while the Hawaiian flag was again raised, and cannons were fired at the fort, on the plains, in the harbor, and at Punch Bowl. It was a day of wild rejoicing.

In the afternoon Kamehameha III, after a solemn procession with his chiefs to Kawaiahao Church, spoke the words that were to become the motto of Hawaii: "*Ua mau ke ea o ka aina i ka pono*"–The life of the land is perpetuated in righteousness. Kalakaua, sitting in the front row of straight-backed pews, would find much to contemplate in these often ambiguously interpreted words as the years passed. A ten-day celebration of Restoration Day followed, and was annually observed.

The last Restoration Day came in 1847 when Kalakaua was thirteen. The missionary element was thereafter to declare the celebrations "too expensive."

The younger children of the royal school rode in carriages and the older children rode horseback, leading the parade–all except Kalakaua. He stood on the sidelines and watched, for he had been badly injured when Amos Starr Cooke had struck him in a moment of anger. He had fallen and dislocated his shoulder. Cooke was not angry solely with Kalakaua but with Moses, who constantly baited Cooke by disobediently joining the sailors on the wharf for drink and carousing. But Moses was next in line to be king, and Cooke did not dare strike him; the blow fell, possibly accidentally, but nevertheless on Kalakaua.[9]

Bitterly, Kalakaua stood with Kinimaka, watching the colorful procession but not taking part in it. The carriage of the king and queen followed the royal children riders.

A thousand special horsemen, five abreast, horses and riders alike wearing gay ribbons and flowers, were followed by 2,500 regular horsemen. The procession arrived at the Nuuanu picnic ground in a pouring rain but with spirits undampened. The delighted native crowds gathered under two open *lanai*, or covered pavilions, which were thatched with ti leaves and thickly carpeted with rushes, and from where they threw flowers into the passing carriages.

Kalakaua held his breath while watching John Ii, a trustee and teacher at the school, who on this day began the ancient games. Someday, he vowed, he would be part of the games. His muscular build easily qualified him. He closely watched Ii, who, standing tall in a dark broadcloth suit and a brilliant yellow cape, came to salute the children before he stepped into the arena. In the tradition of ancient warriors he stood alone, unarmed, opposed by twenty spearmen, each of whom endeavored to hit him. Dexterously catching the first spear, he successfully parried all the rest, which were aimed with furious force at all parts of his body. With the grace of a dancer, he tossed the spears back at his opponents, driving them one by one from the field. Even the *haole*, from under their frame structure, cheered wildly and "applauded thunderously," wrote Gerrit Judd IV, who read about the occasion in his great-grandfather's notes.[10]

When the games were over, Kalakaua was allowed to go with the other children to the "Long House" where the chiefs and king sat on the floor at the far end of the mats and ate with the people, the natives, while the foreigners dined on linen-covered tables in a frame shelter.

❋ ❋ ❋

Kalakaua lived a divided life.

At school he and his classmates were learning of Kamehameha III's great progress toward a constitutional monarchy, of which neither the children nor the Hawaiian king nor his royal council had a clear concept. Many of the "learned" chiefs were opposing the movement on the argument that the Hawaiians were not ready for such freedom. It would bring about the loss of the country, they prophesied. It was American in origin and concept, for Kamehameha III had many missionary and other *haole* advisers.

* * *

The children of the school recited dutifully the Declaration of Rights, written in 1839: "God has made of one blood all nations of men to dwell on the face of the earth in unity and blessedness. God has bestowed certain rights alike on all men, all chiefs, and all people of all lands." They only partially understood the meaning or applicability to their society.

The students were given long hours of study of the first constitution the Hawaiians ever had. They had no understanding of "the transfer of power. . ." *from* the high chiefs *to* an elected legislature—elected for the first time by the commoner. They merely memorized the words.

The greatest of constitutional rights was for the protection "to the persons of all people, together with their land, their building lots, and all their property, and nothing whatsoever shall be taken away from an individual, except by express provisions of the laws."

The Hawaiian *alii*, who knew the commoner had no land, building lots, nor property of his own found the right non-applicable; the commoner who had no understanding of owning land, building lots, or property ignored the right completely. The *haole* who wanted land, building lots, and property thought the right a great forward step into democracy, but they were not willing to accept the "law of the government" relative to land claims. They saw hundreds of ways to gain land from the "lazy *kanaka*" and make it profitable; some worked from an altruistic purpose for Hawaii, but most worked for themselves. Hawaii was unique in allowing noncitizens to take an active part in the government, both to vote and to hold office.

To give the commoner the land that he couldn't comprehend owning, Kamehameha III was prevailed upon through *haole* advisers to institute the Land Reform Movement and the "Great *Mahele*," hailed by the teachers of the High Chiefs' School as the "greatest of Kamehameha's contributions." Previously, all the land belonged to the king, Kamehameha. Now the lands were divided into three parts: the king's land; the high chiefs' land, as recorded in the Great *Mahele* book; and the remaining land, which then became available to the commoners. The king divided his newly-apportioned one-third share into two parts: one for the use of the government and one for his own personal use.

The royal children, Moses, Lot, Liholiho, and Victoria (then three years old) would be heirs to the Kamehameha lands of Kamehameha III, called the "Crown lands," as distinct from the "government lands." Whoever held the Crown was heir to the government lands as well. Other high chiefs' childrens' parents laid claim to their new divisions: Kanaina claimed his portion for Lunalilo, and High Chief Aikanaka claimed his lands for his daughter Keohokalole. Under Aikanaka and Keohokalole, Kalakaua was to share his land inheritance with his two sisters, Kamakaeha (Liliuokalani) and Likelike—but not until much later.

❖ ❖ ❖

The school allowed the children to go home for vacations, so Kalakaua, during the first six years of his life, spent time with Liliha and his grandmother, Alapai, as well as with Kinimaka and Pai. At the knees of these two very different women, Liliha and his grandmother, he learned of a Hawaii that the missionaries shunned.

From Liliha he learned of a world on faraway shores. Although the school taught European and American history, the teachers slanted the lines away from any monarchial splendor, even in their sessions of "how royalty in other lands live." They lived righteously, dutifully for their people. With Liliha all was in ceremonial splendor both at home and abroad.

Liliha told Kalakaua of festivities when Hawaiians had their own happy lives before the missionaries had so much control.

To observe the fourth anniversary of his father's death, Liliha reminisced, Kamehameha II had ordered lavish and splendid ceremonies that would last a fortnight. To Liliha and other high chiefs this was a time of rejoicing, as they loved celebrations and commemorations of their chiefs.

A motley train proceeded from the grass church to Liholiho's bower at Waikiki—a long and lofty *lanai* of slender poles and green branches reared for the occasion. A great banquet was held with both foreign and Hawaiian delicacies. It was followed by hula dancing and competitive sports. Spectators and participants were dressed in feather capes, tapa, and the silks and satins of China.

On the first day's observance the king had saluted (by missionary demand) his pagan father's memory with Christian prayer and toasted that wise old *awa* drinker with heady foreign drafts. He proudly exhibited his new palace in Kona, Hawaii, finished just in time for the celebration. Although it was made of grass like the palace of his forbearers, it was lofty (thirty feet at the peak) and had wooden doors and shuttered windows. There was one great room, its floor covered with patterned mats of native manufacture; but three glittering cut-glass chandeliers swung from the ridgepole, mirrors and steel engravings decorated the walls, and crimson-upholstered Chinese sofas and mahogany tables furnished the place with European beauty. Liliha stressed the grandeur of the palace.

The last day of the festival was the day of processions.

All day singers and dancers by the hundreds moved across the plain, meeting the parade here and there, encircling the

highest chiefs, shouting praise and affection, beating calabash drums, chanting *oli* and *mele*, choruses and responses.

About this day's revels the recently arrived missionary,
Reverend Charles Stewart, wrote solemnly in his journal, ". . .
highly interesting as an exhibition of ancient customs, which,
it is probable, will soon be lost forever . . . There is much reason to believe, that a taste for these ceremonies . . . will be so
far lost . . . even before the lapse of another year . . . that they
will never be repeated . . ."

* * *

Liliha shared even more grandeur with Kalakaua–"modern"
grandeur. Her trip to England was often repeated.

Liliha wept bitterly (Hawaiian tears came easily) as she
told of Kamamalu's (Kamehameha II's favorite wife) farewell
to Hawaii on November 27, 1823.

> "O skies, O plains, O mountains and oceans,
>   O guardians and people, kind affection for you all.
>   Farewell to thee the soil,
>   O country, for which my father suffered; alas for thee!"

Kalakaua's love for celebrations, kingly splendor, and
travel came naturally.

* * *

From his grandmother, with whom he continued to spend
time after Liliha's death in 1842, he learned of forbidden subjects. His grandmother taught him lessons and wisdom
found in the legends handed down verbally from generation
to generation through the *mele*. She told him of the *kahuna*
and their wisdom in healing, bringing forth blessings, and
helping the people to know their history. She was herself a
kahuna (a woman of wisdom) and could pass on the art to
him. She taught him carefully the art of *kahuna-ana-ana*.
These were the *kahuna* who could pray one to death. But a
regularly practicing *kahuna* could save the person. Because
he knew the art and artfulness, he could reverse it. Every-

thing has an opposite, she explained, and to know the good one had to be acquainted with the evil and its ways. The *kahuna* kept the history of ancestors—their genealogies, their beliefs, their customs, and their heritage. One could have no greater honor than to be a *kahuna*.

The stories of these two women, plus the opportunity of learning from Hawaiian teachers, gave Kalakaua a wealth of information, often unclassified and undigested. He developed a hunger for knowledge, especially for the past and the greatness of warrior kings.

* * *

Kinimaka arranged for him to join private sessions held by native historians David Malo and Samuel Kamakau, who were trained at Lahainaluna High School in Maui. These two had been taught by William Richards and other missionary teachers and served as Hawaiian resource persons for the missionary teachers. The two young students were willing to write of "ancient Hawaiian customs and practices" as they had been handed down to them by oral tradition. But they were non-judgmental. As the missionaries gained more information, recorded it, edited it, judged it, and condemned the "savage" and "pagan" customs and practices, the two young chiefs also developed a judgment value of what the missionary teachers taught.

David Malo early warned that the "Big fish were coming up out of the sea to eat the little fish, unless they [the Hawaiians] changed their ways." This warning was incorrectly interpreted to mean, "become more *haole*;" what Malo meant was to listen less to the missionaries, for he wrote later, of them and others, that no early foreigner had been endowed with the wisdom to understand and preserve or build on the culture of the Hawaiians. "First they came sightless, then blinded by self-righteousness, and lastly eyes open to self-interest."

* * *

Honolulu was a vivid place filled with the aroma of human perspiration, fragrant flowers, and sea air.

Kalakaua wandered the streets of Honolulu, then a seaport not much different from seaports the world over in the 1840s, except for the diverse people. He mingled with the brown-jacketed Chinese and the Hawaiian commoner wearing a variety of clothing—top hats and loin cloths, cast-off pants or shirts. The women wore the new *holokus* and *muumuus* that the missionaries had hastily slipped over their bodies. Some were large and tent-like, and others were slim. Not even the clothing could conceal their slender, well-formed young bodies. There were also the elegant European-clad girls from Liliha's house of prostitution, and the high chiefesses colorful in their silks and satins—all bedecked with fresh flowers. Casting a more somber note on the crowds were the dark-clad missionary women with the high-collared men, who waited eagerly for the ships to bring them six-month-old news from home. They cherished and reread many times each letter. The men brought home the barrels of flour or clothing, cast-off and sent by the missions at home.

* * *

Of all, Kalakaua loved the ships the most. He pestered sailors to take him out in the row boats to the ships that he might see the interior of these fantastic monsters with their high masts and winglike sails. The Hawaiians were ahead of the Europeans in canoe building and had made remarkable trips of thousands of miles by the stars. They were skilled navigators. Although Kalakaua knew this, the sail-borne whaling ships intrigued him. Proclaiming himself a high chief, he sometimes persuaded a first mate or even a captain to take him aboard. The persuasive charm that was his all his life captivated the men. He found constant fascination and asked unending questions about the "magic" of the ship. How did the navigational instruments work—the sexton, the compass?

Someday, he imagined, he would sleep in one of the cabins—not the hammocks—for he would always be a captain or a first mate, at least.

A favorite companion of his was Denzo, a young Japanese boy who worked in the kitchen of the school. He had been one of five Japanese boys who had come to Hawaii in a disabled junk in 1841. To Denzo, the oldest of the five boys, Kalakaua listened avidly as he told tales of Japan and struggles of the open sea. The Kamehameha brothers and the Cookes ignored Denzo, a servant unsuitable for friendship, but Kalakaua found him a delightful companion—he was different, he was interesting—characteristics that would always influence Kalakaua in his choice of friends and advisers.

❊ ❊ ❊

Then, in 1848, a measles epidemic struck and Moses died, as did a younger sister of Kalakaua, then *hanai* to the king. Death wailing had been forbidden, but the children were allowed a "silent aloha" for Moses. It was anything but silent. The wailing began immediately, and when one child stopped, under severe threats from Amos Starr Cooke, two more raised their voices louder. It was a terrible experience for the Cookes and a cleansing one for the children.

Shortly thereafter the Cookes closed the High Chiefs' School, called the Royal School after 1846, and Dr. Gerrit Judd decided to take the two young Princes Liholiho and Lot to England. The children of the school were scattered. Kalakaua returned to Kinimaka.

As a thirteen-year-old boy, Kalakaua was confused about his place in the immediate present as well as the future. He had suffered physical and emotional abuse at the school. Then he was deprived of his *ohana* with the death of his grandmother.

The structures of the past were seriously damaged. Where once he would have known his place as a high chief but not as a Kamehameha royal, to be an adviser to the king and to live in moderate affluence, now he seemed to belong nowhere. The lands relegated during the Great *Mahele* and Land Reform Movement tied any that might be his to his grandfather, Aikanaka. He had no money. He had no place in the new society.

He had a growing jealousy of the Kamehamehas and the beginning of an ambition to succeed where they might fail. His grandmother had told him that Liliha, the prophetess, had said that the Kamehameha line would die out and the Keawe-a-Heulu line would succeed. But at thirteen, Kalakaua saw no hope of it.

2 Young Kalakaua

After Kalakaua left the High Chiefs' School of the Cookes, he attended the George Beckwith Royal School. Beckwith and his brother, Maurice, had been teachers at the High Chiefs' School and with the closing of it by the Cookes, almost immediately reopened it as a day school of their own. Susan Mills, founder of Mills College in Oakland, California, later reported that Beckwith, when a trustee of Mills, said: "Kalakaua was an avid student, unfortunately trying to learn everything at once and not digesting the material properly."[1]

During this period, Kalakaua's contact with the royal princes was primarily social. At Moses' death in the measles epidemic, Liholiho and Lot had became heirs to the throne.

In 1849, when the High Chiefs' School had closed, the children had been scattered. Dr. Gerrit Judd, who had entered the king's service as adviser in 1842 and had helped Kamehameha III regain his country after the abortive coup of Paulet, decided the two young princes needed educational broadening in England and the United States. Both looked forward to going to London, for they had heard often of Kamehameha II's tragic trip and of the hospitality of the British to the Hawaiians.

Their trip was entirely successful in England, but disastrous in the United States. Liholiho wrote in his journal that the United States was indifferent and rude to the young Hawaiians. The young princes had not been entertained by the United States government as they had by the British. Then an unfortunate incident occurred in Philadelphia. The princes had been mistaken for Negroes and had been relegated to the last car on the railway.

With their return to Hawaii, they began thinking of the royal succession. Although Lot was the older, Liholiho had been selected by Kamehameha III as next in the succession line; a sharp rivalry began between them—two more different brothers it is hard to imagine.

Lot was taciturn, brooding, resentful of the missionaries, and determined that Hawaii be kept for the Hawaiians. Liholiho was lithe, handsome, gallant, fun-loving, but also aware of the losses his country was suffering. The children of the Royal School were not blind to what was happening to their country. By 1848, the Hawaiian population had dropped drastically from 500,000 to 70,000 as a result of *haole* diseases. The government was rapidly slipping under foreign rule: noncitizens were being placed in high positions of government and replacing Hawaiians. Education was being taken over by the missionaries, and the Hawaiian language had been replaced by English in official circles and in schools. The old customs and traditions were called "pagan" and "heathen" and were rapidly being trampled out of existence.

Politically, Kalakaua's sympathies lay with Lot. Socially, he was included in palace activities and other royal events. His blood sister Lydia (Liliuokalani) lived with Bernice and Charles Reed Bishop, an American banker who had married the great-granddaughter of Kamehameha I, Bernice Pauahi. Bishop entertained lavishly and included Kalakaua in moonlight horseback rides, *luau*, and other youthful activities.

✻ ✻ ✻

At the age of fourteen, Kalakaua returned to his blood father, Kapaakea, who commanded a small militia, having taken over from Aikanaka the Punch Bowl Battery. Kalakaua was placed under the tutelage of Captain Franz Funk, a Prussian Soldier.[2]

Kalakaua loved the military precision and through Funk became strongly indoctrinated in the importance of military protection for a country. There was none to speak of in Hawaii except for the Royal Guard for the palace.

Kalakaua looked back to the days when Kamehameha had unified the nation and gloried in the time of warfare and navy supremacy. Like most Hawaiians he loved the sea, but unlike most Hawaiians he also loved the military—both the pomp and the disciplined form of drill. He loved also the uniforms and medals. By the time he was sixteen he received his army commission as first lieutenant in Kapaakea's militia of 240 men.

In 1853, at the age of seventeen, Kalakaua began his study of law under Charles Coffin Harris. Enchanted by the young Kalakaua, Harris took him into his home to live.[3]

It was Kalakaua's years with C. C. Harris that formulated his legalistic oratory. Harris, an American opposed to the foreign takeover that was occurring in Hawaii, served in the legislature as a thorn to many of the opposition. Harris had a "gift of gab"[4] that infuriated many a legislator. On the other hand, he amused the Hawaiians in the legislature, for they had always been fond of words. Theirs was an oral tradition. He also appealed to their underplayed sense of humor, for the annoyance Harris caused among other *haole* was a delight to them. Harris was called a traitor by the foreign element, but he was hailed by the Hawaiians as a defender of what they held dear.

Harris was a New Englander and a graduate of Harvard. He was also an adventurer who had left the East in search of California gold. But like many, he was disappointed and sailed on a schooner operated by his two brothers to Hawaii. Here he studied Hawaiian, practiced law, became a member of the legislature, and served as a police magistrate.

Kalakaua found in Harris the qualities he most admired; Harris was an adventurer, a spinner of tales, and a Hawaiian supporter.

Harris tried to explain to Kalakaua the inbred hatred the *haole* had for royalty, against whom they had fought for their independence. Kalakaua never really understood this antipathy.

* * *

Under the tutelage of Harris, Kalakaua began to see the results of the Great *Mahele*—the division of land. In its simplest explanation it could be said that until that time all the land was owned by the king except for parcels given by him to foreigners (such as John Young and Isaac Davis, British advisors to Kamehameha I) and to missionaries for churches and homes. With the Great *Mahele*, the land was divided in thirds.

Both the commoners and the high chiefs were vulnerable to land swindles by the foreigners. Their own generosity made them more vulnerable; they gave away land to whoever might ask for it—as Liliha gave her father's land to Hiram Bingham, a missionary, for Punahou School for missionary children.

The *haole*, being far more businesslike in their transactions, wanted definite surveying done. The cases came to the attention of Harris and Kalakaua. Some of the decisions reached by Harris and Kalakaua are still used as precedents for land problems in Hawaii. Surveying was one of the major problems, as often the deed defined a boundary clumsily—"from a stream to a rock." The stream could broaden or dry up, and a rock in drenching rain could move a considerable distance. The seashore property was particularly difficult to ascertain because of the changing tides, yet a popular definition of a land boundary was "*ma ke kai*," which was "usually evident by edge of vegetation or by line of debris left by wash of waves." Harris' interpretation of *ma ke kai* was used as late as 1968 in land cases.[5]

Young Kalakaua early became acquainted with land problems that were to plague him all his life and bring about the end of Hawaiian rule. Yet he never quite understood them.

During this period Kalakaua divided his time between the military and the study of law and the history of Hawaii. He was appointed military secretary and later Adjutant General. For a nineteen-year-old it was not a bad life, though it was a poor one, for salaries were low, and he was yet to receive his portion of the Aikanaka land.

* * *

In 1855, life changed considerably for the young *alii*. Kamehameha III died on December 15, 1854, and after a period of mourning Prince Liholiho became king as Kamehameha IV.

Lot resented Liholiho for superseding him and drew closer to Kalakaua. The two of them were more alike in attitudes as well. They both held to a return to "Hawaii for Hawaiians," while Liholiho inaugurated a smaller version of the Court of St. James. Liholiho would have been totally content to have a British protectorate. He hated the Americans and to some degree distrusted the Hawaiians in office. Yet Kalakaua was appointed his Aide de Camp as well as being chosen to serve in the Privy Council.

* * *

It was a joyous court under Liholiho. He declared that all protectorate and annexation talks in which his father had engaged were at an end. Politically, the country was quiet because there was prosperity—agriculture of various types was coming into its own as well as trade. Hawaii seemed, after a turbulent twenty years, to be safe from outside powers. Internally, the charismatic Liholiho had no problems.

The court set a tone for gaiety, and romance was in the air. Kamehameha IV announced his marriage to his childhood sweetheart of the High Chiefs' School, Emma Rooke. Emma was part British, her father having been High Chief George Naea and her mother Fanny Young, a descendant of John Young. She was also *hanai* to her aunt, Grace Young Rooke, and British Dr. T. C. B. Rooke.

Kamehameha IV had leaned toward the British since his trip abroad in his teens, and there was little protest against his *hapa-haole* (part-foreigner) marriage. Besides, he was *king*.

A slight flurry arose over Liholiho's choice by some of the high chiefs putting forth Lydia Kamakaeha as the "highest chiefess" by blood and *hanai*.⁶ Lydia was Kalakaua's blood sister, and his blood father, Kapaakea, argued vigorously in favor of Lydia. Genealogies of both Lydia and Kalakaua were carefully studied during this controversy. Yet his was to be challenged later. Kalakaua was of a darker color than his sister and had some Negroid features, as many Hawaiians had. It was quickly picked up that he was Negroid, and a rumor began that his father was not Kapaakea but a Negro blacksmith named Blossom,⁷ even though Blossom had not come to Hawaii until Kalakaua was thirteen years old. This early rumor persisted throughout Kalakaua's life, fueled by his opposition.

Kalakaua's importance in the royal circle was increased when he became groomsman with Prince Lot for the wedding of Kamehameha IV and Emma Rooke. They were married on June 17, 1856. The wedding was the most prestigious ever to be held in Hawaii. It was the first royal wedding. It was also to be the last.

An exciting deviation from custom, more pleasing to the Hawaiians than to the American *haole*, was that the wedding ceremony would neither be Hawaiian nor missionary. True to his love of Britain, Kamehameha IV requested an Anglican service. As there was no Anglican churchman in Hawaii in 1856, Reverend Richard Armstrong, a missionary, rose to the occasion and agreed to read "the vows according to the ceremony of the Church of England."

The day was declared a holiday: all offices and most stores were closed. Flags of all countries represented in Hawaii waved, and people thronged the streets, awaiting the royal wedding party.

Three thousand guests—native Hawaiians, *haole*, chiefs, and foreign dignitaries who filled the Kawaiahao Church to capacity—waited inside the stone edifice, festooned with *maile* and other greenery hanging from the ceiling and the galleries and entwined about the columns. The air was heavy with the scent of flowers. Guests waited in breathless stillness for the bride to walk down the aisle.

At 11:30 the bride entered the church. Walking with her *hanai* father, Dr. Rooke, Emma was dressed in a wedding gown of the richest white embroidered silk selected from the then-famous store, Stewart's on Broadway, New York City. The gown, worn with an elegantly wrought bridal veil and a headdress of white roses and orange blossoms, "gave her the appearance and beauty to which Parisian art could have added but little," the papers extolled.

The twenty-year-old bride was then joined by a handsome, uniformed twenty-two-year-old king, who was accompanied by the Governor of Oahu, his blood father. The couple met at "an altar covered with rich figured silk with gold trimmings." There the two knelt on a rich carpet before Dr. Armstrong, who read the vows in both English and Hawaiian.

"All foreign dignitaries and guests were graciously received," according to the newspapers, at the magnificent reception at the palace that evening. Dancing continued throughout the night, with Kalakaua declared the "best dancer in Hawaii." It was at this dance that Kalakaua first became aware of the young Kapiolani.

* * *

Julia Kapiolani[8] was of high chiefly background, her maternal grandfather being the last king of Kauai. She had from her early teens been under the custody of Kamehameha III and had been a member of the court. In 1852, when she was eighteen, she had married Benet Namakeha, thirty years her senior. They had both gone on a missionary expedition to Micronesia. A year later they returned to the court of

Kamehameha iv. Kalakaua was attracted to Julia, for although she was educated in both English and Hawaiian, she spoke only Hawaiian and was thoroughly Hawaiian-oriented. She was described as lovely, shy, and gracious—as her later life proved her to be.

Later that year Kalakaua was appointed to the House of Nobles (high chiefs) and made Aide de Camp to the king. He thus served during the period when Kamehameha iv experienced both great personal problems and joy. On May 20, 1858, Queen Emma gave birth to a new prince and heir to the throne—Albert (named after England's Prince Albert). Great rejoicing took place throughout Hawaii for the birth of the new heir.

He was taken everywhere and parties were almost continuous for the young prince. Shortly after his birth, Julia Kapiolani became *kahu-alii* (nursemaid) to the prince, as she had just given birth to a stillborn child. Her status was that of honor. She was actually of higher lineage than the queen.

It was here in the royal household that Kalakaua saw more of Kapiolani, and fell in love with her, but his love-life was as complicated as his later political life was to be. Shortly after her arrival in Hawaii Kapiolani became widowed, and her path constantly crossed Kalakaua's.

* * *

Although serving under Kamehameha iv, Kalakaua sided with Prince Lot in promoting Hawaii for Hawaiians. On the premise of going to Canada for Prince Lot's health and to study the possibilities of securing trade and preferential treatment of the sugar tariff, Kalakaua and Lot set sail for San Francisco and Victoria, B.C., in 1861. They shared between them another purpose: that of securing arms and artillery for Hawaii. Lot felt that military defense would someday be necessary to secure the independence of Hawaii. Kalakaua, in the past having been influenced by Captain Franz Funk, believed strongly in the importance of military power.

It was Kalakaua's first trip on a steamship-sailing vessel. He could hardly contain his delight and often lost sight of the political purpose of the trip in the sheer pleasure of travel. This proclivity was to be repeated frequently in his life. Neither he nor Lot were successful in their mission—either for trade or artillery.

Even though they lived close to each other, the young men communicated by the written word. Letters and notes between Kalakaua and Prince Lot indicated that the military plans were to be kept secret from Kamehameha IV[9], who was totally convinced that there would be no attack on his kingdom. He was exceedingly popular, did nothing to upset the *status quo* of his father's liberal constitution, and best of all, there was prosperity in the country. The Kamehameha private lands, plus the Crown lands, brought in more than adequate money for the royal treasury. The *haole* had practically no demands made on them in exchange for supporting the royal family, as they would later.

While Prince Lot and Kalakaua had a close relationship politically, a problem existed socially. Princess Victoria, Lot and Liholiho's sister, was next in line for the throne and was *kuhina nui* (premier). She never served in the office, as she was having a personal crisis. She had fallen in love with a married *haole* auctioneer, Julian Monsarrat. The love affair was public knowledge, and Lot, who resented the situation, tried to persuade Kalakaua to become engaged to Victoria. Kalakaua was, however, attracted to Kapiolani. Nevertheless, in the midst of the heat of gossip over Victoria's conduct, Kalakaua suddenly received a note from Victoria asking him to set a date, for they, according to her, were indeed engaged. He wrote his sister Lydia of the surprising turn of events.[10] But he accepted the invitation to be engaged to the princess. It was no small honor for an ambitious young man.

Coinciding with Kalakaua's engagement notice was the engagement of Lydia to Prince Lunalilo, a lineal descendant

of the Kamehamehas. Hence, both brother and sister were to
attend a ball to be given by Prince Lunalilo, during which
engagements were to be announced. Lunalilo was an excep-
tionally popular young man, known as Prince Bill to both
haole and Hawaiian.

Liliuokalani later wrote in her book, *Hawaii's Story by
Hawaii's Queen* , that Victoria made a different decision. In
the midst of the festivities, Victoria, with a vast retinue of
over a hundred men and women, arrived. The music and
dancing stopped, and Victoria imperiously made her way
across a rapidly clearing floor to her host, Prince Lunalilo.
Taking his arm, she called for silence. She then publicly announced her long-standing engagement, indeed from birth,
to Lunalilo. The crowd cheered, for few knew of the other
two supposed engagements.

Victoria did not, however, marry Lunalilo. Her thwarted
romance with Monsarrat (Lot threatened to exile him), her
strong attraction to alcohol, and her hopeless feeling about
Hawaii's future led to her return to her half-sister Princess
Ruth's home, where she stayed until her death in 1866.

* * *

In 1858, at the age of twenty-two, Kalakaua was chosen to
serve in the House of Nobles. The same year saw another
dream come true: through Prince Lot he was invited to join
the Masonic Lodge. Throughout his life he was to be devoted
to the principles of Masonry and later became a Thirty-Third
Degree Mason.

In 1861, after returning from Canada with the partial
financial backing of Lot, Kalakaua joined the expression of
nationalism in the press. He originated the first Hawaiian
language newspaper, edited solely by Hawaiians—*Ka Hoku A
Ka Pakipaki (Star of the Pacific)*.

He collaborated with two strongly loyal Hawaiians, G. W.
Mila and J. K. Kaunamano. The paper stressed the loss of
population and heritage. It was to be the paper of the "com-

mon people" and promoted the use of the Hawaiian language and the keeping of Hawaiian traditions and cultures.

Kalakaua's never-dying interest in the past was brought to the editorial pages in genealogies, *mele*, legends, and histories.

He served at the same time in the position he enjoyed most: as social host for Kamehameha IV, entertaining arriving foreign guests. These events included the presence of Lady Franklin, wife of the Arctic explorer, and her companion, Sophia Cracroft, who described him as ". . . pure Hawaiian, excessively stout, but of most gentlemanlike manners and appearance, dressed exactly after the morning fashion of Englishmen in light grey . . . very dark brown (not black) with an aquiline nose and thick lips—whiskers and moustache and hair much more woolly in its crisp curliness than is usually seen among this people . . . Queen Victoria's Aide-de-Camp could not have acquitted himself better." In letters to friends, she mentioned his charm, excellent English, and dress. Kalakaua, aware of his appearance, did not always appear in military garb but was picturesque ". . . in his A.D.C. traveling costume—a scarlet woolen shirt over the usual white one, black trousers, large black waterproof hat round which was a wreath of natural flowers of the Hawaiian colours (rich crimson and yellow, each in separate masses), white buckskin gauntlet gloves, Mexican spurs, and a very handsome Mexican saddle of stamped leather."[11]

* * *

Kalakaua was to play a sadder but less personal part in the reign of Kamehameha IV. During one of the royal tours to Maui, a scandal broke over the royal household. After hearing rumors that his secretary, Henry Neilson, had been having an affair with the Queen, the inebriated king shot at close range and wounded Neilson. Kalakaua, as Aide, rushed to Neilson's side and carried him into another house for care. Later, when the king discovered the rumors were untrue, he became abjectly repentant and spent the next two-and-a-half years in constant attendance upon Neilson, who after that period died. But greater grief was to befall Kamehameha IV.

On August 17, 1862, the king, annoyed by a tantrum the young prince had thrown, decided to "cool him off" by placing him under a cold water faucet. The child became ill shortly after this dousing. Although Kamehameha IV blamed himself, the cause of the child's illness was a high fever called "brain fever."

The royal couple were Episcopalian and had asked Queen Victoria of England to be the child's godmother, as well as requesting a resident Anglican minister to come to Hawaii. Queen Victoria, upon receiving the request, sent an Anglican bishop to have him represent her as godmother to the young prince. Before the bishop could arrive, however, the young prince's illness worsened.

On August 19, 1862, it was publicly announced that the Prince of Hawaii had become seriously ill. Bulletins were issued three times daily, but what was kept out of the press was that the king considered himself responsible for the illness.

The British Commissioner and Consul-General, W.W.F. Synge, and his wife arrived August 25, 1862, bearing a beautiful christening cup from Queen Victoria. It was Kalakaua's painful duty, as chamberlain to the king, to tell Synge of the prince's illness and later to bring him to the king and queen for an audience. The queen asked Synge to act, in the absence of the Prince of Wales, as proxy for the young prince's godfather. He agreed, and the baptismal service proceeded, with Lot as the other godfather.

The young prince was then officially christened Albert Edward Kauikeaouli Leiopapa a Kamehameha.

Two days later, on the 27th, he died, at the age of four.

Kalakaua's sister, Lydia, had replaced Kapiolani in attendance during the last illness of the Prince; Queen Emma blamed Kapiolani for having "allowed the king near the child" to douse him with cold water. It certainly was not Kapiolani's fault, and she took the blame with great grief.

Kalakaua fell more deeply in love with the beautiful, grieving widow, now that she was being barred from the court and final services for the young prince. He felt a kinship, never having felt at one either with the Kamehamehas.

Kamehameha IV took the blame of his child's death upon himself and never recovered from his grief. He became a recluse and withdrew from public life to continue work on translating the Anglican Prayer Book, a project he had begun after the death of Neilson.

On November 30, 1863, Kamehameha IV died at the age of twenty-nine. The services were Episcopalian and "subdued in contrast to Hawaiian fashion." Prince Lot was to become Kamehameha V.

❋ ❋ ❋

In the meantime Kalakaua's sister, Lydia, married an American, John Owen Dominis, in 1862. She had met him when she lived with the Bishops.

❋ ❋ ❋

On December 19, 1863, Kalakaua's romance with Julia Kapiolani crystallized, and they were married in a quiet, secret ceremony by an Episcopal minister. The news soon became known, and Kalakaua fell under heavy criticism for having married during the mourning period after the death of Kamehameha IV (November 30, 1863).

Kalakaua wrote several letters[12] to Kamehameha V explaining that the marriage had been a "secret one;" he had not even told his sister Lydia. Still, criticism of the young couple grew, fueled by Queen Emma's resentment of Kapiolani and some question of Kalakaua's abortive "engagement" to Victoria.

Julia Kapiolani was born December 31, 1834, in Hilo, Hawaii, of High Chief Kuhio and High Chiefess Kinoiki. She was named in honor of the first High Chiefess to defy the Goddess Pele. The story goes that when Kilauea erupted, the first Kapiolani walked to the edge of the active volcano and pelted the flames with sacred berries that grew on the hillside and were presumed to be the personal property of Pele. She then cried out, "Jehovah is my God." Julia Kapiolani did not follow in the footsteps of the missionaries, but both she and Kalakaua joined the Episcopal Church. Well-versed in Hawaiian history and its tradition, she continued to speak no English and tended to lean toward the old *kahuna* system. Despite this, she often attended the Kawaiahao Church in Honolulu. As a descendant of Kaumualii, the last king of Kauai, the only island that surrendered peacefully to Kamehameha I, she carried a strong line of nobility and vast lands.

On December 7, 1863, Kalakaua had been reappointed to the Privy Council—just previous to his marriage. It was no wonder he felt uncomfortable under the criticism, but apparently Kamehameha V carried little resentment, for he appointed him chamberlain to the king on February 3, 1864.

The same year Kalakaua served unsuccessfully as postmaster general. His duties had not been fulfilling to him nor the minister of interior, who accused him of "irresponsibility and absenteeism."

* * *

Under Kamehameha V, Kalakaua took on more serious challenges than he had under Kamehameha IV, but he continued as social host. Kamehameha V was not known for his social graces, and social entertainments fell to Kalakaua, such as acting as host to the Duke of Edinburgh, also a Mason, at an extensive *luau*.[13]

* * *

Lot was not appreciated by the *haole* for his political acumen. Lot had for some years seen Hawaii slipping away from the Hawaiians. Not only had they lost their land, they had lost their ability to hold what was rightfully theirs in terms of heritage and culture as well. Kamehameha V resented the liberal constitution under which his father had ruled and under which his brother continued to rule. He, like Kalakaua, looked to their roots of a strong Hawaii under Kamehameha I and saw it being destroyed inch by inch by foreign diseases, land-grabbing, and cultural extinction. The dwindling of the native Hawaiian population, which continued despite Queen Emma's establishment of a hospital for natives and foreigners, was discouraging enough. More discouraging was the loss of self-worth and the ability to hold on to and have pride in a culture full of tradition.

Kamehameha V decided the first step to a return of Hawaii for Hawaiians would be a return to a monarchy they could understand. He requested a constitutional convention to change the 1852 Constitution to a more monarchial one. When he received nothing but opposition, he consulted with Attorney General C. C. Harris and Harris' one-time law student, Kalakaua, and found that although critics might insist he needed a constitutional convention, if he had the courage he could follow the wishes of his people.

In May and June Kamehameha V toured the outer islands. He asked *his* people—the Hawaiians of Hawaii, not the politicians nor the foreigners—what *their* wishes were. He found an enthusiastic response, a strong surge against the current restrictions on monarchial power, as stated in the provisions of the 1852 Constitution. Mainly, he discovered the people intensely loyal to him and his purposes.

Back in Honolulu, the king called for a constitutional convention. Nothing but acrimony resulted, not only in the constitutional meetings but also in newspapers, public meetings, and private conversations.

Kamehameha V took matters into his own hands and stated: "I will give you a Constitution." And so he did: the Constitution of 1864.

The new constitution gave greater power to the king and his appointed cabinet, curtailing the powers of the privy council and legislative assembly. It also abolished the honorary office of *kuhina nui* "as unnecessary and expensive." Hawaii was to be governed by this monarchial constitution for twenty-three years, until the Bayonet Constitution of 1887 was forced upon Kalakaua.

Secondly, Kamehameha v sought to reestablish the heritage his people had lost. He chose Kalakaua as his emissary. Sophia Cracroft presented her view of Kalakaua's popularity among the Hawaiian people:

"Buckland [Lady Franklin's maid] saw Col. Kalakaua (who is greatly loved by the natives for his amiable character and because he is one of the highest families of pure descent) seated by an old woman with his hands on her shoulders. She had drawn them forward and was kissing first one and then the other with every sign of affection."

The old men and women, who had vivid memories of the cordial, entertaining, and generous Liliha, welcomed him into their homes, recited genealogies, recounted legends and history. Kamehameha v, therefore, sent Kalakaua among the natives in the back country to find the culture of the past. There seemed to be a resurgence of interest in the past to which the *haole* did not at first protest.

❋ ❋ ❋

Then came a setback. Princess Victoria, sister of Kamehameha v, died on May 29, 1866, at the age of twenty-eight. Because of the Hawaiian custom of lying in state, journalists at home and abroad suddenly brought accusations against the Hawaiians as "heathen" and "pagan" with little hope of redemption. The old Hawaiian ways were severely condemned.

Kamehameha v, who had ambivalent feelings about his sister, was at a cultural crossroads. He had stopped her from being *kuhina nui*, but she never wanted to be co-ruler. As has been noted, she had suffered severely from cultural shock and her abortive romance. As a result, she had returned to alcohol and the "old ways"—ways deemed by the *haole* "heathen" and "pagan," full of "evil" and "eroticism."

Although Kamehameha V had returned the country to a monarchial form of government, he recognized that the culture and customs were not respected. Yet his conscience bothered him, and he decided his sister should have the traditional royal funeral that she would have wanted.

Victoria's body lay in state at the palace for nearly four weeks. The chamber was darkened, and the walls and ceilings were draped and festooned with black. The *kahili* bearers, six on each side, stood as the honor guard under the command of Kalakaua. His sister Lydia, and his wife, Kapiolani, shared the death-watch duties with other high chiefesses, one of whom was in attendance at all times.

The tragedy of the situation was that Kamehameha V forgot the disrespect that could come from the *haole*. The first evening the palace doors had been open for all to view the body and gather in the courtyard. It soon became evident, however, that the foreigners did not respect the living or the dead and turned the scene into one of rowdy desecration, attempting to join the sacred hula dancers and pushing wildly for "front row" views. Kamehameha promptly placed a ban on the *haole* spectators.

Disgruntled, they watched from a distance in a *haole* home, where they could see inside the palace gates. A journalist wrote of the scene with condemnation:

"Hula girls attired in white bodices and full skirts, wreaths of white flowers about their shoulders and garlands of green leaves on their heads danced rhythmically, slowly, in the center of a large assembly. The palace grounds were illumined by candle-nut torches . . . a dozen native women locked arms and swayed back and forth wailing the death songs."[14]

On June 30, 1866, the funeral of the princess took place from Kawaiahao Church. The services were read by Reverend H. H. Parker, later a pulpit slanderer of Kalakaua.

By the 1870s, Kalakaua was beginning to feel the pressure of poverty that nearly all Hawaiians were either now or soon to experience. He wrote, "Auwe to be poor–it is difficult."

❊ ❊ ❊

It is true that the Kalakaua family did not have the riches of the Kamehamehas. His father, Kapaakea, had died in 1856 and his mother, Keohokalole, had inherited part of the lands of her father High Chief Aikanaka. One-half of the lands went to his younger brother, who had died in 1868, and was passed on to his heirs. The lands that came to Kalakaua were few. His government salaries were low and his talent for making money in the *haole* way was negligible.

But as Queen Emma wrote to her cousin Peter Kaeo, Kalakaua was constantly trying "to better himself." "With Taffy's [Kalakaua's nickname] faults we must give him credit for great ambition . . . he has faltered but he keeps on trying . . . this is a good point in him which we must copy. He is not idle, he has stumbled and blundered before the public till actually he really has gained courage amongst them and can speak out and write boldly."[15]

Emma's reference to Kalakaua's "faults," faltering, stumbling, and blundering referred to Kalakaua's disastrous tenure as postmaster and his engagement in newspaper work. Along with his political duties, Kalakaua's dreams and interests were with the arts.

In 1865 he joined Hawaiian John Kapena in publishing *Ke Au Okoa (The New Era)* to protest rising American domination. Kalakaua continued through the years to write for pro-Hawaiian publications. His previous venture in the *Hoku* and this one proved to be financially disastrous. As late as 1870, Kalakaua promoted at his own expense (he received some Aikanaka lands in 1868) *Ka Manawa*–the first daily newspaper written in Hawaiian for Hawaiians. Unfortunately, it lasted only two months due to financial problems. While it stressed genealogies, *mele*, and legends, it also carried local and international news. For the first time, Kalakaua signed his pieces as "Figgs."[16]

In the early 1870s, with a young wife to support, Kalakaua reached for a means to support himself beyond his salaries as chamberlain, attorney (he passed the bar in 1871), and as clerk in the Land Office. He became an inventor–not a lucrative position. Remembering the wonderful ships he had visited during his trip to Canada, he turned his attention to naval defense.[17] He recalled Liliha's visit to Dom Pedro, Emperor of Brazil, and on September 19, 1872, he wrote the Emperor for funds to build a torpedo-proof vessel. Dom Pedro proved to be interested in the young Kalakaua, but not enough to invest moneys in his invention. Kalakaua then wrote Queen Victoria of England.

". . . I flatter myself . . . Among inventors of instruments of naval warfare to have invented a submarine torpedo for the destruction of an enemy vessel advancing on a hostile coast . . . the important feature of the invention is the direct action of destruction and the sure annihilation of anything crossing its way . . . I may safely assert that there is nothing afloat with the thickness of iron armour and carrying a plate of three to four inches thick at the ship's bottom . . . save the invention proposed by me and submitted to the British government."

Long before electricity had found its way to common use, Kalakaua presented to both countries a "fish torpedo to be driven by electricity . . . in contrast to wind and steam."

Among the less ambitious projects was "Kalakaua's improved bottle cover" [stopper] of November 16, 1872–his thirty-sixth birthday. One hundred years later such an invention was to appear and be exceedingly popular.

* * *

Kamehameha v died on December 11, 1872, at the age of forty-two, without appointing a successor and without leaving a will. As a result, the country took on a new aspect.

Much has been said and written about Kamehameha v's possible choice. The most common one has been Bernice Pauahi Bishop, wife of Charles Reed Bishop and childhood sweetheart of Kamehameha v.

According to John Owen Dominis, husband of the later Queen Liliuokalani, who took meticulous notes at the time of the king's death, Bernice *was* asked by the king to be queen. She, however, refused. Dowager Queen Emma was suggested but rejected by the king as having been queen "only by marriage."

Another choice was Lunalilo, but strained relations had long existed between him and Kamehameha v, beginning with their lineal descent relationship and continuing through the abortive engagement of Lunalilo and the king's sister, Victoria. During the reigns of the Kamehamehas, Lunalilo protested that he had never been fairly treated, for he was never appointed to a government position. The reason might be explained by the fact that Lunalilo's excessive behavior in spending moneys, drinking alcohol, and general carousing had caused his father to place him under Charles R. Bishop's guardianship.

Because Kamehameha v died without a will, the Crown lands that should have followed the Crown became disputable. The Kamehameha lands, which had so long supported the royal family, were the thorns that surrounded the rose that Kalakaua felt might be his for the plucking, for as Kamehameha v had died without a successor, the people could "elect" their king.

3 Interregnums

The Kamehamehas were gone. The first part of Liliha's prophecy had come true. Kalakaua had seen the end of the Kamehamehas. But Kalakaua was not king.

The king was to be elected.

There were four possible contenders: Lunalilo; Bernice Bishop, who had already refused the throne; Ruth Keelikolani, who did not speak English; and Kalakaua. Thus, Lunalilo and Kalakaua became the only elective opponents.

Kalakaua was not liked by the *haole*, as he represented to them Kamehameha V with his "old ideas"–a return to the past, Hawaii for Hawaiians. He was not strongly supported by the Hawaiians; in the eyes of many he was not "royal" as the Kamehamehas were.

Nevertheless, during the interregnum Kalakaua put forth his platform in a Hawaiian rhetoric reflecting what he had learned was desirable among the Hawaiians. He pointed to the past, but also touched on the current problems of the times.

"I shall obey the advice of our ancestor of Keaweahuelu, [sic] my grandfather, which he gave to Kamehameha I, to be the rule for his government: 'The old men, the old women and the children shall lie in safety on the highways,' preserve and increase the people, put native Hawaiians into Government offices, amend the Constitution of 1864."

Scant attention was paid to Kalakaua, and Sanford Ballard Dole wrote that Lunalilo intended to proclaim himself king no matter what happened in the legislative election:

"Therefore we supported him, paying little attention to Kalakaua." Kalakaua was fully aware that he was not popular with the *haole* or some of the Hawaiians. It troubled him that he was once again "outside."

Despite the fact that Kamehameha v had been overwhelmingly supported in his new constitution, Lunalilo's promise, based largely on his own personal rancor against the Kamehamehas, was to destroy the 1864 constitution and go back to the one of 1852. This, along with his personal charm and his high lineage—he was a lineal descendant of the Kamehamehas—was to win him the election.

Lunalilo declared that there should be a free election. Although the legislature would elect the king, a popular election was held on January 1, 1873. Lunalilo was overwhelmingly, unofficially "elected" by the people, and the legislature followed the lead. Lunalilo was king.

Lunalilo had been a schoolmate of Kalakaua's and the envy of the children of the High Chiefs' School. His mother, Auhea, the premier to the king, spoiled him outrageously. She visited him constantly, bringing gifts and even sending his *kahu* to the school to be with him. Auhea struggled continuously with Cookes for special privileges—even to the point of insisting she should sleep near her son when he was ill. This is one thing she was irreversibly refused.

One day Lunalilo's *kahu* brought him an unbroken horse. Lunalilo decided he would break the horse immediately before an audience. He jumped on its back and a daring ride followed, one in which Lunalilo was thrown heavily to the ground—but unhurt. His *kahu* was caught immediately, for a *kahu* was responsible for his master and could be punished severely, could even be put to death if his charge were injured.

A crowd of the High Chiefs' School's children, *haole* and Hawaiian spectators, closed in upon the terrified *kahu*, who was in the grip of Lunalilo's father. Into the tense air strode

Lunalilo to demand that the *kahu* not only be released but given his freedom.

This freeing of the *kahu* reflected Lunalilo's generous nature, and the crowd cheered him as "one of the people."

He was a delightful young democratic chief. He won the hearts of the *haole* and Hawaiians alike. He was a devotee of Shakespeare and at the slightest provocation recited long passages. He had an impressive tenor voice, and he sang in the homes of the both the Americans and the British—baiting each with songs and praises of the other. Then he would throw his arms about his host and explain, in not an altogether sober voice, that he had only been joking. Sometimes there was tearful laughter.[1]

❋ ❋ ❋

When Lunalilo learned of his election by the legislature, he walked bareheaded through the throngs to Kawaiahao Church to take his oath of office. His visits to the outer islands were huge successes. People from around the country brought him gifts and piled *lei* of *maile* and *ohia* blossoms upon him. He was their idol. He represented all a king should be: fatherly and beloved of his people for his benevolence—his *mana* (wisdom and strength).

❋ ❋ ❋

Once Lunalilo had been elected king, Kalakaua moved gracefully to read in Hawaiian his own congratulations and the proclamation of the new king to the legislature.

The most surprising appointment by Lunalilo to his cabinet was Charles Bishop, as minister of Foreign Affairs. He had resented Bishop as his guardian, but surprisingly, must have recognized him as a shrewd businessman. All his cabinet members were Americans, except one, Robert Stirling, who was a Scotsman.

Kalakaua was relegated to a minor position during Lunalilo's reign. He served as a fireman and a substitute governor of Oahu during a short absence of John Dominis.

He was finally appointed a member of the Board of Land Appraisers of Oahu, a job he was eminently qualified for after his experience with Harris, but he was allowed only a subordinate position. It was an advancement from his clerkship, but he did not head the Board.

Lunalilo's regime was one full of the gaiety that predominated his life. Music, theater, singing clubs of the *alii* were all promoted. Once again, annexation talk was begun, and a secret mission of Major General John M. Schofield and Brevet Brigadier General B. S. Alexander[2] was sent by the United States secretary of war to "ascertain the value of Pearl River Harbor." Talk was renewed for the cessation of Pearl Harbor in return, possibly, for reciprocity on sugar sent to the United States. Charles Bishop, as minister of foreign affairs, said that such a move would not be a part of annexation; the natives, however, thought otherwise. Queen Emma spoke for them: "The reciprocity treaty, giving away land, is much discussed these days . . . There is a feeling of bitterness against these rude people who dwell on our land and have high handed ideas of giving away somebody else's property as if it were theirs."[3]

Lunalilo remained in the peculiarly fatherly position of listening, for a time committing himself to the proposition, and then withdrawing his acquiescence ". . .no doubt influenced by the fear of revolution among [the] people." C. R. Bishop wrote to Secretary Hamilton Fish of the United States that ". . . reports received from other islands indicate excitement and turbulence of feeling among the Masses [against reciprocity]."[4] Another problem, the segregation of lepers, was a part of Lunalilo's reign, resulting in the establishment of a new Board of Health.

Leprosy was a serious problem in Hawaii.[5] It is not known when or from where leprosy came to Hawaii, although some suspected as early as 1840 that it came from China, there being frequent travel between the two countries. The disease came to public notice in a Board of Health report in 1863 when outbreaks were becoming alarming. Enforced segregation came in 1865 by the Board of Health, when the legislature passed an act to Prevent the Spread of Leprosy.

The lepers were then sent to Kalaupapa on Molokai. Conditions were abominable. The lepers often were starving, as barely enough *poi* and beef were sent each week. There were also non-lepers, close relatives of the ill, who volunteered to work with them, but their help was often such a drain on the food supply that the lepers began to resent them.

Morale was extremely low, as the lepers had nothing to look forward to but getting worse and dying. Government agents often cheated the lepers and furnished them with island-made alcohol.

Under the new Board of Health, persons who had been cheated by agents were repaid and the food supply was increased and varied. A store was established and money given to the leper to buy his clothes rather than receiving cast-offs from agents who doled them out.

Lunalilo also made attempts to change the 1864 constitution, and like the three previous kings, tried to gain a reciprocity treaty with the United States, offering a lease on Pearl River, an action which caused such a storm of fury among the people the attempt was discontinued.

During Lunalilo's reign, Kalakaua figured prominently but negatively at the time of the Barracks Revolt. The barracks of the Household Troops, some sixty men who made up the entire standing army of the kingdom, had for some time resented their drillmaster, Captain Joseph Jajczay and Adjutant General Charles H. Judd. Early in September 1873, the barracks flamed into open revolt. Several soldiers had been punished for disciplinary reasons by violent and angry actions of Jajczay and supported by Judd.

David Leleo Kinimaka,[6] Kalakaua's *hanai* half-brother and a member of the guards, had brought the smoldering resentment to Kalakaua. Kalakaua, who sympathized with the military, sided with the mutineers and advised and instigated them in their refusal to accept conciliatory messages from Lunalilo, who was recuperating in Waikiki from an attack of tuberculosis and alcoholism. Finally the word of the king was accepted. "If you shall implicitly obey this my command, then I shall be on your side, as a father to his children, and I will protect you from injury."

The consequences, however, were serious. Lunalilo abolished the Household Troops except for the band, but not before they had ransacked the barracks. Feelings ran along racial lines: in favor of the mutineers were the Hawaiians and opposed were the *haole*. The incident was humiliating to the government, for it revealed its lack of power and control. The legislature and the king's ministers were flailed by the newspapers. The *Advertiser* stated they were ". . . incompetent in case of emergency," suffered from "dullness of apprehension . . ." "poverty of resources . . ." and consequently "left the country helpless." Fear arose that the government could not cope with any emergency.

If Kalakaua had a few moments of pleasure to behold the embarrassment of Lunalilo, they were short-lived, and the results of the incident were later to boomerang back to him.

After a brief reign, Lunalilo became ill and was sent to Kailua-Kona. He was accompanied by his physician, Dr. Trouseau; his chamberlain, Charles Judd; his father, Kanaina; Queen Emma and others of the *alii*; but not Kalakaua. "The Hawaiian band of native musicians and others did all they could to distract the king from his illness," Liliuokalani later wrote in her *Story*. During this time, he was frequently requested to appoint a successor—certainly not a request which would "distract" him from his illness. His only comment was that he "owed [his] sceptre to the people and [saw] no reason why the people should not elect [his] successor."

Soon it became evident that Lunalilo was failing rapidly. He was brought to Honolulu with his royal court in attendance. When it became evident that the king was dying, Emma's advisors foresaw danger and encouraged Emma to influence Lunalilo in her favor for succession before his death. Emma agreed; however, nothing could have been more unfavorable to Lunalilo, who cared little for the Kamehameha-royal Emma. But her advisors counted heavily on her popularity with the natives and their love for their queens.

Lunalilo died slowly but peacefully at the age of thirty-nine. He roused several times before his passing to express his desire not to be "associated with his Kamehameha cousins." He requested that he not be buried in the Nuuanu Valley Mausoleum, but at Kawaiahao Churchyard, "among the common people who loved him." The night before his demise, he stated he wanted none of the royal trappings buried with him. He had all his kingly insignia destroyed. His final words, in good Shakespearean tradition, were "Alien touch shall not finger my crown or traitor breath stir the feathers upon my raiment."

At eight o'clock on February 3, 1874, the guns from Punch Bowl Hill announced the death of King Lunalilo. Notice was given that the remains of the king would lie in state between the hours of 10:00 a.m. and 2:00 p.m. in the palace. The Honolulu Rifles were drawn in front of the palace as a guard of honor. Within were the ministers of state and the *alii*. It was a royal lying-in-state.

Lunalilo, after a year and twenty-five days of reign, left a Hawaiian nation that was strongly against annexation and cession of any territory and a newly elected legislative assembly comprised of nearly all natives. He also left behind him another interregnum.

More important, he left a will in which his property was to go to Kamehameha v, now deceased, to his father, Kanaina, and then to a home for the old, the poor, the indigent. He said that in leaving his property thus, that he was continuing further along the line of the "law of the splintered paddle:" the law that the wayfarer should be kept safe from marauders. Now the old should not only have the right to lie down on the wayside in safety, but in a home, in peace and contentment. Interestingly, here he resorted to Kalakaua's cry of remembrance of the old ways. Nevertheless, he was the typical liberal king of the people: the man who preferred to leave a country moving further toward bankruptcy than allow the people to think of him as less than a "liberal humanitarian." The disputed crownlands, Kamehameha's and Lunalilo's personal lands, were to be a bone of contention beyond the time of the overthrow, even to the present day.

* * *

The country was now to go into a second interregnum.[7]

The day after Lunalilo died, Kalakaua declared himself a candidate for the throne. The next day Queen Emma did the same. The first real animosity between the Kamehamehas and Kalakaua began to appear.

Kalakaua put forth his proclamation in a dignified, calm statement quite unlike his proclamation given at the time of the first interregnum.

> "To the Hawaiian Nation.[8]
>
> "SALUTATIONS to YOU—Whereas His Majesty Lunalilo departed this life at the hour of nine o'clock last night; and by his death the Throne of Hawaii is left vacant, and the nation is without a head or a guide. In this juncture it is proper that we should seek for a Sovereign and Leader, and in doing so, follow the course prescribed by Article 22d of the Constitution. My earnest desire is for the perpetuity of the Crown and the permanent independence of the government and people of Hawaii, on the basis of the equity, liberty, prosperity, progress and protection of the whole people.

"It will be remembered that at the time of the election of the late lamented Sovereign, I put forward my own claim to the Throne of our beloved country, on Constitutional grounds—and it is upon those grounds only that I now prefer my claims, and call upon you to listen to my call, and request you to instruct your Representatives to consider, and weigh well, and to regard your choice to elect me, the oldest member of a family high in rank in the country.

"Therefore, I, *David Ekamackamacanaia* [sic] *Naloiachu* [sic] *Kalakaua*, cheerfully call upon you, and respectfully ask you to grant me your support.

D. KALAKAUA
Iolani Palace, Feb. 4, 1874."

Queen Emma issued her proclamation the next day:

"*To the Hawaiian People*:

"WHEREAS, His late lamented Majesty LUNA-LILO died on the 3rd of February, 1874, without having publicly proclaimed a Successor to the Throne; and whereas,

"His late Majesty did before his final sickness declare his wish and intention that the undersigned should be his Successor on the Throne of the Hawaiian Islands, and enjoined upon me not to decline the same under any circumstances; and whereas,

"Many of the Hawaiian people have since the death of His Majesty urged me to place myself in nomination at the ensuing session of the Legislature;

"Therefore, in view of the foregoing considerations and my duty to the people and to the memory of the late King, I do hereby announce and declare that I am a Candidate for the Throne of these Hawaiian Islands, and I request my beloved people throughout the group, to assemble peaceably and orderly in their districts, and to give formal expression to their

views on this important subject, and to instruct their
Representatives in the coming session of the Legislature.
"*God Protect Hawaii!*"

Honolulu, Feb. 5, 1874
EMMA KALELEONALANI."

It was evident from the beginning that many of the
Hawaiians and the British preferred Emma. The pro-United
States faction opposed Emma on the basis of her pro-British
leanings, but only halfheartedly supported Kalakaua because
of his strong "Hawaii for Hawaiians" position. Yet he
seemed the lesser of two evils.

Remembering how Lunalilo had virtually proclaimed
himself king, the backers of Kalakaua moved swiftly to
bring in legislators from the outer islands to demand a
proper legislative election. On Oahu, mass meetings were
held and Emma seemed to be the favorite. Emma, like
Lunalilo, promoted a "popular election," but as the voting
took place at her home, the results were disregarded.

The mood of the election was ugly, and the *haole* of
Honolulu requested warships to stand by. For nine days the
campaign raged in the newspapers and in privately printed
pamphlets.

While it seemed that the majority of the *haole* papers favored Kalakaua and negated Emma, some Hawaiian papers
and all the privately printed pamphlets favored Emma. The
latter were printed in Hawaiian and not translated until after
the election.

The *Nu Hou Extra* on February 6, 1874, gave a gentle rep-
rimand to Queen Emma that it was known that Lunalilo
had not appointed her his successor. The writer blamed
"unwise friends" for prompting her to put forth her claim,
and begged her to "be content to be hailed as Queen of Benevolence and Mercy—and not as Queen of a small political

party . . . the Hawaiian people will love her as a benefactress and hate her as a politician."

In the *Hawaii Ponoi Extra* of February 7, Charles Reed Bishop was quoted as saying that although King Lunalilo had been "repeatedly urged . . . to nominate a Successor to the Throne, he had nominated no one whatever," either officially or in private. It ended by proclaiming Kalakaua as having the strongest claims to the votes and confidence of the people . . . "He is the eldest male representative of a Princely Hawaiian family, which is undoubtedly next to the House of Kamehameha, and is entitled to the highest consideration in this country."

This news article was followed immediately by a pamphlet "To the Public" from Queen Emma in which she resorted to establishing her genealogy as superior to "any other person;" she was quoted as having established "Queen's Hospital;" and as being a person of wealth. As "a person of wealth, and extensive lands," being the heir of Lunalilo, she would save a government money . . . "The Queen, if made our Sovereign, would be the person to contribute to that discharge [government debt] by living on her own private income, and dispensing with any allowance from the Treasury."

The *Nu Hou Extra* of February 10, published a rebuttal:

"The unwise friends of Queen Emma have again published a very foolish paper." It denied her being the heiress of King Lunalilo. The refutation went on:

"They say she built the Queen's Hospital. But this is not true. It was built with the money of the people—native and foreign. Her Majesty's name is given to it, because it was built during the reign of her husband.

"They speak of Queen Emma's benevolence to her servants, and to many children whom she educates, which is true and is true of all chiefs, but it must be remembered that she receives six thousand dollars a year from the representatives of the people which enables her to perform her good deeds.

"It is said that we want to ignore her Majesty's desire for the Throne, but we do not, as we are now satisfied that she has been planning for a long time to gain the position . . ." Newspapers raged on: Against a "petticoat government" it was better to have "that garment than a pair of pants, with boots for the purpose of kicking the people about."

One mass meeting followed another with proclamations read from the candidates. Queen Emma had a letter read from High Chief Charles Kanaina, father of Lunalilo, saying that at Kailua-Kona (where the late king had been attempting to recover his declining health), Lunalilo had expressed his intention to appoint Queen Emma, but that his cabinet refused to act. She began making other promises such as that she would "select natives to fill the offices," revise the constitution to conform with the constitution of Kamehameha III, and reduce salaries of government officials.

Kalakaua's second proclamation came out similar to his first, tying him to the constitution and claiming that the Kawaiahao Church mass meeting had selected him as "Successor to the Throne:"

> "His late Majesty died without nominating or pro-
> claiming a Successor to the Throne, and it therefore
> devolves upon the Legislative Assembly, under the
> Constitution, to elect a Sovereign.
>
> "I accept your nomination of myself to this high
> and responsible position of Guardian of the Govern-
> ment, with the earnest hope that Government may be
> conducted wisely, and so as to secure and perpetuate
> our national independence and the preservation and
> prosperity of our race.
>
> "*God Preserve Hawaii!*
>
> KALAKAUA."

The *Gazette* of February 11, calling him for the first time "Prince," indicating he came from a royal household, gave three reasons for him to be elected king:

"1–He has been nominated unanimously by mass-meetings, not only in this city, but in various districts on this and the other islands of the group, clearly indicating the popular preference for Sovereign.

"2–His election will result in providing a Prince to succeed him [his younger brother] even should he leave no children, and thus prevent the recurrence of these dangerous interregnums, which are so demoralizing to the people, and which ought to be guarded against.

"3–A King will be more acceptable and undoubtedly be able to give more satisfaction to his people in the administration of the Government than a Queen could possibly give."

Numerous other circulars, mostly anonymous, were printed in Hawaiian, favoring Queen Emma. They were incendiary in style, but repetitious in content except for a few additions such as the one exhorting women to put forth their claims for Queen Emma:

"Ye wives of the Representatives, beg, coax, and draw the hearts of your husbands. Induce, persuade and lead the thoughts of your husbands to the one you are thinking on. If your husband does not consent to your desire, it will show that he despises you. Husband and wife should be of one mind, not merely companions."

Reassurance was given by Queen Emma's supporters that Emma would not marry a foreigner, and if not a high chief, a Hawaiian commoner.

❊ ❊ ❊

Despite a campaign that seemed to make Emma the favorite, the Legislature elected Kalakaua king by a thirty-nine to six vote. A violent disturbance broke out.

When the announcement was made that Kalakaua was king, cheering began but was silenced almost immediately by the police. Cheering was heard outside, but it was also mingled with yells and cries of rage.

The Queenites or Emmaites incited the crowd against the representatives who had voted for Kalakaua. The cry was that they had voted "against the wishes of the people." When the committee that was to notify the king of his election left the office, the outbreak began. The carriage was attacked and demolished. The rioters used the spokes and other pieces of the carriage to attack the committee. The members then sought refuge in the courthouse. The mob continued threatening their lives despite intervention of the marshal and deputy and many "well-known foreigners." The native police, according to the newspapers, were of "little or no use."

The doors of the courthouse were broken down and the mob surged in. Furniture was broken and thrown from the building. Papers were indiscriminately destroyed. Only the library and the office of the clerks of the court were untouched, as the clerk and the sheriff persuaded the rioters that "the contents were properties of the people."

After destroying property, the rioters began attacking the committee members. The scene of violence continued to threaten the lives of the committee—one person was killed and many were wounded.

While Emma waited in her home, Kalakaua waited for results in Kapiolani's home where were gathered Kalakaua's brother Leleiohoku, his sister Lydia Kamakaeha, and Princess Pauahi Bishop. The news, not only of the election but of the riot, was brought by Charles Reed Bishop and John Owen Dominis (Lydia's husband).

Bishop recommended that protection be immediately called for. To his chagrin, Kalakaua's first official act as king-elect was to call on foreign ships for aid. He must have remembered the Barracks Revolt and its unfortunate results. A request from the king-elect, the minister of foreign affairs, and the governor of Oahu was made to the representatives of

Great Britain and the United States for land forces. In a short time, marines and sailors from the USS *Tuscarora* and *Portsmouth* and BHS *Tenedos* landed and took possession of the courthouse and grounds.

The hostilities gradually ceased. A few rioters were arrested, but most walked off in triumph to Queen Emma's residence. The Queen was cheered and incendiary speeches continued to be made.

A paper supportive of Kalakaua noted:

"In this [riot] connection it should be stated that while the riot was at its height, a member of the House of Nobles drove to the Queen's residence and begged of her to go down to the Court House to use her personal influence in dispersing the mob and preventing the spilling of blood which he represented as imminent. The Queen is stated to have treated this message with indifference, as no concern of hers. Subsequently she promised another gentleman that she would go, but did not go. She sent, however, a note to be read to the rioters, which was addressed to 'My People,' and was in substance to this effect: That if they could not obtain their desires now, perhaps they had better wait until the morrow, when a new election for Sovereign could be had!"

The press lamented the lack of effective police action.

"As no outbreak of this kind had been anticipated, no firearms had been provided. The Marshal had one or two pistols in his office, and two of the Representatives were armed with pistols, but they were not used; and it is perhaps as well that they were not discharged, as the number could have had but little effect in staying the riot, and may have increased it. Had there been twenty-five armed persons in the building at the outset, there would have been no outbreak. It was this entire absence of means of defence that encouraged the rioters . . . They had assembled in the morning at the residence of Queen Emma, and a little before noon marched in squads of a hundred or more to the Court House, where they remained till the election was over, the leaders constantly haranguing the populace. Although there were several hundred engaged in the riot, it will probably be found that the leaders and promoters do not exceed a dozen . . ."

The last of the mob was finally dispersed from Queen Emma's yard by the marines. Queen Emma did not insist on a new election. Shortly after the foreign representatives had acknowledged Kalakaua king, Queen Emma proclaimed her allegiance to him.

There followed days of newspaper speculation about the riot—its cause and the results. Queen Emma was held largely responsible for inciting the riot by permitting a meeting at her home before the election, for not intervening later to stop the bloodshed, and lastly for implying there would be a second election. A great deal of discussion burst forth about the need for police and military protection.

From the *Gazette*:

"We all supposed ourselves to be tolerably well protected by the volunteer companies, which now we find are unreliable. They were ordered out before a blow was struck, but the officers reported that no dependence could be placed on them. Hence, when too late, we found ourselves defenseless, and welcomed the intervention of a foreign armed force. Let us now profit from our experience and provide such means of as can be relied on in any future emergency."

There was no more talk of a second election, and Kalakaua took his oath of office on February 12, 1874, to uphold the Constitution of 1864, which Kamehameha v had instituted. The oath of office was taken not at Kawaiahao Church where the previous kings had taken theirs, but in the Aliiolani Hale. Was it fear of another uprising and Kalakaua dared not go to the Church? According to the newspapers of the period, the choice was made by Kalakaua himself who had said to Charles Reed Bishop that the palace was the proper place for a "Coronation,"[9] but the current palace was not ready as it had been considered for reconstruction for some time. Also, Kalakaua was not a member of the Kawaiahao Church, but a member of the Episcopal Church. As the latter church had entered into the electioneering controversy with Queen Emma, Kalakaua chose neutral ground.

It was an inauspicious beginning for Kalakaua. It left him uneasy about his position, and because of rumors and threats of assassination, he became deeply concerned for his personal safety and that of his immediate and extended family.

4 *The Good Years (1874–1880)*

Even Kalakaua's good years were uneasy ones. His election had been a poor beginning, and he was unsure of himself and his position.

He stood on divisive ground to take his oath as king. Nevertheless, he immediately took up his duties as executive officer. He was described as calm and in control. When he arrived to prorogue his first legislative assembly, the *Advertiser* further reported:

"His Majesty, who was looking extremely well, was attired in a plain black suit, with the star and ribband, and wore the decoration of a Commander of the Order of Francis Joseph of Austria. Both on the arrival and departure of the Royal Cortege, the crowd at the Court House and in the streets cheered heartily." This reception gave Kalakaua some respite from anxiety.

His stature and air of confidence made for a striking royal portrait. He was of large proportions, above the medium height; his copper-colored skin offset by full length whiskers and moustache, dark, curly hair, and fine white teeth. His mannerisms were natural, though dignified; his voice was soft, almost musical. When he spoke English he evidenced a slight New England accent. But most powerful was the character of the eyes; accentuated with prominent bushy eyebrows, they blended the diverse strains of his personality and race—fierce, uncompromising and powerful, though remarkably gentle, embodying the paradoxes of the Polynesian blood that no *haole* could fully understand.

❊ ❊ ❊

At twelve noon, His Majesty, reported the papers, accompanied by his aids, left the palace under salutes from Punch Bowl battery BHS *Tenedos* and the USS *Tuscarora*, and was escorted by the Hawaiian Cavalry. On the arrival of His Majesty at the courthouse the foreign troops and the Honolulu Rifles were drawn up in front of the building and received the king with the usual honors. He rode down in the State Carriage, accompanied by his brother, Prince William Leleiohoku, and brother-in-law, Hon. A. S. Cleghorn (husband of Likelike, younger sister of Kalakaua).

When he entered the Legislative Hall, the audience rose while he proceeded to the president's desk and remained standing while he was present. Prayer was offered by the chaplain of the assembly, after which the king read the following address, in Hawaiian and English, proroguing the assembly:

> "NOBLES AND REPRESENTATIVES:
> "The vacancy of the Throne of Our Kingdom by the demise, on the 3rd inst. of Our much lamented Predecessor, made it necessary for you to meet in extraordinary session . . .
> "By your free choice I am now King, and I hope, with your aid and that of all my faithful subjects, to make My Reign a blessing to my people . . .
> "I desire again to thank you for your partiality and kindness towards Myself, and I pray the Almighty that He will continue to protect and prosper our Kingdom . . ."

His first act as king was to appoint his brother, William Pitt Leleiohoku, as successor to the throne; there would not be another interregnum.

He quickly moved to select a new cabinet, one for which the newspapers of the time, both pro and con, had nothing but praise. It was noted that he chose for his ministers representatives of Hawaiian, English, German, and American nationalities.

Governor of Maui Paul Nahaolelua, new minister of finance, was "one of the few left of the educated petty chiefs having served under Kamehameha III." The seventy-year old Nahaolelua held a family connection to Queen Dowager Emma and was a "just and proper concession to the native Hawaiians."

W. L. Green, minister of foreign affairs, was an English merchant. He was praised for his "culture and enterprising habits . . . believed to be devoid of national prejudices."

Judge Widemann, minister of interior, stood out for his "liberal views," industrious habits, and understanding of the Hawaiians.

Of Judge Hartwell, attorney general, it was said "The cabinet has been strengthened at the expense of the Bench."

After summing up the "personnel" of the new cabinet, the newspapers generally agreed that the country "has a right to expect at the hands of this Ministry, an administration of the Government which shall be characterized by the positive evidence of enterprise, prudence and strength. It will be our province in the future, as it has been in the past, as independent public journalists to closely watch the course of public men, equally prepared to award the need of praise or apply the lash of criticism, as the necessity for either alternative may arise."

For his first justice of the Supreme Court, not surprisingly, he appointed his old friend and mentor, Charles Coffin Harris. The press paid high honor to Harris, and Second Associate Judd. It went on to say:

"For the first time since its organization in 1846, all the seats of the Supreme Bench are occupied by men bred to the law . . . in the maintenance of the purity and integrity of the Supreme Court—the tribunal of last resort—lies the security of our independence, and of all that we hold dear."

Cheered by the newspaper reports, Kalakaua began to feel more comfortable in his garment of king.

He lost no time in attacking a problem he felt was major—one of which he had been long aware but now had come to the public's attention—that of military and police protection for the country. Within two weeks he wrote and proclaimed under W. L. Green as "Secretary of War" seventeen rules and regulations to govern the military forces of the kingdom. These were followed the same day by "Articles of War"—rules governing the Royal Guard and volunteer forces when on active duty. They were clear-cut and comprehensive. The *Advertiser* commented:

"MILITARY REORGANIZATION—By reference to the official documents which appear in to-day's paper, emanating from the office of the Secretary of War, it will be seen that the Military service is to be reorganized, and placed upon what appears to be a basis that will ensure efficiency, economy and proper discipline. The knowledge and experience of Attorney General Hartwell will be invaluable in this connection. Major J. Bates Dickson, who has been appointed as Aid to the Secretary, is no holiday soldier, having seen several years of active service in the late American War."

The speed at which King Kalakaua operated was a surprise to many. But he had yet one final duty before the second interregnum was to be completed. He needed both to organize and step aside for the obsequies of the late King Lunalilo.

* * *

Lunalilo's funeral took place on Saturday, February 28, 1874. Early in the morning a crowd of 6,000 people began to gather along the streets of Honolulu, where the procession was to pass. Stores and business were officially closed.

Shortly after ten o'clock, the Marines and seamen from the four war vessels in port marched onto the palace ground, taking their positions on the west side of King Street. On the east side were different civic groups: firemen, Good Templars, Knights of Pythias, Odd Fellows, and Knight Templars.

At noon the procession began to move through the streets to the mausoleum. An estimated 1,500 persons, including the Royal Hawaiian Band, were present in the procession. The hearse, heavily draped with black, was drawn by four black horses.

In the mausoleum were gathered members of the Kalakaua family, Princess Ruth, Queen Emma, and Lunalilo's father, Kanaina.

At the time of Lunalilo's death, his family had no mausoleum and his remains had to be immured in the Kamehameha crypt to await a second burial, when his own tomb (as he had requested) at Kawaiahao Church was completed two years later.

The newspapers noted:

"The effect of this scene in the mausoleum in the dead quiet of the building was strikingly beautiful, and in marked contrast with the outside, where the wailing was loud and heart-rending, while within all was hushed. Mr. Parker offered a short prayer, and then, in a most impressive manner, with raised hand, he gave the final blessing.

"The seamen and marines drawn up in front of the Mausoleum then fired three volleys, flags were run up to the masthead, the populace returned city-ward, and the funeral of Lunalilo was over."

There was a marked difference between Lunalilo's funeral and Victoria's. The old Hawaiian ways were fading out and western ways were being established.

＊ ＊ ＊

The second interregnum was at an end, and Kalakaua was free to begin, beyond his preliminary work, his reign as King of Hawaii Nei. However, quiet did not descend. The Emmaites were to provide a disconcerting background for several years.

Kalakaua began his reign in a promising way. He was consciously aware of both the natives and the *haole*.

On Monday, March 21, 1874, at ten o'clock, he held his first official audience at the old coral palace. With him were the new heir apparent, Prince William Leleiohoku, the cabinet ministers, and his aids—Governor John Dominis and Charles Reed Bishop.

Each in turn, the ministers tendered congratulations to the king. One can gather no better idea of the Hawaiian government than by recognizing the number of officials who were present. The American minister resident, H. A. Pierce; Britain's commissioner and consul general, James H. Wodehouse; and France's consul, Theodore Ballieu—each addressed the king singly. Consul Edmund Heuck represented consuls for Austria and Hungary, Peru, Chile, Italy, Russia, Sweden and Norway, Belgium and The Netherlands. To the consuls Kalakaua expressed his foreign policy.[1]

"It gives me great pleasure, gentlemen, to receive your congratulations on this occasion. I recognize the importance and value of friendly relations with all the world as a means of promoting the prosperity of my Kingdom. My government will no doubt do all in its power to encourage commercial intercourse between this country and those whose flags you so worthily represent, and I shall be the more desirous to see that commercial intercourse increased, because it involves the necessity of increasing at the same time, the exchangeable products of this Kingdom, by which means alone it can attain the prosperity you desire for it during my reign."

Thirty naval officers were then presented to the king.

Hawaii was a well-established, sophisticated, though small kingdom. One for a king to be proud of, and Kalakaua determined to make it better. He felt an early stir of kingship.

He had made his promises. first and foremost was the increase of his people. The matter of *hooulu ha hui* (increase the race) was closely allied to advancement of agriculture and commerce, a commitment to make a place in the world for Hawaii, to keep the land intact by not ceding Pearl River, and last but most important, to keep Hawaii independent.

❋ ❋ ❋

Kalakaua began his traditional tour to the outer islands to mend fences that might have been broken by the election of a new royal house. He spoke extemporaneously most of the time—speaking in homes, lehua groves, churches, plantations; at *luau*, informal dinners, and any other gatherings. His training as an attorney made him a persuasive speaker; his remarkable understanding of his race, a diplomatic speaker; and his innate charm, a popular speaker.[2] According to contemporary reports in the newspapers, wherever he went he was overwhelmingly received. The scene at Koloa, Kauai, was typical:

There was a slight drizzling rain, but it did not prevent the crowds from gathering. Coming by foot, carriage, oxcart, buggy, horse, they appeared in the festive garb of their best clothes adorned with *lei*, which they took off to hold out to the king and his royal entourage. The entourage included Queen Kapiolani, his sisters, Kamakaeha (Liliuokalani), and Likelike, and their respective husbands, John Owen Dominis, governor of Oahu, and Archibald Cleghorn, a prospering merchant.

They were greeted with shouts of welcome. The king was pressed upon by children singing Hawaiian songs and bearing bouquets of flowers. It was a sight to heighten the heart of the new king. He had not seen such display since he had travelled with Kamehameha v as he toured the islands, asking the people to support his 1864 constitution.

Later, Judge Lilikalani, who was to be Kapiolani's secretary, was the host to the king and his party. The crowds followed the king's party to the home of Lilikalani, which was decorated in greenery and a banner welcoming "King Kalakaua." Kalakaua's heart stirred in eagerness. He was indeed *king*.

As in all places on his tour, *hoo'kupu*, the giving of gifts, was practiced. Hundreds of people pressed upon the king their offerings of fish, flowers, meats, vegetables, and fruits. It was the "offering of mind, soul, and body," Liliuokalani said, "of which nothing was withheld by the people from the kings and queens of Hawaii."

The king spoke briefly to the rain-soaked people, assuring them of his desire to hold their wishes and best interests in his heart. The following morning, March 20, 1874, he addressed them formally from the pulpit of the Koloa Church:

"People of Koloa—Salutation to you all. Coming the first to your island on my first progress after my election to the Throne, it is a great pleasure to me to meet with you and to observe the evidences of your loyalty to myself and to the government of your country. By the will of heaven and the vote of the legislature I have been chosen as your king. I have accepted the responsible position with a firm trust in the help of God and the support of the people to enable me to discharge my duty to the country, to govern wisely, so that the nation may be built up and increase, that agriculture and commerce may flourish, and that our national independence may be secured and perpetuated. But the people must remember that in order to accomplish the desirable ends, the king will require the active cooperation of all his subjects; alone and unaided by you I cannot bring renewed national life and prosperity. Let it be your earnest endeavor then—as it will certainly be mine—to cherish habits of industry, of morality, of respect and obedience to law. Let us work together, actively and earnestly, as lovers of our common country, and God will give us the increase."[3]

From the remote regions of Napoopoo and Kau on the Big Island of Hawaii; to the plantation communities of Ulupalakua and Makawao, Maui; to Father Damien's leper colony at Kalawao, Molokai; the ceremonies, the enthusiastic greetings, the hospitality, the *hoo'kupu*, the kissing of

the hand that characterized the king's visit of Koloa, were
repeated on the successful royal tour. Everywhere the natives
pressed to see their king, and always the king delivered his
simple but stirring message—to increase his people and promote prosperity throughout the land, to secure independence
and make Hawaii a nation of the world.

Everywhere he was hailed with cheers, affectionate
greetings, *aloha*, acclamations, and burning torches. The
waters became alive with canoes carrying torches, and the
night thrilled to music and song that King Kalakaua was
bringing back to his naturally happy people. He and his sister Lydia Dominis joined the groups of people singing and
playing the ukelele, while Queen Kapiolani, it was said, lay
with her head in his lap. It was a comforting scene.

"He was an affable prince [sic]. He had the rare faculty in-
born and cultivated by contact with a great variety of persons
of diverse nationalities at home and abroad, of saying pleasant things in a pleasant way to all whom he met. And it
made no difference whether the rank of the person he met
was humble or exalted."[4]

He spoke of the renewal of the nation: ". . . The extinction of which has been prophesied by some foreigners . . .
Shall we sit by and see the structure of our fathers fall to
pieces . . . if a house be dilapidated let us repair it; let us
renovate our own selves to [this] end that . . . the nation may
grow again with new life and vigor."[5]

He chose as his motto Increase the Race and adopted the
flaming torch his sign. He quoted:

"Our ancestor Iwikaukau said 'When the sun is high in
the heavens, look to me; and by the sign of this flame you
will know me and my seed after me . . .'"

This was a departure from the Kamehameha's call for
thunder, lightning, drenching rain for royal proclamation.

He was extraordinarily careful to keep the rapidly un-
raveling ties between himself and the Kamehamehas and

Lunalilo from disintegrating further. Before he gave his exhortation to the progress of the new regime or his motto, he spoke gently and lovingly of his predecessors. In his address to the people of Lahaina on April 13, 1874, he began:

"People of Lahaina: Before addressing to you the brief remarks which I propose to make on this occasion, I cannot omit referring to some memories of my late lamented Predecessor, who made a short visit here last year, on the journey which he undertook for the benefit of his health. The late King was deeply solicitous for the welfare of his people, but the condition of his health was such that he was unable to carry out his plans for their good. I regarded the late King and his two immediate predecessors with strong affection, for on these sands and among these fields of Lahaina, they and I have played together as boys, in the family of our grandmother, Hoapili Wahine. The recollections of those days long past come before me vividly now.

"And now I have come hither to see you, as my children, and that you may look upon me as your father. I thank you much, people of the district of Lahaina, for the very warm and loyal reception which you have given us, one which neither myself, the Queen nor the members of the Royal Family can cease to remember without pleasure."

He was careful to tie his motto to the roots of the past and to make a connection with the Kamehamehas:

"There are some of the old folks remaining and here present, the people of the time of Kamehameha I, who heard that celebrated saying: 'The old men, the old women, and the children may sleep by the wayside without fear.' That motto remains good to this day. Kamehameha II broke the tabu on social intercourse his word was, '*O ka ainoa.*' Said Kamehameha III, 'The righteous man is my man,' and this sentiment prevails today among us, both foreigners and natives. I believe that if I shall make the main object of my reign the increase of the nation, there may be secured both the stability of the Government and the national independence. Then let my motto be—'The man and woman who shall live correctly and bring forth children; they are my people.' And I charge you parents, take every care of your little ones. And to you children also I say, obey your parents.

"The increase of the people; the advancement of agriculture and commerce—these are the objects which my Government will mainly strive to accomplish."

❋ ❋ ❋

In his speech at the opening of the legislature in 1874 he took care not to blame Lunalilo for the neglect of presenting the suggested amendments to the constitution that had been proposed during his reign. He recognized his tenuous hold on the throne and remembered his defeat by Lunalilo.

"In the Providence of the Almighty, it was not permitted to the King, Lunalilo, to see the accomplishment of his hopes. Scarcely one year of his reign had passed ere he was summoned away."

He went on to say, "The amendments proposed in the Constitution have been published as the law required, and will receive from you the most careful and mature consideration. They were intended to restore certain features of the Constitution of 1852, and of these which re-establishes a separate house of Representatives is the most important."[6]

Regardless of the fact that Lunalilo and Kalakaua had disagreed during the first interregnum on changing the constitution—Lunalilo proposing to change the 1864 constitution to conform with that of 1852, and Kalakaua standing firm on Kamehameha v's constitution—he now discussed the proposed changes to come before the assembly.[7]

He recommended consideration of the tenure of office of judges of the Supreme Court; stated that exclusion of judges from the legislature was in keeping with current policy; he rejected that the king give his reasons for vetoing a bill as unnecessary—as these would already have been stated to the ministers and the house. He warned that careful consideration should be given to removing the property qualifications of voters:

"The limited diffusion of wealth among the masses of the people tend directly to circumscribe, under the present franchise, the expression of the popular will in the return of the members to the House of Representatives."

He urged a codification of the laws, expressed pleasure at the good foreign relations then existing, and congratulated the legislative body on its part in the treaties with foreign nations. He spoke of not ceding Pearl River (Harbor) because that was not "in consonance with the feeling of the people," and he recommended facilities of steam communication with San Francisco and Australia as well as a submarine cable.

He stated emphatically:

"The subject, however, that awakens my greatest solicitude is to increase my people, and to this point I desire to direct your earnest attention. Perhaps some modification of the divorce law may be found conducive to this end. The Board of Health has been required to improve to the utmost the hygiene of the people, but much still remains to be done in this direction, especially to devise means for the preservation of the lives of infants, and I would suggest that some special exemption should be made in favor of those who rear large families."

He closed the assembly with the exhortation that its deliberations "be guided by an eye single to the national welfare."

As desperate as was the need for increasing the Hawaiian race was the need for revitalizing the natives. Kalakaua knew that a mere increase in numbers without hope in a future–in a reason for being, in pride of the past, in an understanding of culture and tradition–would be worthless. This knowledge divided the king into a political man and Renaissance man; the latter was his natural inclination.

The *kapu* system under the *kahuna* reached into all aspects of life—social, religious, ethical and political. He knew from past decades that from the destruction of the *kapu* to the present, the changes in Hawaiian life were more than the loss of physical life. Although the enormous loss of life through venereal disease and leprosy had occurred, the loss of a desire to live had a close parallel.

Leprosy had been introduced to the islands in 1853, and by 1864 had begun to spread. As a response to the proliferation of leprosy, the leper colony of Kalawao on Molokai was established in 1865, and lepers were then judiciously segregated from the rest of the native population.

More than disease, though, was contributing to the decline of the native population. The cultural revolution in the 1820s, the introduction of *haole* culture and religion, were leaving the people increasingly unprepared to cope with social change. Under the *kapu*, the Hawaiian had been industrious, clean, and self-restraining in his behavior. But under the western culture, which he could not understand, he became indolent, dirty, and morally careless.

The answers to these issues—to revive culture, race and pride, to resolve the paradox which seemed so irreparable, stood before King Kalakaua, capturing his imagination, and moving the Renaissance man to the hope of turning back the clock. At the same time he hoped to discover ways and means to give new life to a new culture to his people—to thus increase their desire to live as well as increasing life itself.

When Kalakaua returned from his outer island tour, his heart swelled with pride and a desire to promote his people, to rescue them from the destruction of the past years. But he was troubled, too, because of memories reaching back to his childhood—and before.

He was painfully aware of the changes that had come about. Honolulu served to point up the changed village from the time of his birth in a grass compound at the base of

Punch Bowl Hill. It was a puzzled man—and king—who viewed his capital in 1874.

From the deck of the incoming steamer, Kalakaua saw that Honolulu had changed from a village of grass structures and few *haole* buildings to a town of two church spires, a *haole* business district of wood and brick, of hotels, stores, government buildings, blacksmith shops, brothels, and saloons.[8]

Beyond the business district were houses: wood frame houses from New England, adobe-brick homes, structures of cream-colored coral conglomerate set in cement, houses built on raised posts and sturdy thatched dwellings, as well as grass shacks. There were elaborate homes, mostly belonging to *haole*, but there were a few well-built large Hawaiian homes, such as Archibald and Likelike Cleghorn's "Ainahou," Charles Reed's and Bernice Pauahi Bishop's "Haleakala," and Queen Emma's "Rooke House." Even the cottage on the old coral palace grounds was attractive to his eyes, but Kalakaua envisioned a new palace.

Everywhere were flowers and greenery—passion flowers, lilies, gladiolas, ginger, Mexican creepers, and geraniums. There were fruit trees of the *haole* type and mangoes, banana, and papaya.

On the streets, Kalakaua knew, strolled *haole* and Hawaiian alike—men in shirts and pants, boots and spurs, women in *holoku*, *muumuu*, and long skirts. Along the street sides Hawaiian men and women sold *lei*, fish, papayas, mangoes. Often a Hawaiian group could be seen sitting under a banyan tree eating *poi* and fish. It was a placid scene of diverse peoples: plantation laborer, stevedores, sailors, coachmen, boatmen, house-servants, *haole* businessmen, missionaries and missionaries-become-businessmen, *alii*, unemployed commoners, retainers—all intermingling.

❋ ❋ ❋

But Kalakaua's memory was disturbed by haunting pictures from the outer islands and the environs of Honolulu. Here was an ambience of growth, progress, profit, decay, despair, and death. On Maui, at the Ulupalakua plantation, 1,300 acres of land yielded from four to seven tons of sugar cane per season, a handsome profit for the *haole* planters and their Honolulu-based sugar agents. Entrepreneurs Isenberg and Wright had established a growing plantation complex at Koloa, Hawaii.

On other parts of the islands gross poverty existed. Dilapidated shacks seemed to cling to each other for support. Dirt and filth filled the falling-down huts. The people were old and sick and weary. There were no young, vigorous men or women. The king, as Kamehameha v had done after visiting the devastation, asked, "Where are the people?"

Pau kanaka make was the answer. Done. People dead.

Hopeless in a strange environment with everything they understood and believed in taken away from them, they found solace only in death.

"I have seen many lingering and wasting away," wrote Missionary Titus Coan, "under painful disease and die with little or no emotion or regret. It would seem as if their indifference to life were a reason why they succumb so easily to disease."

The Hawaiian had struggled to assimilate the new and cling to the old. Under the *kapu* system the Hawaiian had laws of economics, conduct, place or position in his world. He understood himself and others. He worked with the supernatural power he believed in and by whose laws he could function. Now, as he was assimilated into the Western ways, he became a bewildered swimmer in a strange and turbulent ocean. He had been deprived of the *kapu* that kept him clean, industrious, healthy, and strong. He struggled to hold on to its symbols of dance, folklore, and the mysteries of old. The Christian God practiced by the Christian man no longer met his needs as the supernatural gods had. His land was gone after the Great *Mahele*, and his sense of *aina* (land) in its higher sense of light, time, water, stability, and the human being had been violated.

He was asked to change his thinking to an entirely different belief system. The happy man who gave his first fish to his god and took no more than he needed—or if he did gave it away—was gone. His sense of *aloha* was crushed against the *haole* acquisitiveness.

But he still looked to his king for his *mana*—for his righteousness. Kamehameha III had made the first mistake of throwing the Hawaiian into confusion with his decree of the Great *Mahele* (the loss of their land) and the Constitution of 1852 (the loss of monarchial power). Kamehameha V, detecting something of the desire of his people and their great loss, created the Constitution of 1864 to restore monarchial rights, strengthening the monarchy and protecting the sovereignty of the natives.

The Hawaiian struggle to retain a little of his essence was resisted by the foreigner's concept of values.

This paradox of two racial worlds, so interdependent and yet so incompatible, had been far from resolved before the reign of Kalakaua. Yet both sides expected the king to solve the dilemma.

It was not that during the 1850s, '60s, and now '70s the *haole* was unaware of the situation. It was that their explanations were too simplistic and often erroneous. To the Spencerian indoctrinated *haole* the explanation of the disappearance of the natives was simply the result of the axiom "survival of the fittest." The old beliefs and customs of the natives were doomed before the march of new technology and with them, the Hawaiians themselves. It was determined: "Many races originally savage have melted away and disappeared before the relenting march of 'civilization'." If that answer were not pat enough, the religionist offered demise as retribution: "Sin when it is finished bringeth forth death."[9]

Yet in 1868, a voice crying in the wilderness was heard from a native politician. "You must rise in your strength and be men; tomorrow you must tell these bloated money aristocrats they cannot make you slaves; that you are bound to hold your taro patches against all comers; that you cry Hawaii for Hawaiians."[10]

Kalakaua knew intuitively that he had inherited not only the Crown of the Kamehamehas, but the leadership of a nation struggling in a paradox. Yet he was like a well-intentioned optimistic, hopeful, effervescent youth thrown into the midst of a solidly entrenched grown up world.

* * *

Within the Kingdom of the Hawaiian Islands in the 1870s existed two seemingly irreconcilable but hopelessly intertwined worlds. In the new world, the *haole* competed and profited. In many cases it was a descendant of the early missionary, in other cases an adventurer from the United States, Great Britain, or Germany who sought future in paradise; the *haole* was the young, vibrant species in Hawaii. Whether through turning a profit from sandlewood, whales, sugar, or merchandise, whether saving souls or selling soap, the Hawaiian Islands offered a satisfying and profitable home to the *haole*.

Though he might have reluctantly viewed the native's ways as crude, barbarous, and sometimes pagan, the *haole* was still dependent on the Hawaiian. In 1872, the population of foreigners was only 3,500, approximately five percent of the total. Economically, the Hawaiian provided the bulk of the social manpower that was the sustenance of the foreigner's continued wealth. Although the 1872 census showed a population of 2,000 Chinese, the Asian immigrants during this period were secondary to the Hawaiian as the major labor force. Politically, the *haole* was dependent on the voting participation or apathy of the Hawaiian—the foreigner lived under a governmental system he could influence but not openly control. To ensure social, economic, and racial tranquility, the five percent *haole* population cultivated the natives' friendship, frequently intermarried, learned the Hawaiian language, cherished the riches of the land, and gradually, sometimes learned to respect the people.

In another world, the old world, lived the native, attempting to assimilate the culture of the *haole* while isolated from the profitable mainstream of the *haole*'s economic and social powers.[11]

Standing on the shifting sands of time, Kalakaua decided first to turn his attention to the needs of the foreigners in his land—the sugar planters. For a number of years the effort had been made to effect a reciprocity treaty, without results.

Kalakaua used his birthday to win both Hawaiian and *haole* to him. To reactivate the negotiations of a reciprocity treaty, Kalakaua in October of 1874 had sent H. A. P. Carter with Supreme Court Justice Elisha Allen to Washington, D.C., with little success. He made the decision that by his going to the United States himself the American government would possibly recognize the status of Hawaii in a more favorable light. He had gained a better feeling about himself, and besides, the Renaissance man in him loved to travel and see different ways of life, dress, and architecture. The suggestion was frowned upon by the foreign element in Hawaii as "too expensive." Nevertheless, Kalakaua decided to go, taking with him his brother-in-law, John Owen Dominis, governor of Oahu, and John M. Kapena, governor of Maui and one of the most outstanding Hawaiian representatives, a former adviser to kings and a student of Hawaiiana.

Kalakaua declared November 16th, his birthday, a national holiday. The return of holidays was welcome to the Hawaiians, who happily honored their king. He kept the revelries at a minimum, testing the waters of the cultural resurgence that was just beginning. To an overflowing congregation at the Kawaiahao Church he gave a short speech explaining his forthcoming trip, one that would please the *haole* and comfort the natives, who remembered the death of Kamehameha II and his queen in England.

"It has been the custom of rulers of other countries to go to foreign lands to obtain assistance, and this is what I desire to do. I am going to visit our great and good friend, the United States. Wise and prudent statesmen think that a treaty can be made with the United States which will benefit both countries. I am going to endeavor to obtain this treaty, which, should I succeed in doing, I think will revive the country."[12]

Thus, His Majesty, with much fanfare, departed for San Francisco on the S.S. *Benecia*.

❈ ❈ ❈

San Francisco overwhelmingly welcomed the "first King ever to visit the United States." Over 6,000 people gathered at the wharf, and thousands more thronged the streets to see the king "escorted by Mayor Otis and a credible military escort of State troops to the Grand Hotel."[13]

He was interviewed by reporters about everything from his experience as journalist and a fireman in Honolulu, to his overland route, to his purpose in Washington, which he stated was in no way to negotiate but "merely to present" reciprocity. He was called "urbane," "gracious," "humorous," "charming," "amusing," and "extremely handsome." Kalakaua handled himself well with the reporters.

The *Chronicle* kept a daily report of his tour of the city, including a reception given by the mayor, a visit with foreign consuls, and a formal reception at the Grand Hotel, where he was entertained by a "most persistent visitor"–Caesar Celso Moreno, who "bombarded him with plans to lay a Pacific Cable," The king "listened patiently." The *Chronicle* noted his visit to the California theater, a serenade by the Second Regiment, and a visit to the *Chronicle* building, as he himself had been a journalist. An unsubstantiated story began to be circulated among the opposition in Hawaii that Kalakaua had indulged in his pastime of gambling, had lost all the money given him for his trip to the United States, and had to be refinanced by the City of San Francisco. Not one word of this story appeared in the *Chronicle*, whose reporters dogged his footsteps day and night. But it was a good story for the opposition to report about the "gambling king."

The *Alta* in San Francisco noted that he "dressed plainly, nothing in his costume denoting royalty." His aids, however, were colorful in dress, wearing military uniforms and bright red sashes. The *Alta* set the tone of welcome for the rest of the country:

"Welcome, King Kalakaua. For the first time in the history of our country, we have a reigning king among us. Luckily, he is a gentleman as well as a king—a well-educated, intelligent, popular *gentleman*—which is a better term than that which designates his rank."

San Francisco loved King Kalakaua, and his trip to Washington was carefully recorded, as well as his welcome there.

The papers across the country kept close account of him, and all were pleased.

The December 15, 1874, *Herald* of Washington, D.C., described the king's appearance:

"The Hawaiian monarch is over six feet in height, dignified and imposing in appearance, and with an ease of manner, suitable to his station. He is not a man one would care to take liberties with, though his whole bearing is pervaded by the bonhommie and good nature which was such a favorable trait in his character before his present exaltation."

He met with President Ulysses S. Grant and with the members of the cabinet "assembled in full dress for the occasion." Kalakaua kept his visit social and did not discuss the reciprocity treaty. Such discussions, he noted again and again, were to be left to H. A. P. Carter and Elisha Allen. Receptions were held and balls were given, all in which

Kalakaua shone as "gallant," "a fine dancer," and "gracious." The New York *Herald* wrote of him with an enthusiasm vying with the San Francisco papers:

"No king in the world could be more warmly welcomed than King Kalakaua, for he rules by the will of the people, and is not a despot, but a kind of republican monarch, such as a third or fourth term President might be to us. We interpret his visit as an evidence of good will to the American nation, and it will be our fault if he returns to Honolulu disappointed in his trip."

At Washington Kalakaua had the honor of being the only king ever to be asked to speak before a joint session of Congress. Unfortunately, the cold weather had taken its toll, and Kalakaua was too hoarse to speak. His prepared speech was read by Chancellor Allen. It was the king, however, who was cheered.

In New York the king attended a children's party, shopped on fifth Avenue, attended a Masonic Lodge meeting, and breakfasted with the editor of the *Popular Science Monthly*, with whom he had previous correspondence regarding his inventions. Possibly, if the editor had known his correspondent would some day be a king, he would have been more interested in the articles the young Kalakaua had written.

He spoke before a temperance league in New York, urging them to open correspondence with temperance leaders in Hawaii. With piquant charm he added that he himself was at one time missionary-temperate "but humanity is weak, you know, and I do not know how they [the missionaries] consider my case now." These words brought smiles and a touch of applause rather than reproach. Kalakaua was at his best when he laughed at himself.

City officials and groups everywhere continued to invite him to speak, but his hoarseness made his remarks inaudible except to those in the immediate vicinity. Still, the people crowded about to see the King of the Sandwich Islands, which were for the first time beginning to be recognized as "Hawaii."

The *Advertiser* in Honolulu quoted the American papers, and King Kalakaua was coming into his own among a foreign population that was beginning to believe in his ability and personality to influence reciprocity for them.

He returned to Honolulu on February 20, 1875, a few days earlier than he was expected, much to the annoyance of Sanford B. Dole, who was to be his official greeter, and others.[14] But hasty arrangements were made, and Dole gave a welcoming speech, while thousands gathered at the foot of Fort Street to greet the king. A quick-forming procession of the military, firemen, and schoolchildren escorted him from the wharf to the palace, where he was met by his wife, Queen Kapiolani, and his sister, Lydia Dominis, who was also welcoming home her husband.

* * *

Although from all indications Kalakaua's trip had been enormously satisfying to the *haole*, there was among the Hawaiians a question of distrust regarding reciprocity involving Pearl River and a closer relationship with the much feared United States—and annexation. The Emmaites were particularly vociferous.

It fell to the king to quiet these fears, and he set out to do so. He made another tour of the islands and spoke of his trip to the United States. He also kept in mind the ever-frugal foreigner who resented every penny spent to further Hawaii as Hawaii.

In his speech known as "His Majesty's Address to the People" on February 20, 1875,[15] he carefully reiterated the steps of his journey from a personal point of view. He spoke of a cordial meeting with General Schofield, who by now it had become known had come to Hawaii to investigate the potential of Pearl River as a harbor. He spoke of the kindnesses that San Francisco had extended to him, adding, for the money-worried foreigners, that "the city assumed the payment of all the expenses incurred during our stay."

Unconsciously, he added fuel to the rumor of his gambling debt. Then, for the generosity-loving Hawaiians, he stated, ". . . and this was but one of many instances in our experience of the generous feeling of the nation toward us . . . Through the kind courtesy of the Road [railway] officials, we were provided with three magnificent cars for our special use."

He spoke of the United States hospitality–hospitality the Hawaiians could admire:

"We were seven days on the journey to Washington. The members of the President's Cabinet came out on the road to meet us–a high mark of respect on the part of the Government–and we were escorted to the Hotel, where rooms had been prepared for us, by the military and bands of music."

Kalakaua included the missionaries in his presentation: he spoke of visiting at New Haven, "where the Rev. Mr. Bingham and the other Pioneer Missionaries to these islands were consecrated for their work."

He spoke of meeting in Boston "the Rev. Dr. Anderson, a distinguished member of the American Board who visited Honolulu in the year 1864. I attended service in the Park Street Church in which Mr. Bingham preached before he sailed for these islands."

He praised the expedient manner in which Chicago had been rebuilt and admired openly the manufacturing cities such as St. Louis. Always he spoke of being received with honor by state legislatures, public officials, and Masonic bodies of Knights Templar.

He called attention to the position of the Hawaiian Islands:

"Our position is a most favorable one, in the midst of the Pacific Ocean on the highways of the world's commerce. California on the East, Australia on the West, Chile on the South, Japan and China on the North: All these countries are progressing, and it will be impossible for us to remain stationary."

For the sugar planters he stated:

"In regard to the proposed Treaty of Reciprocity a subject in which we all feel deeply interested–the people and the Government of America are favorable to it, and the work of negotiation is in the hands of our Commissioners. The latest advice which I have received give the information that the Treaty has been signed by President Grant and sent to the Senate for ratification."

He exhorted the citizens and denizens of his country to industry:

"As I observed the vast wealth and prosperity of that nation, I was impressed with the reflection that it was a result of the industrious habits of the people ... The wealth and greatness of nations is created by the cultivators of the soil and by the men who toil with their hands: and thus has it ever been since forms of government were first instituted on earth. To these considerations let us of Hawaii Nei earnestly direct our attention to the end that by our industries we may be enabled to attract foreign commerce to our ports and freight it [sic] with the products of our country.

"If we take a retrospect of the past, we shall plainly perceive that a failure to put our hands and our faculties to a proper use, has been one of the causes of the decline of our nation. Indolence, while it degrades the individual, saps the life of the entire nation. And therefore there is a vast difference today in the numbers and in the habits of industry of the people, from what was to be seen in the days of Kamehameha I."

He gave them goals for the future, specific and long-term: He spoke of the upcoming Grand Centennial of 1876 in Philadelphia: ". . . In those buildings a separate department is reserved for every nation to be represented at the Exhibition, and a place is reserved for Hawaii. While it is true that we have sent specimens of our products to England, France and Austria, our displays of this description have been but meagre, and it is therefore hoped that the opportunity which now offers will be zealously and industriously improved and that all our merchantable articles of product will be fully represented at Philadelphia, whereby we may become better known in the world's commerce . . ."

For the longer view:

"Let us therefore wisely take care of ourselves; and the best way to do this is to endeavor to make such material and social progress, that the powerful governments whose friendship we now fortunately possess, shall be convinced that we deserve their aid and support. Let us in short, prove to the world that Hawaii is worthy of her position among the independent nations of the world."

Sandwiched into his talk was a small nugget of his own dreams of the kinsmanship with the people of Samoa:

"Colonel Steinberger, who came in the same ship with us to Honolulu, is U.S. Commissioner to Samoa. We do not know the precise nature of his mission, but we do know that it is humanitarian in effect, and that this officer has already displayed his devotion to a remarkable people whom we are proud to call kinsmen . . ."

The Hawaiians were so pleased with their king that "with a facility peculiarly Hawaiian," having at once transformed themselves from an "assemblage convened to hear the Sovereign, into a public meeting, while the Sovereign was still present," passed several resolutions:

"Resolved, That the thanks of the Hawaiian People be tendered to our beloved Sovereign, King Kalakaua, for his mission to the United States, and for the favorable impression which he has made in that country regarding Hawaii.

"Resolved, That the thanks of the Hawaiian People are hereby tendered to the American Government and People, for the hospitable manner in which they entertained our Sovereign, and for the kindly service of a national war vessel to convey him to and from San Francisco.

"Resolved, that these resolutions be printed in the Hawaiian and English newspapers, and that a copy of them be sent to the American Government through its Minister Resident."

Kalakaua could be justly satisfied with himself. He had presented to the people his beginnings as a monarch who hoped to stimulate his country in agriculture and commerce, to further international relations and to make a place in the world for an independent Hawaii. He had begun to encourage his people to rise from their apathy and become active in affairs of the country and of the world.

❊ ❊ ❊

Upon his return from the United States, the at-home and private man, Kalakaua, decided to rewrite the Hawaiian national anthem. The anthem written by his sister, then Lydia Kamakaeha Dominis, for King Kamehameha v, was too missionary for his taste. It was referred to by the American newspapers as the "Hawaiian National Hymn." In 1876 he enlisted the help of Henry Berger, Hawaii's Royal Bandmaster, to compose the music to a song better suited as an anthem.

Heinrich Berger had come to Hawaii in 1872 on "loan" from the German government. He stayed four years, then returned to Germany as his loan was recalled. However, in 1876 Henry Berger was back in Hawaii to form the Royal Hawaiian Band, and Kalakaua recruited him for the final composition of the Hawaiian anthem:

HAWAI'I PONO'Ī

Hawai'i pono'i,	Hawai'i pono'i
Hana'i kou mo'i,	Nana I na ali'i,
Ka lani ali'i	Na pua muli kou,
ke ali'i.	Na poki'i.
Makua lani e,	Hawai'i pono'i,
Kamehameha e,	E ka lahui e,
Na kaua e pale	'O kau hana nui
Me ka ihe.	E ui e.

HAWAII'S OWN

Hawaii's own,   Hawaii's own,
Look to your king,   Look to your chiefs,
The royal chief.   The children after you,
The chief.   The young.
Royal father,   Hawaii's own,
Kamehameha,   O nation.
We shall defend   Your great duty
With spears.   Strive.

It was a rousing song far different from the "hymn" his sister had written under Kamehameha v: *He Mele Lahui Hawaii.*

THE HAWAIIAN NATIONAL ANTHEM

Almighty Father lend Thine ear,
And 'list a nation's prayer,
That lowly bows before Thy throne,
And seeks Thy fostering care.
Chorus: Grant Thou Thy Peace, thr'out the land,
O'er these sunny, sea girt Isles,
Keep the nation's life, oh Lord,
And upon our Sovereign smile.
Guard him with Thy tender care,
Give him length of years to reign,
On the throne his fathers won,
Bless the nation once again.
Give the King Thy loving grace,
And with wisdom from on high,
Prosperous lead his people on,
As beneath Thy watchful eye.
Bless oh Lord our country's chiefs,
Grant them wisdom so to live,
That our people may be saved,
And to Thee the glory give,
Watch Thou O'er us day by day,
King and people with thy love,
For our hope is all in Thee
Bless Thou us who reign'st above.

❀ ❀ ❀

Several personal problems befell Kalakaua shortly after his return from the United States. During his trip, Leleiohoku, his younger brother and successor, served as regent.

Leleiohoku, youngest son of Kalakaua's parents, had been taken in *hanai* at birth by Princess Ruth. He had been, according to the newspapers, "well educated, of correct morals, and a promising heir." His sister Lydia Dominis wrote:

"He was a very popular young man, about twenty years of age, having been born on the 10th of January, 1854 . . . He had the same love of music, the like passion for poetry and song, which have been so great a pleasure to me in my own life, as well as to our brother, King Kalakaua. He had a taste for social pleasures, and enjoyed the gay and festive element in life. During the absence of the king, there were three separate clubs or musical circles engaged in friendly rivalry to outdo each the other in poetry and song. These were the friends and associates of the prince regent, those of the Princess Likelike, and my own friends and admirers . . . but candor compels me to acknowledge that those of Prince Leleiohoku were really in advance of those of his two sisters . . ."[16]

Leleiohoku had made no important governmental decisions during his regency. His reign had been one of "social pleasure."

❀ ❀ ❀

On October 16, 1876, Princess Likelike, Kalakaua's youngest sister, gave birth to a baby girl, Kaiulani. Likelike had been married to Archibald Cleghorn, a Scotsman, in 1871. Kaiulani was baptized in the Episcopal Church as Victoria Kaiulani Kalaninuiahila Kalapapa Kawekuii Lunalilo Cleghorn.

Immediately upon her birth her mother sent word to Kalakaua demanding that Kaiulani be proclaimed "next in line for succession." There had been some domestic problems in the royal household centered on Kalakaua's devotion to the children of Kapiolani's sister, Kinoiki Kekaulike, and High Chief David

Pikoi: David Kawananakoa (8 years old), Kuhio Kalanianaole (6 years old) and Edward Keliiahonui (5 years old). Queen Emma wrote flora Jones that "Mrs. Dominis and Mrs. Cleghorn [Likelike] constantly worry about the elevation of the boys above them."[17]

Kalakaua did not immediately proclaim Kaiulani successor to the throne, but the Hawaiians did. Guns were fired from Punch Bowl Hill and the people proclaimed throughout the streets "a new royal princess–the Hope of Hawaii." The enormous love the Hawaiians have for children, coupled with the birth of a new royal child, resulted in *luau* and celebrations. But Kalakaua was taunted by his sisters, Likelike and Lydia Kamakaeha, that the Hawaiian people had to override the king and declare the "rightful heir." However, the natives had a strong nudge from Archibald Cleghorn, Kaiulani's father, Liliuokalani later admitted.

But at the time, the Emmaites seized upon the "victory of the natives," and the story did Kalakaua no good.

❊ ❊ ❊

On April 9, 1877, six months later, Leleiohoku died of pneumonia. Princess Ruth, as his *hanai* mother, immediately claimed it her right to succeed her son. However, Kalakaua moved quickly, and on April 11, 1877, proclaimed his sister Lydia Kamakaeha Dominis heir apparent under the title of Liliuokalani. Princess Ruth was a Kamehameha, and immediately the Emmaites moved to point out that Kalakaua had again ignored the wishes of the people. (Actually the "people" never raised a whisper for Ruth).

One last Hawaiian problem was to befall Kalakaua. Lunalilo had requested that his remains be placed in the Kawaiahao Church grounds, so they were moved from the Nuuanu Mausoleum to a newly erected tomb on the church grounds in 1877. A request was made to Kalakaua by a group of Hawaiians to have a twenty-one gun salute given at the time of the second funeral. Kalakaua refused, saying a royal funeral had been given Lunalilo in 1873. Stormy weather ensued, and during the burial twenty-one distinct thunder claps were heard. "What man withholds the gods give" was the comment of the Hawaiians.

Kalakaua was uneasy about the three events and the ammunition it gave the Emmaites and many of *haole* opposition who fought Kalakaua on their own premises.

Something must be done for the "people"–for the natives. And Kalakaua had plans.

5 The Divided Man

In the next few years Kalakaua was to become the divided man—the political man and the Renaissance man: the king of the Hawaii of the *haole*, and the king of Hawaii Nei, Hawaii for the Hawaiians. For every advance he made as the Renaissance man, he slipped back two as the political man.

The Sugar Treaty opened Pandora's box, as well as bringing great financial prosperity to Hawaii. The prosperity among the *haole* sugar planters and businessmen brought a resolve among them to govern Hawaii. It also brought Claus Spreckels, the most ruthless and selfish businessman Kalakaua and Hawaii were to know during this period.

Claus Spreckels was born in Lamstedt, Hanover, Germany, in 1828. He grew up in a poverty-stricken household under harsh conditions. He was expected to do the work of an adult from the time he was five. At eighteen he came to the United States, where he entered into the grocery business. Successful, he came West to go into sugar refining as a laborer. He learned quickly and soon took over the business, becoming a millionaire by the time he was forty. He opposed the reciprocity treaty with Hawaii and the United States. But when it was passed, he was quick to take advantage of it by coming to Hawaii, arriving on the same ship that brought the news to Honolulu.

He founded Spreckelsville in 1878 and marketed through N. G. Irwin Company Monopoly. With his money he was soon to ensnare Kalakaua in his net.

Before Kalakaua was to become entwined with Spreckels, he resolved to do something for his people, the native Hawaiians, something that would bring back to them a reason to live. He would cut through the surface veneer of the *haole* culture and bring on the greatness of the past. His first step was to call forth the banished *kahuna* who held the history, tradition, culture, and genealogy of the past. It was to be the beginning of the much maligned *Hale Naua*. But Kalakaua would also bring his country into the nineteenth century of commerce and rural and city improvements.

He would complete the long-planned palace. He would reintroduce the hula, the *mele*, the *oli*. He would educate young men to be statesmen the world over, but they would not be ignorant of the games and arts of the Hawaiian youth. They would be *Hawaiian*. But it all took money. And only the *haole* had money. Even the *alii* were short of money, and the former retainers (commoners) were often destitute. His sister, Liliuokalani, came to him asking that her husband, John Dominis, be given a better-paying position, for money was short, and every day she was beseeched by former retainers asking for help. These came from their mother's and grandfather's lands, which had been sold. She never sent anyone away without something, even if it was only an "all-purpose" coconut.[1]

Kalakaua continued to dream and plan. He would travel. His trip to the United States lived vividly in his memory. He had made a good impression on the foreigners who had no personal interest in Hawaii. He had been highly praised and acknowledged as the head of his country. He would travel the world and bring to his ravished land men and women of cognate races; thus he would increase his people. But he would do more. He would let the world know that Hawaii was an *independent* nation, self-governed, open to commerce and social interchange with all people.

These ideas were heady wine, and he needed to share them with someone who had dreams such as his. Such a man came to Hawaii–Celso Caesar Moreno–and such a man was already there–Walter Murray Gibson. Thus, there were for him two men of dreams and ideas and one man of money. All three were to bring him both his dreams and his downfall.

Celso Caesar Moreno had first spoken to Kalakaua in San Francisco, where the newspapers reported the king had listened patiently. Some interest must have been provoked, because Moreno arrived a welcome visitor in Hawaii, with proposals that dazzled the king.

Celso Caesar Moreno was a flambouyant, handsome Italian, arriving in Hawaii from China. Glowing reports of this "Gentleman from Genoa" appeared in newspaper accounts.

Both Kalakaua and Moreno were dynamic men, and it is not without reason that Kalakaua said he was "surprised how exactly they agreed." The big, burly six-foot adventurer was probably what Kalakaua would like to have been had he not been cast in the role of a king. Later, W. L. Green spoke gently of Kalakaua's having been "taken in," saying that "shrewd men in Washington and elsewhere had been deceived to a great extent by his [Moreno's] arts."

Green was correct in his surmise of Moreno's "arts" in the United States and elsewhere. Celso Moreno, educated by a Catholic bishop and a graduate of the University of Genoa, was knowledgeable and persuasive. He had persuaded the United States Congress on August 15, 1876, to give him and others the right to lay and maintain a submarine cable on the Pacific coast to connect American and Asiatic countries. His limitations were raising the capital in three years. For this purpose he went to China, and although again failing to raise the moneys, he convinced influential Chinese of a plan to set up a steamship line between China and the United States, and on the way, to bring laborers to Hawaii. Moreno had arrived with the first shipload of coolies in Honolulu in November, 1879.

Moreno began presenting his ideas to King Kalakaua. Using his United States "rights" for laying a cable, he proposed instead a cable between Hawaii and San Francisco. The concept was not bad; it was the million dollars he wanted that was promptly defeated by Minister of the Interior Wilder.

Importation of opium was a second idea of Moreno's. After much discussion in the legislature, the bill was passed. At this time Kalakaua vetoed the bill, but later allowed a modified bill to pass.

A loan bill of $10 million was a third Moreno project. Here he was supported by Walter Murray Gibson, who was soon to come into the political limelight, but the bill was opposed by the cabinet.

Two king-makers were now active in Hawaii. The king's dreams of a better Hawaii were to continue in a fomenting society of problems.

❋ ❋ ❋

A shadow had been cast over Kalakaua's future by breach of loyalty among the Hawaiians in the Queen Emma-Kalakaua election. It was further lengthened by the constitutional right of the king to choose and dismiss his cabinets—a right Kalakaua stretched to its breaking point. There was coming to the fore racial antagonism in who should run the country—the Hawaiians or the *haole*. On one side were the Hawaiians and part-Hawaiians, and on the other side were the *haole*. Approval had been given to the first cabinet appointees, as there had apparently been a balance of races. Well-thought-of Paul Nahaolelua represented the Hawaiians. There had long been the feeling that Hawaiians should be represented in the cabinet; but there was also a strong feeling among the *haole* that native Hawaiians should serve in subordinate positions until "properly educated."

From the time of Kamehameha III (1852) to 1887, by right
of the 1852 constitution, the king could choose and dismiss
his cabinet. During the first two or three years of Kalakaua's
reign, cabinet changes occurred because of disagreements
among the ministers. One such disagreement occurred over
the Loan Act of 1874. It was not the first legislative act for a
loan, but it was for the largest amount.

It is possible that the Hawaiian Kalakaua had a limited
concept of what a loan meant. Hawaiian *aloha* tended toward
an outright gift rather than a borrowed sum. Only partially
alerted that such moneys would not only have to be repaid,
but repaid with interest, Kalakaua saw the loan as a solution
to his financial problems, as did some other Hawaiians.[2]
Some of the *haole* also favored the loan, fully aware that the
moneys would have to be repaid.

Kalakaua had difficulty in orienting himself to a new
concept in which money was power.

Brought up in a tradition in which the high chief had the
greatest *mana* or "power and wisdom," he now faced a culture
in which the man with the greatest amount of money was
the "highest." It was the opposite of his traditional beliefs.

A loan or the return of it with interest was foreign to the
king, as was the idea that support from the taxpayer could be
resented. The king had made it possible through the reciprocity treaty for the planters to make fortunes. It seemed
only fair and right—worthy of gratitude—that some of these
moneys went to support the king's plan to enhance his people
and his country.

The country was no longer wealthy. Land, the life blood
of Hawaii, had been sold or given away. Also, a far greater
problem arose in 1880. It was the first time that government
money had to be used for the royal household.[3] Until this
time there had been enough money from the high chief
lands of the current king to pay for the personal needs of

the king and the royal family. Queen Emma had used this argument in her campaign.

As has been mentioned, at the time of the Great *Mahele* (1843), the lands of Hawaii were divided: a third to the king, a third to the high chiefs, and a third to the common people. The lands belonging to the king (Kamehameha III) were then divided into halves—one half for the king's personal use and one half for the use of the government, known as the Crown lands. It was thought by many that the Crown lands were to follow the holder of the Crown. Of course, at the time of Kamehameha III it was never expected that anyone except a Kamehameha would hold the Crown. Therefore, after the death of Kamehameha V, who left no will, much of the Crown lands was claimed by Kamehameha heirs.

Because most of the Crown lands often remained Kamehameha lands, and even the personal lands of Kamehameha V were withheld from the government, the money from Crown lands for Kalakaua's use was almost negligible. He had to fall back on money received from the use of the lands of High Chief Aikanaka, lands which had been divided after the death of Aikanaka between his younger brother, Moehunua, and his daughter Keohokalole, Kalakaua's mother, whose lands in turn were given to her remaining children—Kalakaua, Liliuokalani, and Likelike.[4]

* * *

Only Spreckels had money to offer the king, but he would demand his pound of flesh in time.

Spreckels needed water rights for his tract of land in central Maui. He petitioned the cabinet. The cabinet and Chief Justice C. C. Harris were willing to work out an accommodation for Spreckels. But Spreckels was impatient; he demanded immediate action and approached Kalakaua with a plan: dismiss the cabinet, and in return the king would receive a $10,000 gift and a loan of $40,000 at seven percent interest.

C. C. Harris wrote that "it is the first time money has been used in this Country to procure official favors and now with the king . . ."[5]

Kalakaua had stepped upon a slippery road to secure moneys. Therefore, cabinets that did not agree with him were removed, until he appointed who he thought was the perfect premier–Celso Caesar Moreno.

The final blow fell.

* * *

Many of the Hawaiians, who liked Moreno and looked at him as an "Italian friend and savior," approved the king's action, but businessmen, the foreign diplomats, and the white community disapproved violently. The native supporters of Moreno published a manifesto that revealed their sympathies:

"To all true-born citizens of the country, greeting: We have with us one Celso Moreno, a naturalized and true Hawaiian. His great desire is the advancement of this country in wealth, and the salvation of this people, by placing the leading positions of Government in the hands of the Hawaiians for administration. The great desire of Moreno is to cast down foreigners from official positions and to put true Hawaiians in their places, because to them belongs the country. They should hold the Government and not strangers. Positions have been taken from Hawaiians and given to strangers. C. C. Moreno desires to throw down these foreigners and to elevate to high positions the people to whom belongs the land, i.e., the red skins. This is the real cause of jealousy on the part of foreigners, viz., that Hawaiians shall be placed above them in all things in this well-beloved country. C. C. Moreno is the heart from whence will issue life to the real Hawaiians."

The opposition, however, was far stronger than the affirmation of Moreno. Kalakaua had opened the 1880 assembly with praise of Moreno for the loan concept, a loan which would be used for buildings, equipment, manning two forts at Diamond Head and Koko Head, and for several warships to protect Hawaii. The loan was also to support hospitals, boarding schools, harbor improvements, railroads, roads, and irrigation works.

Robert Hoapili Baker, who introduced the measure, sought also to extend suffrage to more natives and promote equality by the repeal of the laws prohibiting the sale of liquor to natives.

Moneys from the loan were to open the doors to Asia by a trans-oceanic cable between the American and Asian continents via a Honolulu-China steamer.

The loan failed to pass, but appropriations for a coronation, the establishment of a Board of Genealogy of the Chiefs of Hawaii, National Coinage Act, construction of Iolani Palace, and a bill to subsidize education of Hawaiian youths in Europe passed. Then Kalakaua moved too fast and inexpediditiously.

The Wilder cabinet, which had not supported the king's plans for the loan, was peremptorily dismissed by the king. No reasons or complaints were given. Moreno was appointed minister of foreign affairs and premier.

Acrimony broke out in Honolulu. Placards denouncing Moreno flooded the city. Talk of abdication, crowning Queen Emma, lynching Moreno, and the ever present threat of annexation by the United States were rampant. Even Queen Emma, Princess Ruth, and Princess Pauahi Bishop supported the king's opposition.

Over 2,000 excited people at Kaumakapili Church resolved:

"His Majesty has thereby acted inconsistently with the principles of the Hawaiian Government as a Constitutional Monarchy as established and handed down by the Kamehamehas and their successor Lunalilo, and that his action therein is hostile to the permanence of Hawaiian independence, the perpetuity of the Hawaiian race and the security of life, liberty and property in the Hawaiian Islands."[6]

Rumors came to the king and, remembering the election riots, he ordered the volunteer companies disarmed, arms stacked in the palace, and the Household Guards posted around the palace and the barracks, where he slept. These were frightening times for Kalakaua, who was threatened with assassination and/or loss of his country.

The British and French commissioners, together with the American commissioner, who remained "noncommittal" but sided with the French and English, refused to recognize Moreno. This action was followed further by German, British, and American residents signing a petition against Moreno. Following the Monday mass meeting, headed by Sanford Ballard Dole and held at the Kaumakapili Church, the resignation of Moreno was demanded.

Comly, the American Commissioner, went to Kalakaua explaining that Moreno's so-called commissions from the United States were defunct by the time he presented them as valid and his achievements were grossly exaggerated.

Kalakaua, in fairness to Moreno, called him to the palace and presented the case against him. Kalakaua also explained that peace must be made between Comly and Moreno, or Moreno would be dismissed. Moreno went to Comly, who was dining with Dr. John S. McGrew.[7] A passionate argument broke out between Comly and Moreno. Infuriated, Moreno returned to the palace, where Kalakaua informed him he had no choice but to dismiss him.

Kalakaua by this time had recognized the liability of keeping Moreno in office.

Comly received a note from the king within hours that Moreno had resigned. The committee, however, now feeling the success of their pressure, decided to humiliate the king further and demanded the removal of the entire cabinet. Even Comly thought this was a mistake; he wrote in his dispatch to Washington: "A little tact would have given the king time to 'feel good in,' and then the people might have had their way. But these old Puritans don't know any halfway between damnation and election."

The Hawaiian language newspaper, *Ko Hawaii Pae Aina*, stated that "The Constitution does not grant the subject a right to express his opinion of censure [censure of Kalakaua had been rampant in newspapers] on His Majesty the King."

The political heat of criticism and show of power by the foreigners weighed heavily on Kalakaua. Comforting words in the Hawaiian paper had little or no effect upon the *haole* population that was beginning to become obsessed with the idea of removing the king from office. They were led largely by Lorrin A. Thurston.

Thurston was to become one of the king's deadliest enemies. He was the son of the missionaries Asa and Lucy Goodale Thurston. He had studied at Columbia University and had been admitted to the Hawaiian bar in 1878.

It is amazing that in the midst of animosity that could be cut with a knife, Kalakaua had not foregone his many plans. He had begun to choose and educate young men to go abroad to study as potential future leaders in Hawaii. Among these he chose three—Robert Napu'uako Boyd, James Kaneholo Booth, and Robert W. Wilcox—to go to Italy with Moreno. He, in the face of opposition, appointed Moreno ambassador to Italy and sent the young men with him.

Kalakaua believed the best way to accord diplomatic relations with foreign countries was to understand their customs and speak their language. He was only too aware of the problems the language barrier was causing in Hawaii. Although nearly all governmental procedures were conducted in English, Kalakaua often translated these programs into Hawaiian for a better understanding of his native subjects.

Over the next few years Kalakaua became engaged in an extensive educational program abroad for numerous young men and women, which was to continue until 1886. Besides his nephews, the young princes David Kawananakoa, Jonah

Kuhio Kalanianaole, and Edward Keliiahonui, who were
sent to St. Matthews School, San Mateo, California, there
were August Hering and Maile Nowlein, who were to attend
schools in Italy. Henry Kapena, Hugo Kawelo, and John
Lovell studied in Glasgow, Scotland. Joseph A. Kamau'oha,
Mathew Makalua, and Abraham Pi'ianai'a were educated in
England. Thomas Puali'i Cummins, Henry Grube
Marchant, and Thomas Spencer entered schools in the
United States. James Kapa'a was tutored in Canton, China.
The program's two youngest students, James Haku'ole and
Isaac Harbottle, 10 and 11 years old respectively, traveled to
Tokyo where they were immersed in the Japanese culture.[8]

"These young people were sent abroad between 1880 and
1886, supported by a reluctant government to spend money.
In the face of enormous opposition of the *haole*, but with the
help of Gibson and, to a degree Moreno, Kalakaua carried
out his plans. He 'personally' selected the participants in his
education program and probably planned to groom these
young Hawaiians to become future leaders in his monarchy.
Several of the youths were descended from Hawaiian *alii*
(nobility). Several were the offspring of leaders in Kalakaua's
government. As members of Hawaii's leading social families,
some of the students had mingled with visiting dignitaries
and literati. Most of Kalakaua's proteges had attended
Honolulu's best private schools where they had studied Latin
and the Classics. They were young Hawaiians with a heritage and background to indicate that they would benefit
from an education abroad."[9]

The students could pursue medicine, law, engineering,
surveying, stenographic work, teaching, carpentry, or drawing.

Amid the threatening, grumbling roar of the *haole* population, Kalakaua also continued to plan for his palace and his
trip around the world. He also spent many hours in helping
his wife, Queen Kapiolani, with her plans for the maternity
home which was later to bear her name. The idea for the ma-

ternity home—an attempt to save infants and increase the race—was begun after Kapiolani's visit, representing the king, to Kauai.[10] Kapiolani, often travelling alone with an entourage or with her sister-in-law Princess Liliuokalani, met with and counselled mothers on the care of children.

❀ ❀ ❀

Kalakaua's first major step in increasing prestige for Hawaiians (the *haole* said it was only for his own ego) was laying the cornerstone of the new Iolani Palace on December 31, 1879, on Queen Kapiolani's birthday. The cornerstone was laid with complete Masonic rites. Kalakaua was a Thirty-Third degree Mason in the Scottish Rite and a Knight Templar in the York. He had been told by the Order of Free Masons to "follow the ancient Masonic rites prescribed for proper cornerstone ceremonies," and he did so.

Present at the ceremony were members of the royal household, representatives of the Hawaiian chiefs, legislative and other political—foreign and domestic—representatives, as well as throngs of natives and *haole*.

While the *haole* decried the king for his extravagance, John Makini Kapena, a recognized scholar of Hawaiiana and a cabinet member (1878) spoke:

"In our brotherhood of Masonry each member is taught the symbolical meaning of the three rounds of the ladder, which the Patriarch Jacob saw in his dream. They are: Faith, Hope and Charity.

"I need hardly apologize to the craft assembled here today for comparing these three great rounds with the peculiar characteristics of the sovereigns of this Kingdom who have been members of the Royal craft. Kamehameha IV as Faith, Kamehameha V as Hope and his present Majesty as Charity. For Liholiho, Kamehameha IV, believed the people might be saved by curing the diseases—as witness his exertions in procuring the erection of the Queen's Hospital as proof of his Faith.

"His Majesty Kamehameha v hoped for the perpetuity of Hawaiian independence. The stately government house with its enduring walls stands before you as a proof that his leading sentiment was Hope.

"To his present Majesty we apply the title of Charity. It is the noblest virtue. Charity, springing from an earnest desire for the prosperity of his people, induced him to leave his Kingdom and to brave the wintry cold of the Rocky Mountains and to face the icy precincts of the world renowned cataract of Niagara with the only object in view of securing for his people the boom of Reciprocity and we have all observed how he and his queen have labored in all weathers throughout the Islands for the welfare of his people. In the words of Paul to the Corinthians I may say 'and now abideth these three, Faith, Hope and Charity, but the greatest of these is Charity.' In the words of our order:

"'For our faith may be lost in sight; Hope ends in fruition: but Charity extends beyond the grave through the boundless realm of eternity.'"[11]

Grimly, the *haole* heard such high praise of a reckless king who was about to spend vast sums of tax money for a new palace. The old palace, they thought, was certainly sufficient for a high chief king—as the *haole* often conceived of him.

The original Iolani Palace was a one story coral building with a wide veranda. It had wide reception halls, *lanai*, and a throne room. The family lived in the cottage nearby. Kalakaua had already begun his much criticized entertainments with receptions and dinners. A divided concept existed among the *haole*. On one side was the complaint of too much display and on the other side, fostered by letters home and journalists, was given the picture that the "high chief king" was "primitive."

The dinners at the palace were not, as some American newspapers reported as late as the time of the overthrow of the Hawaiian government, "poi and dog." A typical menu is one taken from a dinner given for "Capt. Tupman and the officers of the HBM *Reindeer* on Tuesday evening spoken of by those present as having a triumph of taste and art, and reflecting much credit on Mr. R. von Oelhoffen, His Majesty's Butler. It is said to have been, in all its appointments, far superior to anything before served in Honolulu. The bill of fare, printed on white satin ribbon and enclosed in a bouquet of artificial flowers placed on each plate, may be a matter of interest to readers here and abroad, and we therefore transcribe it in full: "Iolani Palace, March 16, 1875:

MENU
Anchovies Marionette

SOUPS
Mock Turtle, Nivernaise

FISH
Uhu, stuffed

REMOVES
Fillet of Beef aux Champignon
Roast Goose

COLD DINNER
Aspic de Canard
Mayonnaise of Chicken
Shrimp Curry and Rice

ENTREES
Sweet Bread a la Santa Cruz
Chicken Saute a la Croutons
Roman Punch

GAME
Salami of Duck
Plovers en Papilotte

PASTRY
Charlotte Russe
Confectionary
Biscuit Glace Sauce Shandau

DESSERT
Fruits
Strawberries and Cream

CAFE"[12]

* * *

With Moreno gone, Kalakaua was to turn to the second man, Walter Murray Gibson, who could not only oversee the building of the palace but who would strongly support Kalakaua's controversial trip around the world.

Walter Murray Gibson overlapped Moreno's stay in Hawaii. He arrived eighteen years earlier (1861), but did not come into government until 1872, when he was elected to the legislature. Gibson had supported many of Moreno's projects. Although he attacked the ministry, he supported Kalakaua's program of raising the prestige of the monarchy and the Kalakaua dynasty, perpetuating the genealogy of the Chiefs of Hawaii, national coinage, education of Hawaiian youths abroad, the coronation, the building of a new palace, and financial support of the royal family.

Walter Murray Gibson was another colorful immigrant to the islands. He equalled, if not surpassed, Moreno in his background and experience. He claimed royal lineage and told of being kidnapped at birth, thus preventing him his rightful heritage. He had travelled the world with unjust imprisonments and many other personal adventures. King Kalakaua, who preferred people about him who were entertaining, rather than commonplace and tedious, found in Gibson a delight.

Gibson had arrived in Hawaii in 1861 as a missionary of high standing in the Mormon Church with commissions from Brigham Young and introductions to the rulers of Japan and Malaysia. He planned only to rest briefly in Hawaii before continuing on to direct the missions in Malaysia. He found, however, a ready reception, and decided to stay. His early years in the islands were marked by a masterful reorganization of the numerous native converts to the Mormon Church into a congregation and theology of his own making. He was able to convince the new saints, only recently abandoned by their *haole* missionaries when Young had recalled them to Utah, to turn over all their wealth and property to him. With this considerable income he proceeded to purchase the major part of the island of Lanai and set up a small kingdom in the name of the Latter Day Saints (Mormons).

Upon investigation by three emissaries sent by Brigham Young, he was excommunicated and his followers drifted away to their original church home. He had, however, managed to gain an island home in the process.

Gibson was a "tall, thin old gentleman of sixty with white hair and beard, a mild, cold blue eye, a fine patrician nose and a tolerably port wine complexion . . . [his] voice was soft and low, and confidential to a rare extent. He was an unquestionably eminent-looking veteran, of smooth address, silky manners, and a somewhat fascinating mode of speech, in the estimation of the susceptible and sympathetic—a fine old fellow, I should say; wise as a serpent, but hardly as harmless as a dove," a journalist wrote of Gibson after he became Kalakaua's premier.

He entered politics through his election to the legislature and through his newspapers, *Nuhou* and *Elele Poakolu*, and writing for the *Pacific Commercial Advertiser*. He was to be appointed premier and minister of foreign affairs in 1882.

❊ ❊ ❊

After Moreno's ignominious departure, Kalakaua confided in Gibson his desire for the new palace and placed in Gibson's hands the overseeing of its construction while he took his trip around the world.

Although one of the major problems of the period was the building of Iolani Palace, the concept of a new palace was not an original idea of Gibson's or Kalakaua's.

From 1866 to 1868, during the reign of Kamehameha v, moneys (Kamehameha [Hawaiian] as well as public) were set aside in the sum of $60,000 for a new palace. The 1866 legislature had designated $40,000, and then the 1868 and 1870 legislatures had raised the amount to $60,000.[13] Even at that time, the old palace was beginning to crumble, and if Kalakaua said it was "not fit for him and Kapiolani," he was entirely correct. It was nearly completely termite destroyed. Even Kalakaua's Scottish brother-in-law, and architect, Archibald Cleghorn, declared it was too far gone to repair.

The two bachelor kings, Kamehameha v and Lunalilo, may have found it endurable, but Kamehameha v did recognize the need for living quarters, as well as for official rooms. He planned to call his proposed structure "St. Alexander Palace" in memory of his brother Kamehameha iv (Liholiho Alexander). However, as it was said in 1870 that it was to be built on the site of an old *heiau* (temple). It needed a more "sacred name"—that of Iolani. Kalakaua agreed.

Gibson's excellent executive and managerial talents were the basis for the actual building of the palace, but the conception was Kalakaua's, encouraged by C. C. Harris, dating from the time of Kamehameha v. The $60,000 set aside in 1870 for the new palace was diverted by the more "republic" minded *haole* in government to a government office and legislative building, which was renamed "Aliiolani Hall" by Kalakaua, and of which the final cost was $120,000.

Hawaii without doubt needed a new palace.

A second plan of Kalakaua's, opposed by the *haole* as "another extravagant idea" but supported by Gibson, was the trip around the world. Gibson was himself somewhat of a world traveller; and after hearing the adventurous tales of Moreno's travels, as well as Gibson's, Kalakaua was receptive to such an idea. However, his receptivity dated further back than Gibson or Moreno; it came from the tales of Liliha and her trip to England.

He came by his desire to travel honestly—sea travel was in the blood of the Hawaiians. The number of Hawaiians who travelled far and wide in the 18th and 19th centuries is staggering. There is nothing wrong with travel, unless one is a public official and might spend someone else's money. However, Kalakaua had a little of his own money to support a large part of his adventure. It was Gibson who helped give him a purpose on which the *haole* population might look favorably–immigration. The planters needed workers and favored immigration, and the Hawaiians recognized that their population was decreasing. The divergence came with the type of immigration: the planters wanted cheap labor, while Kalakaua and Gibson wanted people of like values and background for intermarriage with Hawaiians. "Increase the Race" was now the cry of both Gibson and Kalakaua.

It was to be carried around the world along with the message that Hawaii was an independent kingdom of stature worthy of inclusion among the world powers.

6 The King Around the World

Despite the heated animosity found among the *haole* in Honolulu, Kalakaua continued to plan his trip around the world.

King Kalakaua was the first ruling monarch in the history of the world to circumnavigate the globe. When he first made known his bold plans, there was great fear among his native people and his household.

Kapiolani could not forget that Kamehameha II and his wife Kamamalu had ventured to England and had died there. Her fear was excessive, and she desired prayers from her people, not only the Episcopalian and missionary Christian prayers, but *kahuna* prayers also. The people responded by filling the air every night with prayers, *mele*, and songs.

Kalakaua realized that he also needed to reassure his people of his intentions, for rumor was rife that the king was going to "sell" the country to the highest bidder and that all types of unwelcome foreigners would inundate Hawaii as laborers for the plantation owners. Kalakaua, with Kapiolani and often accompanied by his sisters, Princesses Liliuokalani and Likelike, visited all the outer islands, assuring the natives that his project for immigration would be for those people who would have the same values as the Hawaiians and would be a cognate race to "increase the Hawaiian population." He wanted to bring to Hawaii not "slaves for the *haole*" but people to increase the race. He did not want a nation of a few millionaires with the remainder living in poverty, he said. He hoped that by increasing the population, he would also level the wealth.

Night after night, the people thronged to the seashore as his vessel came in. Bonfires glowed for miles along the coastline and torches were held high. There was something magnificent about the king who was going to make their little nation known around the world. There was also something touchingly Hawaiian about the king, who sat among them strumming his guitar or ukelele and singing songs with his two musically talented sisters. His wife, Kapiolani, it was reported, "lay on her side by his side" and listened to her chief assure and entertain both her and their people.[1]

Often, the royal party ate on the deck of the *Likelike*; then the king would send food and gifts to the people on shore. On the Big Island of Hawaii the royal party travelled on horseback over 100 miles. The band at Hilo greeted them with the song dedicated to Kapiolani, "She of the Lovely Eyes." In some of the remote places, the natives crawled on their hands and knees to greet the king, but Kalakaua always gently commanded them to rise. Louise Coffin Jones, a member of the party, wrote "There was no native so poor or humble but had some token of *aloha* to offer."[2] All were received alike and welcomed to an evening of song and dance and refreshments.

Kalakaua, who was himself a *kahuna*–a Hawaiian priest of knowledge and mysticism–joined in the chants with the *kahuna* who came to him to wish him God-speed. Hulas were written and performed for him.

Many news articles tried to negate the popularity of his trip and carried comments such as the one in the *Hawaiian Gazette* of December 12, 1880:

"The King returned from his tour in Hawaii on Sunday morning. We hear it was intended to receive him with a salute and a turn of military; but the gallant defenders of our shores are apparently not addicted to early rising, for by the time they reached the wharf, the 'Likelike' was in. The consequence was that no salute was fired and that an official got wigged for his dilatoriness."

No doubt, the military, precise-minded Kalakaua was not pleased.

While the missionaries shivered at the "blasphemy of the *kahuna* priests" and the "lascivious hulas," the queen grew quiet and comforted, and the king, deeply touched, became more determined to hold his nation intact and bring to it people of similar backgrounds.

Just before leaving, Kalakaua spoke to a huge crowd at the Kawaiahao Church to reassure them and state that an additional object of his travel was to avail himself of the experience of other nations for their benefit. This comment was the king's usual calm reply to the howl of the newspapers that he was taking a trip only for his own pleasure. The newspapers fueled the fires of fear created by the death of Kamehameha II and Queen Kamamalu with a ditty written by Theodore Hook:

"Waiter! Two sandwiches! called Death

And their wild Majesties resigned their breath."

The legislature opposed the trip until it was finally decided the king should pay for it with his own money.[3]

Kalakaua chose as his companions his close friend, John Kapena, a Hawaiian active in the government and the king's companion in an earlier newspaper adventure; and George W. MacFarlane, a Britisher, whom Kalakaua greatly admired and felt would be important to his journey, as much of his itinerary covered lands of the British Empire as well as England itself. However, the *haole* legislative members substituted the court chamberlain, Charles H. Judd, and William Armstrong, both Hawaiian-born Americans of missionary stock. A fourth member of the group, whom Kalakaua chose at the last moment, was Robert (Ropert) von Oehlhoffen. He was considered a buffoon and court jester by Judd and

Armstrong. However, Kalakaua had an excellent reason for adding Robert. He was a linguist, a German baron, who knew well the foreign court customs.

Curtis P. Iaukea describes his training with him previous to his own anticipated but abortive trip to the United States in 1874 with the king:

"I immediately began taking daily instruction in matters of etiquette from Robert von Oehlhoffen . . .

"Von Oehlhoffen was running a restaurant in conjunction with the Royal Hawaiian Hotel bar at the time. A man of striking appearance, with graceful manners, von Oehlhoffen was a meticulous person and a strict disciplinarian. Each gesture had to be learned with just the proper flourish and just the right degree of deference. The smallest detail of serving the royal table was a matter of great importance to him. In this spirit, with rigid attention to detail, he drilled me each day in preparation for the duties that would be expected of me during the King's forthcoming trip. What the duties were to be, those of a page or valet, I did not know. Nevertheless, I was put through the training, and rigorous it was."

Later, when Iaukea was sent as a representative of the Hawaiian Islands to the Russian Court for the coronation of the Tsar and Tsarina (1883) he wrote:

"I watched this glittering pageant and the secretaries and supernumeraries of representatives of governments attending the coronation. Among them the United States Mission, headed by Mr. Hunt, was the most numerous with respect to secretaries and attaches while I, with my lone secretary, represented the most distant and certainly the smallest nation. I was confronted with the problem of gaining as much recognition as possible for my country in the face of overwhelming odds. It was now, if ever in my life I thought, that I thanked the fates that had put me in 1874 into the hands of 'Count' Robert von Oehlhoffen. His strict discipline and meticulous training and observance of customs of diplomatic procedure were now standing me in very good stead for I was able to gain recognition equally with other nations represented by impressive delegations.[4]

For these reasons, Kalakaua chose well. However, Robert was deeply resented by Armstrong, who took every opportunity to ridicule him as a drunkard. It was true Robert leaned heavily to drinking and at times put on his own show, which the king accepted with good humor.

It was suggested by Armstrong, who was to travel as commissioner of immigration, that the king travel incognito, for no foreign country could be expected to pay extended homage to such an insignificant king of such a small country as Hawaii. This statement was made regardless of the fact that Hawaii had fifty-six diplomatic and consular representatives overseas, who received only the briefest of notices that the king would be in their countries incognito. As Kalakaua could afford only a small retinue—three persons—he agreed that he should travel as "Prince Kalakaua" or totally incognito, taking with him no royal regalia. Kalakaua, however, knew the extent of his own popularity and the knowledge of his country better than Armstrong did, so he included in his wardrobe a feather cape—aside from that he chose only the most unostentatious suits of black broadcloth and a few decorative insignia.

On the other hand, Armstrong demanded for himself and Judd the finest of uniforms. Although Judd was a colonel and might wear a military uniform, Armstrong had no right to one. The uniforms, costing $700 each, were elaborate, with gilt braid of embroidered gold taro leaf, sashes of red, a sword belt, trousers with gold stripes, and gold bars and stars on the collar.

Thus, the simple king and the ornate retinue left Honolulu and a wharf crowded with well-wishers on January 20, 1881, aboard the *City of Sidney* for San Francisco.

On approaching the Bay of San Francisco, the ship's captain urged the king to hoist the royal standard, which Robert immediately produced, and it was raised. Kalakaua was no longer incognito.

San Francisco was enthusiastic in its welcome to its favorite king. The city had not forgotten the debonair, charming, elegant king of 1874. A twenty-one gun salute was fired, and the *Chronicle* was again at the heels of King Kalakaua to report his every move—private or public. He was met by a closed carriage—closed because it was raining—to take him to the Palace Hotel. Thousands of umbrellas bobbed on the street as San Franciscans turned out again to greet the king from Hawaii.

He was invited to visit the legislative assembly at Sacramento and was given a dinner in his honor. Orators reminded him of the importance of Hawaii in the Pacific, and one shouted "Kalakaua the Colossus of the Pacific." The newspapers took up the cry and, after an interview with the king, went on to say that from the time of Kamehameha I the desire to unify the Pacific under the Hawaiian leadership had been cherished.

Returning to San Francisco, the consul general of his Imperial Majesty the Emperor of China gave a banquet for the king and his party, and the king's projected trip around the world was no longer a secret.

Armstrong described the event:

"It was said to be the costliest dinner ever given by the Chinese in America. Twenty tables were covered with heavy embroidered crimson satin, with fringes of gold bullion and silver stars, heavy silk scrolls hung from the ceiling, upon which were inscribed words from the wise sayings of Confucius; American, Hawaiian, and Chinese flags were intertwined on pillars; the Consul, in a gorgeous costume of silk, sat with the king on his right hand. On receiving his Majesty at the door he had ignored the delicate and artistic pumphandle hand-shaking of Christendom, and placing the closed fist of one of his own hands in the palm of the other, shook them together with the enthusiasm demanded by the rank of the guest. The dishes served were the prize of China: bird's nest soup, white snow fingers, imperial fish brains, preserved bird's eggs, shark's fins, fish maw, tender bamboo shoots, stewed duck with Teintsin sauce, chicken with Satow dressing, turtle stew, melon and many other kinds of seeds, sweetmeats, pear-wine, and many *bonnes bouches* unknown to Parisian restaurants. Chopsticks were laid beside the guests' plates, but forks were also furnished, as a liberal concession to the crude habits of Western civilization.

"The Consul toasted the King, and, as the spokesman for all Chinamen, thanked him for the just treatment they had received in his kingdom; there was but one place in Christendom, beyond the lines of the British Empire, in which all Chinese immigrants could live without fear of unjust assault; it was, he said, in the King's dominions."[5]

Kalakaua, on leaving San Francisco for his first foreign port, wrote Kapiolani:

"Kalakaua to Kapiolani en route to Japan, February 16, 1881.

"i To catch a glimpse of yonder shore,
My eager eyes I strain,
And pray that I was there—once more
Let me not pray in vain.

"ii The surf, its silvery crests display,
On that far shore, I love—
When back, I make my homeward way,
No more I'll care to rove.

"iii Dear waiting one, I think of thee,
The maile round thy neck!
O, tell me wild and angry sea,
How long you'll hold me back?

"iv Since then I cannot meet you now,
Divided by the main,

Let me tell you fondly how
I hope we'll meet again.

"v A love like thine, so real and true
My devious way will guard,
And when the rounded world I view,
Thy love is my reward."[6]

On February 8, 1881, the royal suite left for Japan on the *Oceanic* from San Francisco, arriving at the Bay of Yedo on March 4th. Again Armstrong advised Kalakaua not to be "pretentious" by displaying the royal standard, but the captain of the ship and Robert overruled him, and the standard was flown. Immediately a twenty-one gun salute was given. The sailors stood in line, with each man extending his arm to the shoulders of the next one; flags of all nations were flown from stem to stern. Other warships, following the lead of the Russian ship, fired salutes until 273 cannons roared and thick smoke enveloped the scene.

Kalakaua had some knowledge about Japan. During his years at the High Chiefs' school whaling ships had come into the Hawaiian ports, and castaway Japanese had come to Hawaii from the closed Japan. Five newsworthy Japanese boys had come to Honolulu from a disabled junk in 1841, and Kalakaua became acquainted with the oldest of the boys, Denzo, because he had been taken on as a servant at the High Chiefs' School.[7] Kalakaua, always eager for news of far-off places, listened enraptured to the tales of Denzo. Other stories of closed and "heathen" Japan also infiltrated the High Chiefs' School through the Cookes. In 1854, Commodore Matthew Perry negotiated a treaty with Japan, opening the country to commercial intercourse with the United States. It awakened the interest of the Hawaiian newspapers to the strategic position Hawaii held.

In 1860, the Japanese ambassadors of the first Embassy to the United States stopped at Honolulu. Kalakaua, as aide to

Kamehameha IV, helped with the entertainment of the group. Kalakaua, always an avid reader, was thoroughly equipped to talk with the embassy group. One of the Japanese castaways–the brother of Denzo–was now Captain Nakahama of the Japanese Navy, and reminiscences were in full force between the captain and young Kalakaua.

The officials spoke Dutch, but little English, except for the youngest, sixteen-year-old-Tateishi Onejro,[8] who spoke English well and who satisfied Kalakaua's curiosity as well as his own. During the ambassadors' stay Kalakaua was engaged in planning and attending ceremonies, receptions, dinners, balls. He was also to make the first contact of political alliance with Japan. As Privy Council Secretary, he drafted under Foreign Minister Wyllie's direction a treaty with Japan, which although rejected by the ambassadors, was taken back to Japan.

Kalakaua had a strong liking for the Japanese, regardless of the antipathy the *haole* had for the race, and had eagerly looked forward to his visit to Japan. Hawaii's Consul R. W. Irwin, the great-grandson of Benjamin Franklin, who had married a Japanese woman, together with the American Minister Bingham conferred with Foreign Minister Inoue, and Japan was ready to welcome Kalakaua.

A splendid barge came to the *Oceanic* with a welcoming committee to take the royal party to shore, where the naval band played "Hawaii Pono'i." The royal party travelled through the streets of Yokohama, which were filled with Hawaiian and Japanese flags and people who bowed to the royal carriage.

The Japanese Emperor received and shook hands with the king in Tokyo. In the audience chamber they met the empress, who was dressed in Japanese style, while her attendants wore European styles. Kalakaua wrote his sister that he watched her "quietness" and that he much admired her wearing "the costume of her people."[9]

It soon became evident that Kalakaua and the emperor shared the same belief of tracing their ancestry back to the gods and goddesses.

It was during this time that Robert, who was treated as a member of the royal party and given his own chambers and servants, became drunk and wore the feathered cloak. It impressed the Japanese, annoyed Armstrong and Judd, and amused the king.

For ten days the king and his suite were entertained at banquets, presided over by the Imperial Prince. Armstrong promoted himself to "minister of state," and Robert demoted him to the king's barber.

The newspapers carried articles daily of geographical descriptions of Hawaii and stories of the first foreign king to visit Japan. The *Asahim Shimbun* was greatly interested in the king, particularly about why he allowed foreigners to travel with him rather than natives. It was speculated on whether the white man had already taken over Hawaii.

It may be that Kalakaua, forced by these speculations, carried out a long thought of plan. He escaped his chamberlain and now "secretary of state" and met in private with the emperor. During the interview, Kalakaua proposed the creation of a federation of the Polynesian people with the Asian, with Japan at its head. Secondly, he proposed a marriage alliance between his five-year-old niece, Heiress Presumptive Kaiulani, with the fifteen-year-old Prince Komatsu. These proposals the emperor was to "take under advisement" while the lavish entertainments continued. The emperor later turned down both proposals. It was not the custom of the Japanese royal house to allow interracial marriages, and Kaiulani was not only Hawaiian, but also of Scottish blood. The suggestion of the federation was ahead of its time, considering the western powers' opposition to Japan.

The one success of the visit was an amicable treaty, which was the first to welcome Japan into the nations of the world. Judd presented to the minister of foreign affairs:

"The Hawaiian government is willing to incorporate in a treaty a full and complete recognition of the integrity of the Japanese Empire, and it will relinquish all claims of whatever nature which may arise out of what is known as the extra-territorial rights in the existing treaty."

The instrument of this treaty was not executed, owing to the strenuous remonstrances of the European governments. Seventeen years after this negotiation, the humiliating clause that excluded Japanese sovereignty from seaports of foreign nations known as "treaty ports" was removed from all of the treaties, and the complete integrity of the Japanese Empire was recognized by all nations. Thus, Kalakaua was first to welcome Japan.

Kalakaua discovered for himself two deficiencies. He was presented by the emperor with Japan's most distinguished order, the Order of the Chrysanthemum, first Class with Collar. He was the first monarch to receive it in person. Kalakaua found himself woefully deficient in Hawaiian generosity and reciprocation. He had no orders to give in return. When the story of this incident reached Honolulu, the *Advertiser* said the king would have been saved such embarrassment by traveling officially and carrying with him the proper gifts for such occasions; but the *Gazette* declared the fault lay with those who insisted on recognizing him as royalty when he was traveling incognito.

However, Kalakaua felt that Hawaii should have orders to present to the other host nations he was to visit. He therefore carefully drew up fourteen articles to govern the rules of the recipients of such orders.[10]

Another deficiency that troubled Kalakaua was Hawaii's military power. His country was practically defenseless. Although he himself was aware of the need of defenses, he had been unable to promote any military or naval defense. He found it embarrassing as he viewed the standing armies of Japan. This lack of defense was to be one of the most embarrassing situations for him throughout his world tour.

Nevertheless, the scholarly, inventive, and creative Kalakaua enjoyed all the scientific advances, museums, arts, theaters, and landscaped beauty of Japan. The generous Japanese loaded him with gifts of every sort, including two monumental bronze vases and a Buddha figure.

After leaving Tokyo, the royal suite travelled to Kyoto, Osaka, Kobe, and Nagasaki, where entertainments continued. Throughout Japan, Kalakaua became more and more convinced that the Japanese were a cognate race of the Hawaiians. He wrote in his journal:

"Adieu Japan—beautiful Japan—I felt as if I would have a continued longing to see this interesting country with its kind and hospitable people for a long, long time. Aloha Nui!"

* * *

Kalakaua expressed his wish to visit China, but he was opposed by Armstrong and Judd. The Chinese laborers had long been in Hawaii and were resented by the *haole* for their industrious and quick rise from field workers to shop owners. Celso Moreno had been to China before he met and spoke with Kalakaua and had become his minister of foreign affairs in 1880. During that time, Moreno had told Kalakaua of a modern China that had legations in Berlin, Paris, Washington, Tokyo, Madrid, St. Petersburg, and Lima. This was a China that was attempting to modernize its country with steamship lines, cables, and education of Chinese youth abroad (120 students had gone to the United States and 30 had been sent to England and France by 1881). However, Armstrong thought of China as "heathen," as he thought of Hawaii. And worse, the Chinese had no white men to guide them.

Nevertheless, at Shanghai the American Consul General called on the king and urged him to visit Peking as the first foreign king to enter the Forbidden City. He was not, however, to do so. At the time, the emperor was a child and had no official right to invite even the first foreign king to visit his land. No previous preparations had been made before the visit to China, so it was impossible for the king to visit Peking.

However, Kalakaua found at his disposal a large steamer, the *Pautah*, for his trip to Tiensin. At Tiensin, the suite was welcomed by the viceroy, General Li Hung Chang, whose offer of apartments was refused. The party preferred staying aboard the ship that gave them royal accommodations and "excellent food."

The Vice Consul was full of questions, and again came the crucial queries about an army and the foreigners in Hawaii. As in Japan, Kalakaua and his retinue were lavishly entertained, and the people thronged the docks to see the king. Crowds followed the suite and pressed against the windows of places where they ate.

After leaving Shanghai from the second visit, the suite travelled on the *Thilet* to Hong Kong on April 21, 1881. There the British Consul took over the affairs of the group. As in Shanghai, the newspapers carried news of the king, and again banquets were held.

In Hong Kong, Kalakaua allowed Armstrong to "speak" for him at a banquet. Armstrong, in a most officious manner—for he did not like the British—recalled Captain Cook's incorrect behavior and the foolishness of Paulet in interfering with the Hawaiian government. It was the last time Armstrong spoke for the king.

Nevertheless, the British entertainment was elaborate.

"A formal reception was given at Government House by Lord and Lady Hennessy who said: 'His Majesty's bearing and conduct would not be excelled by any sovereign.'" The *China Mail* reported that the King of Hawaii was welcomed "with something more than the official politeness and respect accorded rank."

Interviewed by the *St. James Gazette*, King Kalakaua told of his desire to recruit citizens for rebuilding his kingdom, which moved that journal to note that in times past kings had gone forth in quest of a kingdom, and nations in quest of a sovereign, "but perhaps never before has a king gone forth in search of a people for his kingdom . . . It is sad to report that the touch of civilization has proven fatal to Polynesia."[11]

News articles of the king and his trip around the world were picked up by the foreign papers. The *Daily Telegraph* in London, under the skillful hand of Sir Edwin Arnold, carried stories of the "gallant," the "venturesome," the "remarkable" king. Already Europe was being awakened to the king's tour.

* * *

Before the entourage departed from Hong Kong for Siam, even Armstrong noted for the first time in his journal that the king was a man of breeding and position. "After four days spent in royal receptions, tiffins, and garden parties, irrespective of barracks and docks, the King, with parades and numerous salutes, embarked on the 'Killarney' for Siam.

"When the Governor bade him good-bye at the gangway he said to me that the bearing and conduct of the King could not be excelled by any sovereign; and he only voiced the sentiments of the cosmopolitan city of Hong Kong. The voluntary expression of gratitude by the Chinese merchants to the King for the justice and the impartial administration of the law in his kingdom was an event of which any king might be proud."[12]

Siam was a delight to Kalakaua. All the suite responded to sights of the river, the forests, the tall coconut palms. It was Hawaii. It was home. They were there in the warm month of May.

Again, no courtesy was expected, as Hawaii had no treaty with Siam nor any representative there. However, the

Siamese consul in Hong Kong had alerted the Siamese court to the king's impending arrival. Thus, the suite was met with a royal salute and a royal barge covered with a canopy of yellow silk and gold embroidery. They were taken in a royal carriage with a cavalry escort to the courtyard of the prince, the twenty-seven year old Souditch-Chou-Fa-Chulalou Korn, King of Siam. Chulalou Korn was the son of the King of Siam, who was portrayed in *Anna and the King of Siam*. The king greeted them in a large marble-floored reception hall. Dressed in a tunic of gold brocade, he remained seated and then ordered a chair to be placed at his side for the king. They were entertained by dancing girls in diaphanous dresses with ropes of pearl.

Nothing was too good for the suite; in their apartments were eight body servants for the king and five to each of the suite.

A great banquet was given in the king's honor, and Kalakaua was made Knight of the Grand Cross of the Crown of Siam and presented with a robe of gold-embroidered satin. Again the king had nothing to give in return.

Kalakaua was caught up in the Buddha worship and invited priests to come to Hawaii. It was brought home to him that the Hawaiian religion had nearly been totally destroyed and there existed only the ruins of the *heiau*, rather than the magnificent pagodas. Of course, the *heiau* had never rivaled the pagodas, but were simple structures of worship. Nevertheless, they were rapidly being destroyed.

Kalakaua and the Siamese king had long conversations about European literature and chemistry and inventions. The Siamese king questioned whether the white man was ruling Hawaii, and Kalakaua again spoke of his desire to increase his race through immigration. It was then that the two rulers discovered they shared Malay blood, and Kalakaua had found another cognate race.

Kalakaua found a likeable and inspiring companion in the young king. Chulalou Korn was the real founder of a modern Siam. During his reign, after reaching his majority, he abolished the feudal system and slavery, and introduced administrative reform, postal service, modernization of the army, the telegraph, and the first railway. King Kalakaua and he discussed at length the modernization of a country without the destruction of traditions and heritage. Going slowly, at a pace the natives could understand and to which they could acclimate themselves, was the answer. This was not happening in Hawaii. Modernization was moving at the pace of the foreigner, not the native.

Nothing was spared to entertain the Hawaiian king and the suite. They were given the rare privilege of seeing the interior of the royal chapel, the chambers in which the Siamese king fasted and prayed before his coronation. They mounted and rode the royal elephants. They were entertained at the theater where Siamese girls danced to Siamese music, and, of course, there were banquets.

The two kings found much in common. When the Siamese king mentioned that he could not understand the missionaries because their conduct did not concur with their stated beliefs, Kalakaua was in complete accord.

* * *

In Singapore, the party was officially saluted, in intense heat, and the governor made plans for their stay and entertainment. At a banquet, the governor toasted the king, saying he had seen many of the Polynesian race and their good nature, and that chivalry was conspicuous among the Maoris of New Zealand, whose language was similar to that of the Hawaiians. Kalakaua's interest in the Maoris was awakened, and later he spoke to his sister's brother-in-law, Charles Reed Bishop, about immigration. But Bishop, although he often travelled to New Zealand and Australia, was disinterested in promoting immigration. Although officially Armstrong was commissioner of immigration, nowhere in the Asiatic countries did he make the slightest move toward discussing it.

While in the Singapore area, the king and his party visited the Maharaja of Johore, who ruled in a district fourteen miles from Singapore under the British protectorate. Again royal receptions and entertainment were found, and Kalakaua in a conversation with the Maharaja discovered the striking comparison of word-similarity between the Malaya and Hawaiian. Kalakaua was particularly well versed in the subject because of his acquaintance with Abraham Fornander, who had compared forty different languages with Hawaiian.[13] Kalakaua again felt a kinship with the country he was visiting.

The *Straits Times* of Singapore highly praised the "knowledgeable king from Hawaii who was widely conversant on all topics be they astronomy, politics, language, religion or history."[14] Here Kalakaua made his first acquaintance with Islam, offered it welcome to Hawaii, and accepted as a gift the Koran.

Entertainments continued in a grand manner in India and Egypt, where the king was the guest of the Egyptian Khedive.

The *Al-Ittihad Al-Misre (Egyptian Unity)*[15], which carried some English translations, praised Kalakaua's manners toward the Hindus and his acceptance of all religions. It told in detail of his trip to the Orient and his projected trip to England where he would be the guest of the Queen.

The French as well as the English papers commented favorably on the king, placing him above some of the European monarchs in intelligence and education: "A man of noble presence, with a benevolent expression."

The Masonic Fraternity of Alexandria asked him to address them and recorded that the king "surprised them by his knowledge of the history of their Order."

The suite saw the pyramids, the museums, and the mummies, which fascinated Kalakaua enough to write Kapiolani,

who later found the same fascination in Washington, D. C.
It was evidence of a reverence for the dead that Kalakaua felt
the *haole* seriously lacked. Kalakaua had already begun to
preserve Hawaiian burial grounds. The king, who had the
Hawaiian love for horses, was overjoyed by the Arabian
horses. One was offered to him, which he did not accept because the other members of the royal suite vigorously objected.

❋ ❋ ❋

Kalakaua, a devoted student of the Greek and Roman classics,
was transported during the portion of the journey approaching Naples. The summer heat was just beginning at the end of
June, and Armstrong warned that "no one would be at home."
As they were now nearing "civilized" countries, Armstrong expected no tributes to be paid to the "pagan" king as had been
paid in the "heathen" countries they had left.

However, he had counted without Celso Moreno, who
had arrived in Italy and made plans for the king, and secretly
had agreed to meet the king there. As the party anchored in
Naples, the mayor of the city and other officials, led by
Moreno, welcomed the king while the two aids to the king
stood helplessly and furiously by; they spoke no Italian.

Kalakaua was quickly whisked off by Moreno, leaving his
suite on the deck of the steamer. They hastily followed, finding him at the Hostel des Estrangers. They entrenched
themselves with vows never to let the king escape again. The
king was highly amused by accounts of their search for him.

Moreno had made arrangements for the king—and his
now constant suite—to be received by King Humberto and
Queen Margherita, who conversed with the king privately.
The King and Queen of Italy were not ignorant of Hawaii,
of the three young men Kalakaua had sent to study there, nor
of Moreno, for the newspapers carried extensive accounts of
all. *La Nazione* called the young men the "children of the
king," something to which Kalakaua proudly acceded as *hanai*,
but members of the suite quickly corrected.

It was discovered that Moreno had also made some inroads with European nations, pleading for support of Hawaiian independence. This too was quickly quelled by Armstrong, who stated "they" could find themselves in difficulty with the United States if they took such steps.

On July 3rd, while in Rome, the suite had the unusual privilege of having an audience with the Pope at the Vatican.

"A door opened, and his Holiness, Leo XIII, a thin and spare old man with an extremely pale face, entered and slowly moved across the room, while all bowed in reverence, to a chair on a dais raised a few inches from the floor. In front of him another chair was placed for the King; around the Holy Father the Cardinals were grouped, and we of the suite stood near the King.

"The Pope began the conversation at once in Italian, which was interpreted by Cardinal Howard. He asked many questions about the Hawaiian kingdom. The Cardinals joined, and soon showed that they were well informed about the condition of the native Catholics in Hawaii, of whom there were almost as many as there were Protestants. The Holy Father said to the King: 'Will you present your companions?' The King presented us. The Pope asked: 'Are they natives of your country?' The King replied that we were, and the sons of Protestant missionaries. Cardinal Howard laughed, and said, 'Then they are in the opposition.' The Holy Father smiled. There was no solemnity in the interview; it was only a pleasant chat.

"'Do my people in your kingdom behave well?' asked the Pope.

"'Yes,' said the King, 'they are good subjects.'"

"'If they do not behave,' said the Pope, 'I must look after them. Why do you have a white Minister in your government?' he continued.

"The King could not make a brief explanation and turned to me. I answered, for him, that the kings of Hawaii chose educated white men, who were better able to deal with the foreigners, who held most of the wealth of the country.

"Cardinal Howard asked: 'Are there any Catholics in your government?'

"I answered: 'No, the American Protestants entered the country before the Catholics did, and have kept control of public affairs; but no efficient Catholic is excluded from high office by reason of his faith.'

"There was often a pleasant twinkle in the Holy Father's eyes, and he smiled while he spoke . . .

"After an interview which lasted twenty minutes we kissed the Holy Father's hand and rose. He said to the King: 'Your country is far away. I shall pray for your safe return. . .'"[16]

Kalakaua had been advised to bypass Paris, as "We," according to Armstrong, "had no love for the French nation," and continue on to London. Kalakaua had also been warned that France was a Republic. It would not take kindly to a king's visit. Later he was regaled by his suite for his "undiplomatic gesture"—and he returned for a brief visit, interrupting his stay in London. He was kindly received in France, despite Armstrong's sentiments.

Armstrong now began to take his job as commissioner of immigration seriously. Both Moreno and the king had issued statements of Hawaii being desirous of immigration of persons who would come to Hawaii to be permanent citizens. But each move the king made was checkmated by Mr. Armstrong who, signing himself "Minister of State," declared in public statements and private letters to officials that none but laborers were wanted in the islands. Some of these published statements were sent by Robert to the *Advertiser*, which editor Gibson, amused by Armstrong's "new and unexpected title," published with the comment that "he is obviously endeavoring to hinder any immigration except that of cheap plantation labor although his instructions from the king are that he is to bring families for repopulating the Islands."

Kathleen Mellen later wrote, "Under his newly assumed title 'Minister of State' Mr. Armstrong continued his propaganda against the migration of Europeans to Hawaii." The Hawaiian newspapers reported that in Belgium he said, "field workers for sugar plantations alone are needed . . . there is slight opportunity for artisans or traders." In Berlin he urged the *Berlinger Zeitung* to give this statement wide circulation: "I wish that emigration to the Hawaiian Islands be rather discouraged than encouraged and this I declare formally and publicly." The paper said that Germans "are not under any circumstances to emigrate to the Sandwich Islands."

When Mr. Armstrong's statement reached Honolulu, Gibson, via the *Advertiser*, charged: "This is treason that belies the real needs of the country by discouraging . . . enterprise that would benefit Hawaii."[17]

The pessimistic Armstrong, always reluctant to admit the charm that King Kalakaua exuded over people, believed the entertainments were now surely at an end.

But again he was wrong. Although he remembered the British royal visits and contacts with Hawaii, he was surprised that the small "slice of bread" cast on the waters should bring such effusive returns. The Duke of Edinburgh had visited the Hawaiian Kingdom during the reign of Kamehameha v and been offered entertainments that were overseen by Kalakaua and his sister Lydia Kamakaeha (Liliuokalani).[18] There also was R. F. Synge of the Foreign Office, whose father had been British commissioner in Hawaii during the reign of Kamehameha iv, and last but definitely not least Queen Victoria, who had consented to be godmother to Prince Albert and who was friendly toward Queen Emma. As both Kalakaua and the Prince of Wales were grand masters of their Masonic Lodges, the king was again welcomed, fêted, and toured.

Every newspaper in England caught the glamour of the king. The *Morning Post*, the *Guardian*, *Illustrated London News*, the *Times*, and the *Evening Standard* could not get enough glimpses of the king—at the Royal Italian Opera where the operatic coloratura soprano Adalena Patti sang, at services in Westminster Abbey, at an interview with Queen Victoria, at garden parties, receptions, banquets, and balls. *Punch* had to have its say, but in a remarkably quiet way for a *Punch* that had its shots at royalty and all unsuspecting visitors:

> "He's really a most intelligent wight,
>   Who's looked on many a wonderful sight,
>   And travelled by day, and eke by night,
>   O'er rivers and seas and dry lands;
>   But wrongly, it seems, his name we say,
>   And print it too, in a horrible way,
>   He ought to be called King Kalakua,
>   This King of the Sandwich Islands."

The interview most interesting to Kalakaua was with Sir Edwin Arnold, editor of the *Daily Telegraph*, who had followed his progress across the world. Sir Edwin had just had published his "Light of Asia" (1879) a poem about the life and teachings of Buddha, which he presented to the king. Sir Edwin became so intrigued with Hawaii that he planned a visit there, as he did during Liliuokalani's reign.

He lunched with Princess Mary Adelaid, who made sure her children were present to meet a king of "such good manners." In Scotland, where he went to see his niece's father's (Cleghorn) homeland, he was taken to Edinburgh Castle to view the Scottish regalia. He was entertained with cake and wine luncheons, where the Lord Provost of Edinburgh Sir Thomas J. Boyd toasted his health with the words: "I give His Majesty a cordial welcome to the capital of Scotland. Since His Majesty's arrival in this country, our attention has been drawn more than formerly to the kingdom of Hawaii, over which His Majesty rules, consisting of the rich, interesting and beautiful Sandwich Islands, in the centre of the Pacific Ocean; and especially we are pleased to think of the vast progress in civilization which their people have made during the present century. In the last seven years, when His Majesty has been King, further progress had been made, and during that time great material prosperity has been also experienced in a largely increased revenue . . . We must all greatly admire the public spirit and love of his people's good shown in his thus going through the world in their best interests."[19]

* * *

Although not of Oriental regal splendor, the remainder of Kalakaua's trip to Europe was one of gracious entertainment and welcome.

"Throughout Europe he was honored by royalty and hailed by the common people who lined the streets when he went abroad and serenaded him at night. The extent of his learning was a source of constant amazement to everyone. The Vienna *Wiener Zeitung* said: 'He evinced a surprising knowledge of all technical sciences, art collections, music, and he is a thorough gentleman in dress, manner, speech. His kindness is such as to make him beloved by everyone who meets him.'"

He had met the Crown Prince Frederick in London and had been assured of a welcome in Berlin by Prince William—and so he was. The military preciseness and reviews led the king to remember his own interest in the military and to buy six field artillery pieces in Austria. The king was delighted to learn that the Hawaiian band, as well as its German-born bandmaster, Henry Berger, was known throughout Europe. "Hawaii Pono'i" was played wherever the king went in Europe, as it had been in the Orient.

In Vienna, Kalakaua responded to the gaiety of music and dance and *joie de vivre*—newspapermen followed him much as the reporters of the *San Francisco Chronicle* had. Everything was news—what he ate, what he said, his dress, his manners, and of course, his waltzing ability. *Die Presse* could not praise him highly enough. In Vienna the king was the best of the "Merry Monarch."

Kalakaua was a favorite among reporters. In Spain the *Diari de Barcelona* praised his manners and quoted *Le Journal le figaro* of Paris, saying he was "the best educated, most elegantly mannered ruler in the world." In Portugal, Kalakaua took the opportunity to praise the immigrants in Hawaii that came from the Madeiras and Azores.

The last leg of Kalakaua's trip around the world was to the United States, which took place in the fall of the year. New York, like San Francisco, loved the king; his journey through Pennsylvania and Kentucky was brief. In San Francisco he was happily received and banqueted. The ever-present *Chronicle* reported his trip, his impressions, his triumphs, and his decorations. It was a fitting end for the king's trip, but the bitter Armstrong had to have a final negative word: "... as the royal party boarded the *California* at San Francisco on the last lap of their journey, Mr. Armstrong reminded the king that 'he was merely a grasshopper in the pathway of an elephant,' saying, 'Your people are dying out and will soon be extinct.' Replied the king coldly: 'Well, other great races have died out ... The best way is to let us be. What good have you done my people . . . bringing leprosy, disease, forcing rum upon us . . .'"

Armstrong concluded: "The king did not understand the law of evolution." The missionaries, he added, were "growing tired of irresponsible Polynesian rule."

Hawaii did not have Armstrong's view, and as Hawaiian papers had quoted many foreign papers during the king's absence, on October 29, 1881, the wharves were crowded, the city decorated, and the people joyous to have their king back after nine months. The palace had been torn down for rebuilding, and a joyful Kapiolani greeted him at a smaller building named "Kinau Hale," while the people massed and buried the king in *lei* of flowers and scented vines.

7 King's Return and a New Palace

While the king was gone, his sister, Liliuokalani, was regent. She governed with few major problems. An outbreak of smallpox in Honolulu caused her to halt communication between the islands in order to contain a possible epidemic. Immediately she and the ministry were attacked, showing that opponents did not need Kalakaua to vent their restlessness or their eagerness to cause trouble in the little kingdom. "Dismissal of the cabinet and want of confidence" became again the familiar cry. Liliuokalani stood firmly by her ministry and held the position of confining the epidemic to Honolulu. It soon came to an end.

Privately, Liliuokalani used her position to join Queen Kapiolani and the queen's sisters, Poomaikelani and Kekaulike, as well as her own sister, Likelike, in domestic projects. The queen's two main projects to which she gave her own money and time were a home for girls of parents who were lepers and the maternity home for women. Liliuokalani worked also for her own two main projects: the school for girls similar to that at Mills College, not for girls to learn to be domestics but to learn the arts and politics; and a bank for women. *Alii* women held great wealth in land, but often it was "bought" at bargain prices by the *haole* or dissipated in marriage. Liliuokalani believed women were quite as capable as men of controlling their own affairs, especially if with a bank of their own. She found little support for the latter as her *hanai* brother-in-law, Charles Reed Bishop, owned Hawaii's only bank and intended to keep it that way.

Kapiolani held salons and teas at the palace to raise money, and the princesses and Liliuokalani arranged for musicals and "ice-cream suppers."

When Kalakaua returned from his trip he was surprised to discover his enterprising women; however, he apparently entered into the activities with good humor. An incident is related by Isobel Strong Field, Robert Louis Stevenson's stepdaughter, in her book *This Life I've Loved*:

At a benefit garden party given by Queen Kapiolani, Mrs. Strong was asked to tell fortunes by cards. "The King was much amused by my cards, always presenting himself first to have his fortune told, and bringing many clients to my tent. Once the cards predicted that he would be mixed up in a quarrel very soon. A little later I passed him in the garden.

"'You are not leaving already, Your Majesty?' I asked.

"'Oh, no,' he said. 'I thought I'd just run in and find fault with the Queen. You see I must have a quarrel to prove that your cards are always right.'"[1]

The king appeared amiable, but he remembered his trip with both pleasure and resentment.

❊ ❊ ❊

If the king's trip had annoyed—as it had—the thrifty New Englanders, this annoyance was small in comparison to the beginning of the outrage King Kalakaua felt toward the missionary-oriented *haole*. The remembrance of his turbulent childhood and High Chiefs' School experiences fueled his bitterness.

He had written his sister Liliuokalani from Cairo in June 1881, during the news of the smallpox epidemic in the islands:

"As you are a religious and praying woman, Oh! All the religious people praise you! But what is the use of prayer after 293 lives of our poor people have gone to their everlasting place. Is it to thank him for killing or is it to thank him for sending them to him consequently I never allowed myself to be ruled by the Church members nation for in my opinion it is only a mockery. The idea of offering prayer when hundreds are dying around you. To save the life of the people is to work and not pray. To find and stop the causes of death of our people and not cry and whine like a child and say to god 'that it is good oh Lord that thou hath visited us thus.'"[2]

During his stay in Europe, where he was wined and dined and saw a "modern" life of joy and gaiety, he wrote from Paris, in August 1881, asking rhetorically if "all these people" were going to hell:

"Surely not! But what a contrast to our miserable bigoted community. All sober and down in the mouth keeping a wrong sabbath instead of a proper Sunday, the Pure are so pure that the impure should make the Sunday a day of mockery, with such rubbish trash that we have so long been lead [sic] to believe, it is a wonder that we have not risen any higher than the common brute."[3]

* * *

On his return, his ears were ringing with the questions asked him in his travels, not once but many times: "Has the white man already taken over your country?" "Why do you not have natives in your government?" "What is the strength of your army?" "Your navy?"

These had been sensitive questions and had aroused further questions in the king's mind about the *haole* in his country, and particularly those who called themselves the "Missionary Party."

Armstrong had done nothing to endear himself or his contemporaries to the king. He had set forth, in his own words, to "educate the king," and had succeeded only in exasperating him. He had continuously ridiculed him and his ideas. Kalakaua, who was a wide reader of philosophy and theology, as well as of history and political science, did not take kindly to Armstrong's negation of the king's invitation to other religions, such as Buddhism. His attitude was negative toward any and all of Kalakaua's observations, comments, and new ideas for Hawaii's incorporation with the world.

There was more than a beginning of an active resentment in Kalakaua against the Missionary Party. Growing parallel along with it was an equally strong resentment among the *haole* against the king and his money-spending proclivities. Kalakaua did not return to a unified Hawaii, but to one that was ripping apart.

The name the "Merry Monarch" was to attach itself to Kalakaua, not in a complimentary manner as it had been in Vienna, but as derogatory: He was being called a womanizer, a gambler, and an inebriate.

While in Vienna, Kalakaua had met a "lovely Danish woman." The meeting and consequent relationship gave rise to so much gossip that the queen heard about it. In typical Polynesian fashion, Kapiolani met the situation by composing a *mele* about an affair with a beautiful woman—but now ended,[4] and that seemed to end it for the royal couple but not for the *haole* gossip. There were whispers of the "woman of Vienna," "of Italy," and of wherever the king had been.

Among his detractors, however, Kalakaua had already gained the reputation of being a "womanizer."

Kalakaua was extraordinarily attractive to women. Newspaper accounts spoke of women in New York breaking out of the ranks of welcoming committees to fall on their knees to kiss his hand. He would gallantly take their hands and raise them to their feet; then he would hold both hands and express "in a most democratic fashion" his appreciation.[5]

The visits he paid to Mills College, Oakland, California, to his friends Susan and Cyrus Mills, as guest lecturer during his trips to the United States, bear record of the young ladies "nearly fainting" in his presence.[6]

Thurston wrote: "An educated American woman said, 'Whenever I attend a public reception or meeting of any kind, at which the King is present, I simply tag around after

him, feasting my eye on him and his actions. He is so un-
affected, kindly, and genial in his conduct and association
with all classes; he has such a manner of kingly dignity about
him, and at the same time is so jovially companionable, with
that hail-fellow-well-met air, and so appreciative of his lis-
teners, that he appears to be almost an ideal man.'"[7]

Ida Pope, a frequent visitor to the palace, wrote to her
sister, "They say he is a womanizer, but I feel he is merely
gallant."[8]

In the attack on his personal habits as well as his political
shortcomings, he was also accused of being a gambler and a
drunkard.

Kalakaua used his boat house for his private drinking and
gambling parties. The diversity of comments depended on
who was invited to attend and under what circumstances. At
the boat house were men of all walks of life—the butcher, the
baker, the lawyer, the doctor, the naval officer, the high officials, the friends and the enemies of the king.

Claus Spreckels, who had bought his way into the king's
favor, often gambled and drank with him. The gaming table,
legend has it, was to be the scene of the end of the Spreckels-
Kalakaua relationship.

The version claims that Spreckels, in a poker game, held
four kings against the king's four aces, but proclaimed he had
won because he actually held five kings, for in the palm of his
hand he also held the king of Hawaii—from that day on
Kalakaua never spoke to Spreckels.

This moment was not actually the end of Spreckel's
association, but certainly, if true, became a determining
factor for the end.

Later Spreckels was to say that Kalakaua could only be
reached at the gambling table or while he was drinking. "The
gin bottle was his divinity."[9]

An admirer of Kalakaua's ability to hold his alcohol was
Robert Louis Stevenson, who was the king's friend and com-

panion, and who called him "the finest gentleman I ever met
. . . a very fine intelligent fellow . . . but what a crop for drink!
He carries it, too, like a mountain with a sparrow on his
shoulders." All sorts of speculations were made by the *haole*
about how the king could drink so much and not become
drunk. The most popular answer was that he ate a great deal
of poi first and thus "lined his stomach against the effects of
drink." Many a poi-stuffed *haole* stumbled home, while the
king, erect and courtly, walked away. Poi was not the answer.

* * *

Another of Kalakaua's dreams was to come into being
shortly after his return from his trip around the world: the
palace was completed.

The palace was a fitting place for the Renaissance king of
a small but vibrant kingdom.

Four architects had been instrumental in fashioning the
building. Its style was termed "American florentine," but several features made it resemble many governmental-colonial
residences built in tropical and sub-tropical climates during
the Victorian period: wide verandas, proliferation of windows
and doors, and solid brick.

Kalakaua had not been idle in the process of building the
palace. He brought in many new elements, such as the use of
concrete, new to masons throughout the world. Experts had
been brought ten years before to work on the Aliiolani Hale.
Their skills were again put to use. Modern plumbing was
installed in four full bathrooms, with a copper-lined bathtub
of seven-by-two-by-two-feet for the king. Wash basins were
of Italian marble, and in the butler's pantry were sinks of
copper. Guests had two "water closets" available, and even
the staff had bathtubs, showers, and toilets in the basement.

Although gas chandeliers were installed, Kalakaua, upon
his return from his trip, resolved to import electricity—a marvel
he had witnessed in Paris. (It was not until 1886, however, that
electricity was installed in the main rooms of the palace.) Less

than seven years after Thomas A. Edison invented the incandescent bulb, arc lights were to be displayed on the veranda of the palace, even before the White House had lights.

In 1880, Kalakaua's sister, Likelike, ordered the newest of gadgets for her brother—a telephone. The first one installed in the palace was a simple instrument that allowed the king to talk with his wife in her apartment across the hall. A more modern telephone used for talking with individuals throughout the city came in 1883.

Kalakaua's interest in new and practical things also brought about the use of water from an artesian well.

* * *

The palace was indeed a thing of beauty, especially the etched glass figures on the glass-paneled portals, which Kalakaua had had designed in San Francisco.

In the Grand Hall were portraits of former Hawaiian kings and queens. In the niches below the paintings were objects reminiscent of the king's travels—often gifts to the king from his foreign hosts—vases, brass, statuettes from all over the world.

The Blue Room was for informal entertaining. Chairs and sofas upholstered in blue lined the room, which featured a grand piano for the musically talented Kalakaua family. Blue satin drapes trimmed with velvet over lace curtains enclosed the room.

The State Dining Room had a table that seated forty guests, with capacious chairs at each end that were upholstered in leather and topped with carved crowns—for the king and queen. Chairs and sideboards were carved with the distinctive quatrefoil design of Gothic-Revival; the chairs were upholstered in fabrics and leathers. Heads of nations of the world who recognized the importance of Hawaii had sent portraits of their rulers and of men of distinction from England, France, Prussia and Russia; these portraits, which had come to Hawaii as early as 1830, hung in the dining room.

The Throne Room, the most elegant of all the rooms, was done in burnished red with the throne chairs at one end. Handsome crystal chandeliers hung from the ornate ceiling. Escutcheons lined the walls. Gilded oval frames lined with velvet and covered with locked glass doors displayed four of the Hawaiian royal orders and twelve foreign orders conferred on the king.

The king's bedroom was at the back, where the privy council met. Upstairs, however, was the king's private suite, with the queen's across the hallway. Each had three spacious rooms with bathroom and dressing room attached. The king's room was blue and the queen's red. Connected to the queen's room were guest rooms, decorated in yellow and blue. The private rooms and the library represented the Victorian culture and were filled with mementoes from the old palace and the private residences: books, magazines, and papers.[10]

It was a small palace—more nearly a mansion—compared to the palaces of the Orient and Europe where Kalakaua had visited, but it was a palace of which a Renaissance man could be proud. It was also a palace that stirred pride in the Hawaiian heart. Not so in the *haole* heart.

Fury increased with each additional dollar spent. The budget of $50,000 rose to over $300,000.

Entertainments began immediately. The first luncheon was given for the members of the legislature, and the first dinner was given on December 27, 1882, for Kalakaua's Masonic brothers.

❊ ❊ ❊

At the beginning of 1883, Kalakaua stood as a glamorous monarch before many of his people and as a very unpopular king before the *haole*.

Although he had a strong ally in Walter Murray Gibson, whom he had appointed premier in 1882, he faced another storm of disapproval from Spreckels' actions. Spreckels on his own had managed to secure from Princess Ruth a vast

piece of land for $10,000. Ruth actually had no legal right to
the land, as it was Crown land, and the government wanted
the agreement annulled. Spreckels then made a bargain with
the cabinet. He would give up his interest in the Crown
lands for a royal patent in fee simple for his 24,000 acres on
Maui. The plan was agreed to by the land commissioners,
Charles H. Judd, Edward Preston (an attorney who held up
his legality of the Crown lands), and Walter Murray Gibson.
Preston, during the time of negotiations, was appointed
attorney general in Gibson's cabinet.

It was not long before the rumor began that Spreckels
controlled the government; both Kalakaua and Gibson owed
him money, and the card game anecdote became popular.

Kalakaua, standing in low favor with the *haole* population,
but with Gibson's blessings, made his second disastrous
proclamation: He wanted a coronation! Nine years after he
became king!

A drawing of Kalakaua. *Homolulu Publishing Company.*

Honorable High Chief David Kalakaua. 1868. *Hawaii State Archives.*

King Kalakaua wrote the "Hymn of Kamehameha I," now called "Hawai'i Pono'i," for which Henry Berger composed the music. 1874. *Baker-Van Dyke Collection.*

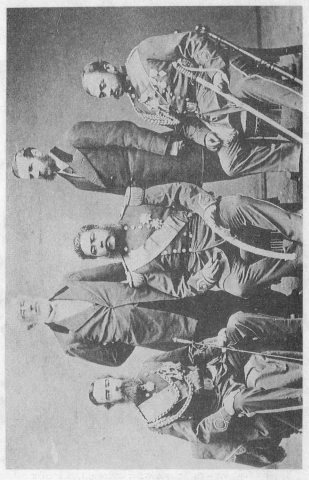

Kalakaua and
his Reciprocity
Committee in
San Francisco.
1875. *Hawaii
State Archives.*

Members of the Household staff of King Kalakaua. 1887.
Baker-Van Dyke Collection.

Kalakaua in full uniform. 1890. *Hawaii State Archives.*

The Kalakaua Dynasty. *Hawaii State Archives.*

Queen Kapiolani in her coronation robes. 1883. *Baker-Van Dyke Collection.*

Princess
Liliuokalani.
*Hawaii State
Archives.*

Prince
William Pitt
Leleiohoku,
heir to the
throne,
brother of
Kalakaua.
*Hawaii State
Archives.*

Princess Kaiulani. *Hawaii State Archives.*

King David Kalakaua and Robert Louis Stevenson. *Baker-Van Dyke Collection.*

Luau given by Henry Poor at his Waikiki home for the King and the Stevenson family. 1889. *Hawaii State Archives.*

A visit to Cook's Monument at Kealakekua Bay. King Kalakaua in white suit; to the right, Princess Liliuokalani; next to her, John A. Cummins. 1886. *Baker–Van Dyke Collection.*

King Kalakaua and a group of friends at a home along the South Kona coast of Hawaii. 1889. *Bishop Museum.*

King Kalakaua in center. Hulihee Palace, Kailua-Kona. 1890. *Baker-Van Dyke Collection.*

A visit to Parker Ranch and Col. Sam Parker. Queen Liliuokalani, top row; her husband, John Dominis, on her left; Sam Parker, front row center. 1891. *Baker-Van Dyke Collection.*

King Kalakaua with group in Hawaii. 1916. *Bishop Museum.*

The City of Honolulu gets ready to welcome Kalakaua back from his first world tour. 1881. *Hawaii State Archives*.

Newspaper clipping of King Kalakaua meeting President Grant at the White House. 1874. *Baker-Van Dyke Collection*.

Parade for King Kalakaua's 50th birthday jubilee, November 16, 1886, at the corner of King and Fort St. *Baker-Van Dyke Collection.*

8 Coronation

Kalakaua felt the coronation was necessary, as Liliuokalani explained later: "It was necessary to confirm the new family '*stirps*'—to use the words of our constitution—by a celebration of unusual impressiveness.[1] The Kamehameha dynasty would be officially gone and the Keawe-a-Heulu (Kalakaua) dynasty established. "It was wise and patriotic to spend money to awaken in the people a national pride," Liliuokalani wrote. It was, however, not that simple. There were to be problems among the *alii* (Queen Emma, Princess Ruth and the Bishops did not attend the coronation) as well as opposition from the *haole*.

Despite the strong opposition, Kalakaua moved forward with his plan. Two gold crowns encrusted with precious stones modelled after those of Russia were ordered from England at the cost of $10,000. Gowns for the queen and princesses were made in Paris, London, New York, and San Francisco. To the *haole* horror, no expense was to be spared for the coronation to be held February 12, 1883.

To the Hawaiians the coronation was looked forward to with great anticipation. For over thirty years the Hawaiians had been deprived of "celebrations." The younger generation knew of extravagant festivities such as the Restoration Day only from tales told by their parents, and of even greater holiday-celebrations from their grandparents. But the only holiday they knew of first hand was Kamehameha Day, June 10th, which Kalakaua had proclaimed in 1882.

❊ ❊ ❊

Early in January, crowds began coming to Honolulu for the coronation and the two weeks of festivities that were to follow. The rich, the poor–the young, the old–all came to see their king crowned. It was an event they had never dreamed could become a reality.

Although much criticism was laid on Kalakaua for his nine-year delay, there were reasons for it. In the first place, he had not taken his oath of office in the Kawaiahao Church, as Kamehameha IV and Lunalilo had (Kamehameha V was not publicly inaugurated). Secondly, and certainly of as great importance to Kalakaua, a new Hawaii was to replace the old. The cry of "advancement" was heard everywhere. The Hawaiians must be "progressive." The progress was usually to mean in industry, commerce and material advancement. Kalakaua now saw that a new type of coronation, such as the "civilized" countries of the world had, was as important as modernity in other avenues.

There remained, however, the beliefs in the natural phenomenon the Hawaiians held. Kalakaua had chosen from his lineage the bright red sun or the torch as his symbol–the once regarded heavy rains were not auspicious for a great event of birth, death, burial, or coronation.

Yet for several days preceding the coronation, drenching rains fell in Oahu. Kalakaua was questioned concerning such, and Kapiolani was greatly disturbed–Was her "beloved Chief" not to be recognized by the weather? Kalakaua said that the rains heralded the demise of the Kamehamehas–perhaps even mourned their departure–but on February 12, 1883, Coronation Day, the rain would stop and the sun would shine on the new dynasty.

Nevertheless, Kalakaua took steps to see that the material structures designed for the coronation would be properly cared for. An additional covering of corrugated iron was placed on the roof of the amphitheater. All the work was

done between four and six o'clock on Monday morning—
Coronation Day.

The newspapers grew lyrical in describing what followed:
"At break of day a change of weather occurred. The sun
shown forth with its wonted brilliancy. The reeds were
spread over the line of march, and by nine o'clock the school
children were marching towards the rendezvous. At the appointed hour the procession started, and entering the Palace
gates, the schools and societies took up the respective positions assigned to them.

"The brilliant weather continued, and strange to say, the
morning star was seen in the heavens at 9 a.m., shining con-
temporaneously with the sun. The Hawaiians regard this as a
happy omen. At 11 a.m. the sun was obscured by clouds, and
remained so until the very moment of 'crowning' was being
solemnized. Like a mechanical transformation scene to take
place at an appointed minute, so did the sun burst forth as the
clock struck twelve, and immediately after their Majesties had
been crowned."[2]

The school children, various orders and societies, as well
as the general public, were escorted to their seats by ushers.
"Within the Amphitheatre the Members of the legislature,
Departmental Clerks, and District Judges, with their wives,
were seated in Section 1. Next to them were the ladies and
gentleman residents of the Islands, besides many visitors
from other lands. On the left of the entrance were seated the
Delegates, Free Masons, Odd Fellows, Knights of Pythias,
Red Men, Foresters, members American Legion of Honor,
Good Templars, Knights of Jerusalem, Paolu Association,
Y.M.C. Association, Church of Latter Day Saints, and
Honolulu fire Department." The children, numbering about
1,100, were seated in chairs on the broad space between the
pavilion and the amphitheatre. In addition to the 4,000
people that were comfortably seated within the amphitheatre
and on the platform, there were crowds of spectators, princi-

pally Hawaiians, extending to the palace gates on either side. Seven thousand spectators were within the palace grounds. The solemnity of the occasion held them spellbound.

The pavilion, today the bandstand, in which the coronation ceremony was performed was octagonal with a domed roof. It was situated directly in front of the main entrance to Iolani Palace and about fifty feet from the stairway, by which it was connected by a platform. The pavilion, about twenty-five feet in diameter, bore on each of the eight sides the name of the Kings of Hawaii with the years during which they reigned, from the time of Kamehameha I to Kalakaua. Each name and duration of reign was encircled in laurel wreaths supported by two crossed palm leaves and surmounted by a crown. Over the front entrance to the pavilion were the following words: "February 12th, 1883, the day on which His Majesty King Kalakaua was crowned." The ceiling was decorated with paintings in oil and fresco work, with the Hawaiian coat-of-arms painted in the center on a white net work.

On the outside of the pavilion, each of the eight uprights supporting the roof were ornamented with emblazoned shields, representing Russia, the Netherlands, the United States, Hawaii, Germany, Austria, Italy, and Holland. On the bridge leading from the palace to the pavilion were two vases of modern Papeiian style; on each vase were two monograms, gilded on blue background. Under the monograms were depicted six dancing girls in different attitudes. The handles of the vases had the form of a "K." The pavilion was surrounded by a spacious amphitheatre for the spectators. It seated about 3,000 people, and it was entirely filled. The outer walls were adorned with the armorial bearings of Spain, Portugal, Belgium, Great Britain, France, Peru, Hawaii, Chile, Japan, China, Norway, and Sweden.

The front of the palace was also decorated, the colonnades being draped in scarlet and white. On each of the pillars was His Majesty's monogram, alternately arranged in red and green. On either side of the main stairway, the Hawaiian coat of arms on a white background was depicted. In addition to the work of the foreign artists, Hawaiian skill had been liberally displayed in the artistic arrangement of evergreens.

Upon the palace veranda on the right of the entrance were seated foreign representatives, and on the left were the government representatives and commanders of ships in port.

A guard of honor was formed in front of Iolani Palace. At ten o'clock, at points assigned, the band formed on the right, in front of the line facing the pavilion.

At ten-fifteen the King Street Gate of the palace ground was thrown open to admit all who had received invitations. At eleven o'clock the sun was obstructed by a cloud and a hush fell over the waiting crowd. The sun remained hidden when their Majesties began their march to the pavilion, preceded by nine-year-old Princess Kaiulani "dressed in a light blue corded silk trimmed with lace, pale blue ribbons in her hair."

The cloudy sky remained, as if also hushed by the solemnity of the occasion, as the procession, "headed by the Marshall of the Kingdom (W. C. Parke) and the honorable Marshall of Household, (J. M. Kapena) moved to the pavilion.

"At the appearance of His Majesty's Chamberlain the heralds of old and new Hawaii—conch shells and trumpets—proclaimed the approach of their Majesties."

Following the chancellor, who was to administer the oath, came Her Royal Highness Princess Liliuokalani, with her ladies in waiting, and Governor John Owen Dominis. She "wore a Parisian toilette of gold brocade, the front part of white satin embroidered with gold, and a heavy crimson velvet train; the head-dress was a wreath of gold leaves and white feathers tipped with pearls; gold necklace with a diamond cross, and diamond earrings."

Following her was her sister, Her Royal Highness Princess Likelike, with her attendants and her husband, Archibald

Cleghorn. There followed the sisters of Kapiolani and other ladies of governmental importance.

Still in the cloudiness of the day, their majesties approached the pavilion. The king wore the white uniform of the Guards, with a white helmet, and plume of white, red, and blue. He wore the Grand Gordon, Star and Collar of the Order of Kamehameha I; the Star of the Emperial Order of the Chrysanthemum of Japan; the Star of the Order of St. Michael and St. George of England; the Star of the Order of the Conception of Portugal; and the Star of the Order of Hawaii.

The robe of the queen was "of rich cardinal velvet, heavily embroidered in an elaborate design of fern leaves in gold, with ermine border, gloves and slippers, embroidered in green, a coronet of diamonds, bracelets of diamonds, emeralds, rubies and amethysts, and she carried a superb hand-painted fan trimmed with lace."

The ceremony began with the singing of the Episcopalian Choir. The Marshal of the Household declared the king's accession and right to the throne by his lineages, "*wohi*" (*mana*), and numerous foreign and domestic royal orders.

Princess Poomaikelani then advanced and presented to the king a *Puloulou* and a *Palaoa* borne upon a cushion, Ke Kukuioiwikauikaua, and the Kahili of the King Pili, as symbols of ancient supreme chieftaincy, which, being accepted by His Majesty, were placed beside the throne and remained there throughout the ceremony.

The chancellor then advanced and, standing before the king, said:

"SIRE—is your Majesty willing to reaffirm your previous oath?"

The king answered:

"I am willing."

The king then left his throne and, advancing towards the chancellor, raised his right hand and said after the chancellor:

"I, DAVID KALAKAUA, King of the Hawaiian Islands, having on the twelfth day of February, in the year of Our Lord one thousand eight hundred and seventy-four, in conformity with the provisions of the Constitution of the Kingdom, been duly elected by the Legislative Assembly of the Hawaiian Islands in the Legislature of the Kingdom assembled, to the Throne of this Kingdom;

"And having on the following day taken the Oath prescribed by Article 24 of the Constitution, do hereby of my own grace and motion solemnly reaffirm the same, and

"I do hereby solemnly swear in the presence of Almighty God to maintain the Constitution of the Kingdom whole and inviolate, and to govern in conformity therewith."

The king signed the oath and returned to his throne.

Chancellor Judd placed the sword of state in the king's hands as the "Ensign of Justice and Mercy"—it was an exact counterpart of that of England, fine Damascus steel inlaid with gold with the Hawaiian coat of arms and the motto of the realm. The hilt, guard, and cord tassels were of gold, beautifully engraved.

After taking the sword, the king returned it to the chancellor, who unsheathed it and carried it "naked during the rest of the solemnity."

Princess Kekaulike advanced with the royal mantle and placed it in the hands of the chancellor, who placed it on the king's shoulders saying: "Receive this ancient mantle of your predecessors as the Ensign of Knowledge and Wisdom." The mantle, worn by the Kamehameha I, was a semi-circular cloak about four-feet long, covering an area of twenty-five square feet when spread out, and was made of the small golden-hued feathers of the Oʻo. Oʻo birds were snared but released again after the two feathers were plucked from them. These feathers, each about the size of one's little finger nail, were fastened to a fine network of fibre made from the bark of the Olana, in such a manner that they overlaid each other.

At least 5,000 of these feathers were used in the cloak, and, only two taken from each bird, which had to be snared in the dense woods, where they were by no means abundant. It was evident that "the first cost of the cloak was very great, and that the keeping of it in order an endless task." This mantle was only worn by the reigning sovereign.

The chancellor then put the ring on the fourth finger of his Majesty's right hand, saying: "Receive this ring, the Ensign of Kingly Dignity." The chancellor delivered the sceptre to the king, saying: "Receive the royal Sceptre, the Ensign of Kingly Power of Justice."

All of the proceedings took place in the dimmed light of a hiding sun. Then Prince David Kawananakoa advanced with the crowns. The choir sang the anthem:

> "Almighty Father! we do bring
> Gold and gems for the King;
> Pure gold for the true Chief,
> The symbol of true Love.
> Gems of the hidden mine,
> Gleaming forth a glory;
> The glory of the unfolding Isles,
> That grow in wealth, and peace—
> That come to crown their King,
> The heir of the farthest ages
> Chosen by the Almighty Father!
> To Whom the honor and the glory. Amen,"

The Honorable President of the Legislative Assembly then took the king's crown and raised it up before the people and placed it in the hands of the chancellor, saying:

"I present this Crown to the rightful King of these Islands, approved by Acts of the Legislative Assembly in the Legislature of the Kingdom assembled of the years 1880 and 1882."

The chancellor placed it in the king's hands, saying: "Receive this Crown of pure gold to adorn the high station wherein thou hast been placed."

The king raised the crown and placed it on his own head.

At that moment, the sun broke through the clouds like a spotlight and illuminated the whole scene—some said that a "single star appeared in the heavens" just previous to the brilliancy of the sun. In any event, the lighting effects were superb.

A sigh escaped the crowd and some fell to their knees.

The chancellor, after a momentary pause, took the second crown and placed it in the king's hands, who rose and placed it on the queen's head, who after a slight moment of confusion as it caught in her diadem, reverently bowed to receive it, the king saying: "I place this Crown upon your head, to share the honors of my throne."

Criticism soon followed that Kalakaua, in a Napoleonic fashion, had crowned himself and his queen; however, for the chancellor to have done so, he would have had to cast his shadow upon the king, and Kalakaua, remaining true to the lingering native belief that no shadow should be cast upon the king, circumvented the situation by crowning himself and Kapiolani. The same year, the Russian Tsar in his coronation similarly placed the crown on himself and then on the Tsarina.

On that Monday, however, the crowd remained in stillness and awe as a prayer was offered, after which their Majesties arose and resumed their places upon the throne. At the conclusion of the prayer, signals from the palace towers announced the event, and a royal salvo of guns was fired from the battery and men-of-war in port. The choir sang an anthem dedicated to the king.

The coronation ceremony completed, the king and queen, attended as before, retired to the Grand Hall, where the disrobing took place.

The procession left the pavilion; homage was paid in private to the king by the foreign and domestic members of the government.

"On the conclusion of the ceremonies, the band, conducted by Henry Berger, played Meyerbeer's celebrated 'Coronation March,' and as the people dispersed there was a general feeling of approbation expressed with successful manner in which the whole proceedings had been conducted. flags were displayed in every direction, and the harbor presented an unusually gay appearance with four full-dressed men of war, and twenty-two merchantmen. The inter-island steamers and schooners also put forth all the bunting they possessed."[2]

❋ ❋ ❋

The fine new palace gleamed in night light as the guests of the coronation ball moved through the garden past the sentry who stood by the iron gates.

A liveried official helped the ladies from their carriages. Everyone was amazed to see the new "electric arc lights" pour out upon the verandas. The ladies hurried to the cloakroom before joining their husbands in the wide hall. Here the guests were announced by the chamberlain as they stepped into the ballroom to be greeted by the king and queen. With them were the princesses and the "little princes"–the three teenage boys of Princess Kekaulike.

The guests passed before the royal hosts, bowing and curtsying. As Isobel Strong Field (a guest) wrote: "I had been getting nervous as I viewed this array of royalty, but following the example of others before me, I made a very low curtsy almost to the floor before the King, who gave me his hand to rise, saying a few words of welcome that I was too agitated to remember. Another bow equally low to the Queen, and then lesser and lesser ones until the three little Princes received hardly more than nods and I was free to join the others, remembering just in time to back away from royalty, which wasn't very easy . . ."

The ball began with a royal quadrille and was followed by general dancing. Later a supper was served with "exquisite dishes cooked by a French chef and trays of champagne."

Isobel Field ended her description of the ball with, "Though nearly all of the Missionary party came to the ball, bowing like the others before the Royal family, they left early; so did the older and more serious of the guests. The rest of us stayed on until nearly morning when we danced the 'galop' to a lively *hula*. Then came the strains of Home Sweet Home and the ball was over."[3]

Coronation festivities continued all that week and the following week, and celebrations included the *hookupu*, the presentation of gifts to the king, each giver contributing his best, whether of the fruits of his land or the finest examples of his talents and skills. "On the 24th, at noon, the Grand Luau at the palace began. five thousand guests were fed and the feasting, hulas, and singing continued until 11:30 p.m."

On Wednesday, February 14, 1883, the statue of Kamehameha I, erected in front of Aliiolani Hale opposite the palace on King Street, was unveiled by King Kalakaua. The statue had been ordered by the legislature in 1878 from an American sculptor in Italy to commemorate the Centennial of the discovery of the islands by Captain James Cook on January 18, 1778. Kamehameha the Great was supposed to have dated his career from that period. The first statue was lost off the Falkland Islands, and a replica had been ordered to be ready for unveiling during the coronation week. The replica still stands on King street before the State Judiciary Building, across from Iolani Palace. The original, eventually recovered, was erected at Okala, Hawaii, the birthplace of Kamehameha I.

The festivities continued for two weeks. Every day the natives moved about the streets in happy throngs. They were colorful in their many-hued *holoku* and bright shirts, always wearing flowers—in their hats, in their hair, and garlands of *lei* about their necks. There were thousands of *luau* with the forbidden hula, the dancers wearing full blouses and skirts and flowered crowns and anklets, held all over the islands in respite from missionary discipline.

Kalakaua, during the two weeks of festivity, took time to visit his native subjects, to encourage them to be happy, to "increase the race," and as was his custom, he joined them in song.

❋   ❋   ❋

The *haole* resentment grew. "Fuss and feathers" was the verdict pronounced upon the coronation: *expensive* fuss and feathers.

Liliuokalani noted in her *Story* that there was much for which the *haole* could have been grateful. "Honolulu had been benefitted in the meantime financially, the merchants and traders of every degree reaping a bountiful harvest from the free expenditure of money by every class." She then spoke of the benefit the coronation had for the Hawaiian people.

"The people . . . went back to their homes with a renewed share of dignity and honor involved in their nationality and an added interest in the administration of their government."[4]

9 Political Downfall of Kalakaua

It was noted that certain members of the *alii* had not attended the coronation; Queen Emma, the Bishops, and Princess Ruth had been conspicuously absent. Stress was placed on the fact that Kamehameha *alii* did not support Kalakaua.

These festering sores came to a head in a peculiar way shortly after the coronation. Kalakaua was attacked by what the newspapers called "a skillful genealogist," as not being of "sufficient *alii* lineage to be eligible for the throne." The contention was that Queen Emma alone was eligible.

It will probably never be known who the "skillful genealogist" was, but it is improbable that he was in the service of Queen Emma. Early in 1883 Emma had suffered a slight stroke, and neither her health nor her desires would have thrown her into the verbal newspaper fray that followed and became vicious and libelous.

Kalakaua picked up the gauntlet, not in his own defence, but to cast aspersions on Emma's reputation and genealogy. He thereby began losing his standing among the native Hawaiians, who still revered Queen Emma.

Only in the newspapers and on the streets was the case "tried;" varying papers carried both sides of the story, labeling it "the genealogical trial."[1]

Kalakaua was first attacked as having no *wohi–mana* of ancient kings and gods–on the basis that neither Keohokalole nor Kapaakea, his blood parents, had *wohi*. Neither did his *hanai* parents, because they carried him, it was said, "on chest, backs, arms, and laps." Keohokalole was fearfully slandered in every possible way. It was said that she had not been allowed to sit at the table of Kamehameha III–an absurd statement, for Keohokalole was one of the councillors of Kamehameha III; she was also the last of the high chiefesses to be honored at *Puna*.[2] The stories went on, becoming even more absurd: the Kalakauas never ate with Kamehameha V. The "trial" grew more and more vicious: it "was told" that before his death Kapaakea had denied being the father of all Keohokalole's children except Liliu Kamakaeha.

The old story of Kalakaua's negro blood was revived. Someone was supposed to have testified that she had seen Keohokalole in sexual relations with Blossom, a Negro blacksmith, and from the union had come Kalakaua. Later studies revealed that the Blossom family came to Hawaii in the 1850s when Kalakaua was in his teens.

John Ii began to break the libelous statements and probably could have ended the "trial" had not Kalakaua interfered. Ii stated that Kamehameha I had been placed as *hanai* in the keeping of the Keawe line and that as a result, a close relationship of the royal lines existed to the time of Kalakaua.[3] But Kalakaua turned his attack on Emma. Emma was accused of changing her genealogy, a Hawaiian "sin," to become "more royal."

The "trial" rumbled on, laying seeds of dissension for the Kalakaua family among the Kamehameha descendants. If it was *haole*-instigated, as was suspected by some, it was succeeding in dividing the Hawaiians further. If division could be achieved among the *alii* of various royal lines from the "conquered" islands, the Hawaiians would be a nation divided against itself. The "genealogical trial" was laying the groundwork for such a division.

But suddenly, the *alii* grew tired of the haranguing in the papers, and after a consultation between Princess Ruth, an acknowledged princess of the Kamehameha line, and

Princess Kekauluohi II, an acknowledged princess of the Keawe line, the two decided to put a stop to it.

While leaving a church service at St. Andrews Cathedral, the Keawe princess stepped aside to allow Likelike, Liliuokalani and Kaiulani to precede her, showing that she gave them royal deference. They were then invited to her home.

This visit took place at noon and, just before the arrival of the princesses, the high chiefess ordered the flaming torch of Keawe to be lit in front of her home.

After the Keawe princesses arrived, Kekauluohi II walked to the torch and extinguished it. Thereby she proclaimed, without a single word, that she recognized the exalted birth of the Princess Kaiulani.[4]

It was the stamp of approval for the Keawe-line-torch symbol belonging to the Kalakaua family.

The genealogical trial came to an end.

Despite a persistent rumor that Emma and Kalakaua never spoke, a story was told by Isobel Strong Field that casts a dubious light on the tale.

The Strongs were invited to a reception and dance aboard the USS *Adams*. The guests were a little nervous from whispers that Queen Emma as well as Kalakaua would be present.

"Guests came pouring over the side, and then, exactly on time, for the King was always punctual, the ship shook with the boom of cannon that announced his arrival . . . As His Majesty stepped on the deck, the ship's band burst into *Hawaii Pono'i*. Kalakaua and his handsome equerries, Captain Haley, the Hawaiian Major and several others, all in flattering uniforms, made a fine-looking group. We, the assembled guests, opened a lane to the companionway, the men bending from the waist, the women sinking in deep curtseys as the King walked slowly along, bowing graciously to right and left, his companions gazing straight ahead haughtily ignoring our presence.

"Breathlessly the crowd below watched His Majesty mount the companionway; when he reached the quarterdeck he was greeted by the Captain who motioned toward the throne where Queen Emma stood. Kalakaua stepped forward, a gallant figure in white and gold, bowed low to the lady in black, and offered her his hand, which she took and was about to kiss. With a quick, dexterous movement he gave her a little whirl and a push that seated her on the throne. Queen Emma's surprised face was almost comic when the King bowed again before her. Then she smiled sweetly, he leaned over and they talked together with such evident friendliness that we all felt like applauding. After that the two were friends and I often saw Queen Emma at the King's formal parties."[5]

This meeting was far more in keeping with the *aloha* that existed among the *alii* despite their differences.

❊ ❊ ❊

Kalakaua was to stumble on for the next four years to inevitable disaster. His passionate advocacy for things and customs Hawaiian came with two liabilities. first, a discomfort with and naivete about politics, which often left him unwilling to find a middle ground and alienated some of his most likely supporters, ultimately limiting his influence. And second, a completely different understanding from them (and lack of in the *haole* mind) of money and its use. Kalakaua felt that the moneys made in Hawaii by the *haole* were a result of the land and the reciprocity and could be spent for the good of the country and the Hawaiians.

Despite the Great *Mahele*, land ownership in the *haole* sense was foreign to the Hawaiian. Land could not be given in sole ownership to another. Land was *aina*–land, sky, sea, air, trees–all of which could not be divided. Land was their being, their soul. What profit came from the land through reciprocity was at least to be shared.

With his improper sense of a loan and lack of understanding that money could be god, Kalakaua went disastrously into debt—both personally and nationally.

Nevertheless, it is difficult to know why such a talented and gifted man was to enter into such foolish adventures as Kalakaua did between 1884 and 1887—escapades that were to bring him as king to his knees. Liliuokalani spoke of his "overvaulting ambition."[6] Unlike MacBeth, he had much to spur him on. Besides his love and desire for promoting Hawaiian culture and tradition, there were Walter Murray Gibson and Claus Spreckels.

❋ ❋ ❋

There is little doubt that Spreckels was totally selfish, self-centered, arrogant, and ruthless, while Gibson shared with the king the love for the things Hawaiian. Liliuokalani wrote: "He did it all for the king." If not "all," certainly he was less selfish and egocentric than Spreckels.

In the early 1880s, Hawaiian money was in shambles. Bits and pieces of Spanish, German, English, and other moneys were used in exchange. The American dollar was, however, the closest money came to stability.

It was not surprising then, that when Spreckels introduced his idea of coinage it was quickly accepted by Kalakaua, though less quickly by the legislature.

Claus Spreckels had insinuated his way into Hawaiian life—and the king's—for several years. He succeeded, as has been noted, in putting the king and Gibson into his personal debt. He came to Hawaii to engage in sugar planting, construction of sugar mills, laying of railway lines, and improving irrigation projects—all to his own financial benefit. Early in Kalakaua's reign, although rice was the second-most important agricultural crop, it was discouraged as an export by the *haole* because it was primarily controlled by the Chinese. Consequently, everyone turned to sugar, and the benefits accrued from the tariff remission went almost entirely to planting interests in Hawaii.

The problem of lack of capital for expansion of the sugar industry was a major one.[7] It was hoped that American capital would invest. In 1880, Hawaiian banker Charles Reed Bishop wrote E. H. Allen, who represented the Hawaiian kingdom in Washington:

"The U. S. govt. and people have unquestionable [sic] been the best friends of Hawaii and Hawaiians; they think and say,–and rightly too,–that they have given us a good bargain in the treaty; and yet the Capitalists large and small do not take advantage of it. Hundreds might have come here with money, strong hands and clear heads and started plantations, thus getting every advantage that the treaty offers equally with those who were here; but instead of doing so they have most of them kept away, croaking, growling and threatening, while the people here have put in every dollar they had or could borrow–having faith in the honor and good will of the U. S. Govt. and Congress pledged in the treaty, in the honesty of their purposes and in our virgin soil and fine climate. There is a good deal of San Francisco capital used here; some invested in planting; but more loaned, and some of it on very hard terms for those who have used it or are using it. What more we want is, that more Americans, east and west, should become pecuniarily interested in our business planting. They could make money by it, increase the trade with their own people and greatly strengthen the influence and improve the prospects for the extension of the treaty."[8] None of note came, except Spreckels.

The depression of 1879-1880 was blamed on "loose management of a majority of sugar planters," indebtedness of planters, and labor problems. The result was the formation of Hawaiian Sugar Planters' Association and the "agency system," forming a link between the sugar market, labor market, and the "whole economic milieu in which they had to operate."9

The agency system has been discussed pro and con by many writers, but the essence of the discussions seems to be that the labor situation was not solved by the agents. Nevertheless, when King Kalakaua proposed his trip around the world to secure laborers as well as immigrants to live in Hawaii, he was vigorously opposed. And although American capital was desired, Spreckels was highly suspect, mostly because he loaned the king money.

He became the arch rival of the planters, but they also feared him and at times considered him to be a battering ram for their own interests, as in the 1880 Princess Ruth Keelikolani case in which she sold her Crown land to Spreckels for $10,000. These were the lands Kalakaua had claimed were not hers but belonged to the Crown. Although Kamehameha III and IV had dealt with the lands as if they were their personal property, in 1864 it was decided that the lands belonged to the continuing kings and were inalienable. Princess Ruth, as half-sister to Kamehameha IV and V, declared that she owned half the Crown lands. Kalakaua upheld the treatise that the land belonged to the government and the king. Three *haole* attorneys upheld Ruth's right to sell and Spreckels' right to purchase as legal.

Haole planters also suspected that if the remainder of the Crown lands became available through Spreckels' case, they could stake further claims for themselves; therefore, they supported him at first. They also considered him a strong moneyed ally in lobbying in America for the extension of the sugar reciprocity treaty.

❊ ❊ ❊

The summer of 1883 brought Gibson strongly into government. During this time, Spreckels presented his schemes of Hawaiian coinage. The currency on the islands was a mixture of foreign moneys out of which finally the American money became the standard of exchange, issued by the Bishop Bank, the only bank in Hawaii.

In 1880, a statute authorizing the minting of Hawaiian coinage had been issued, but only a commemorative five-cent piece honoring Kalakaua had been struck. It was not favored by Hawaiians because the motto of the kingdom had been misspelled on the obverse side of Kalakaua's profile.

In 1882, the Loan Act was passed authorizing the government to borrow up to $2 million at six percent interest to cover the budget deficit. The bonds were issued, but none of the high interest commercial concerns in Honolulu would touch them. The deficit rose dangerously, until Spreckels was attracted to buy the bonds for six percent. As an individual, he was to contract the United States mint for coinage of dollars, half-dollars, quarters, and twelve-and-a-half cent pieces in the amount of a million dollars.[10] This transaction did not go smoothly; it involved law suits, injunctions and much general turmoil.

The authors of the *Fantastic Life of Walter Murray Gibson* wrote (pg. 145):

"Downtown Honolulu did not cheer Gibson's deal in silver. Local commercial companies feared the intrusion of Spreckels, just as had the sugar planters a few years earlier. They were troubled at the prospect of having a politician like Gibson asserting authority over their monetary system. They were piqued that the government's bond issue, confidently declared dead for lack of takers, had been bought off by such fiscal legerdemain. They were most disturbed to see coins bearing the silver likeness of an upstart tinhorn king displace the American eagle and the face of Liberty. A riotous coronation and a gingerbread palace were bad enough, but there was no end of mischief that Gibson and company could do if allowed to play around with money itself."

Law suits and legislative debates continued with Sanford Dole, W. O. Smith, and others until finally the Hawaiian

Gold Law of 1884 limited United States and Hawaiian silver coinage to $10 legal tender. Larger debts had to be paid in American gold coins.

It was estimated that Spreckels had made a profit of $150,000.

Spreckels left Hawaii in 1886, but he came back intermittently and was entertained by Kalakaua, although their friendship had lessened considerably, and he himself entertained lavishly. He finally sold his Hawaiian holdings to two missionary descendants, Alexander and Baldwin, who were to become in later years one of the "Big five." They also took over as a subsidiary the Matson Navigation Company, which found its origin in Spreckels' fleet of sailing vessels between Hawaii and United States.

* * *

By 1884 it would have been difficult to know who was more hated–the king or Walter Murray Gibson. Before Gibson had won the attention of the king, he had reaped the wrath of the businessmen. He had steadfastly worked against the opposition for sanitation, health, political independence of the kingdom, and survival of the Hawaiian race. Now he was to promote one more "scheme."

Gibson's last "scheme to glorify the king," as it became known, came when he approached Kalakaua with the possibility of Hawaii being a protectorate of the Polynesian Islands in the Pacific. Again, this was not a new idea to Kalakaua, because during his trip around the world he had approached the Emperor of Japan with the idea of a unified Pacific in which the Emperor would be the head. When the Emperor refused the offer, Kalakaua decided the leadership fell to him.

This idea had deep roots, usually attributed to Charles St. Julian, a reporter for the *Sidney Morning Herald*, who had never seen the Hawaiian Islands. St. Julian perceived the Hawaiian islands as a pivotal point in the Pacific Ocean. He made his ideas known as early as 1851 in a pamphlet.[11]

Correspondence between St. Julian and Minister Wyllie is voluminous, but in essence what St. Julian tried to do was "achieve four principal objectives: (1) to secure the annexation of territory to the Hawaiian Kingdom; (2) to promote the development of organized local government in certain island groups with the aim of organizing them into a Polynesian Confederation under Hawaiian hegemony; (3) to achieve for Hawaii a recognized 'moral protectorate' over unprotected natives of all island groups lacking their own government, with the right to intervene on their behalf when necessary; and (4) to enhance the prestige of Hawaii in Australia as much as possible."

Although Kalakaua no doubt knew all about St. Julian—and probably liked his proposals—his acceptance of Hawaii's place in the Pacific went back to Kamehameha I, who had been called the "Napoleon of the Pacific" and who dreamed of uniting the Pacific islands; and to Kamehameha II, who also insisted on the title, although he did nothing to justify it. A Hawaiian primacy in the Pacific was deeply rooted in Hawaiian ambitions and dreams, going back even to the god Lono, who, legend had it, ruled "all the Pacific Islands."

* * *

The Gilbert Islands in Micronesia asked for protection from the Hawaiian government against encroachment of foreign powers in 1882. Nothing came of this request, except a wrecked ship, *Julia*, which cost the Hawaiian government considerable money. While Gibson was premier, this plan for Hawaii to become the protectorate of the Polynesian islands of the Pacific was attempted. It brought a heavy, dark cloud over Kalakaua's reign. The plan, which included "interfering in the Samoan Government as a first step to conquer and unite the Pacific Islands," was considered the most irresponsible and lacking in thought of all Kalakaua's and Gibson's schemes.

The plan was actually fairly well thought out on paper, and the intentions were good. It began with a Monroe

Doctrine-type of program in 1883, with Gibson sending a protest to the leading nations–the United States, Great Britain, France and Germany–that Hawaii would "protect" the smaller Pacific islands against annexation.

The motives behind the protest are still unclear, but five possible assumptions about Gibson's desires, except for the first one, show both Hawaii's concern for its smaller neighbors and the ever-present wishes of Kalakaua to promote Hawaiian prestige and to protect Hawaii itself from annexation: (1) to pave the way for a later expansion by Hawaii of its domain; (2) to safeguard the independence of, and promote self-government among, Pacific islanders; (3) to attempt to boost Hawaii's international prestige; (4) to bolster indirectly Hawaii's own independent status so as to assure its continuance; and (5) to insure the retention by Hawaii of sources of labor supply.[12]

When on November 10, 1884, a German agent forced the Samoan king to sign an agreement virtually handing over Samoa to Germany, King Malietoa sent a plea to the Hawaiian islands for aid.

As a result, H.A.P. Carter was sent to the United States and then to Europe to test the waters of the great powers. His interviews and correspondence with Secretary of State Thomas F. Bayard were guarded but generally encouraging. Carter proposed that Hawaii be included in a nation-of-treaties conference to be held in Washington to consider the annexation or protectorate of any of the Pacific islands. It was suggested that Hawaii send an emissary to Samoa to evaluate the situation there.

Bayard responded that he would witness "with pleasure any initiative and participation of Hawaii" in attempting to achieve a general guarantee of the autonomy and neutrality of unappropriated island groups. "It would be most fitting that Hawaii should join in such an arrangement, if it be practicable . . . We desire no domination in the Pacific for ourselves nor can we be expected to sanction, a doctrine whereby any one among the Powers equally interested in trade and intercourse with these regions, might roam at will over the Pacific seas and absorb the jurisdiction of Islands, because unprotected or unadministered, thence to announce to other nations, whose rights are at least coequal, [sic] the terms on which such islands may be visited or traded with."[13]

Pleased with Bayard's response, Carter went to London on November 14, 1885. Bayard was an anti-imperialist, but in Europe imperialism was on the move. England and Germany agreed to partition New Guinea on April 25, 1885; and on December 17, 1885, Spain and Germany made their claims to the Caroline Islands. Established later by papal arbitration, Spain held the Carolines, with Germany reserving the right to a coaling and naval station. The previous October, Germany had taken possession of the Marshall Islands and the Brown and Providence groups. Pressure was being exerted by New Zealand and Germany against Samoa, and by Australia and France against the New Hebrides.

In the face of such movements it is surprising that Carter pursued his tour to Germany, where Count Herbert von Bismark, Germany's foreign minister, told him that Hawaii's proposal was "too late to affect Germany's actions, although if the proposal had come earlier, before annexation orders, Germany might have considered the proposal."

As to the Gilberts, Bismark called Carter's attention to an Anglo-German agreement delimiting influence in the Pacific.[14]

Carter, in the face of adversity, continued with reports to Great Britain, gaining Dutch support but a negative reply from France. Then Great Britain replied, as had Germany, that if the proposal had come earlier it might have received acceptance.[15]

Carter wrote Gibson that he believed that, as a whole, the mission and its motives had added to Hawaii's international prestige.[16]

Lord Rosebery further encouraged Carter, when he returned to England, by stating that Great Britain would not be opposed to a scheme whereby the independence of the Marshalls, Gilberts, and part of the Carolines "should be secured by a self denying agreement among the Powers in order to afford their inhabitants the opportunity of forming settled governments with the assistance and advice of Hawaii."

In Hawaii, however, Carter's mission met with nothing but sharp criticism. Gibson's plans and Kalakaua's desires were derisively called the "Empire of the Calabash." Animosity continued to build toward Gibson and Kalakaua. The *haole* population preferred that all "expansion" movement be to its benefit.

Gibson nonetheless pursued his plan through Carter. "Since American and European statesmen had approved of Carter's previous mission, Gibson said, Hawaii again asked all the Powers interested in the Pacific to abstain from further annexations 'until a fair time has been given the experiment which the Government of this country desire to make.' This experiment, he continued, would be the dispatch of an Hawaiian Commissioner to Polynesia and the placement of consuls or other agents on various islands, all with the aim of promoting self-government. Should the replies to this appeal be favorable, he stated, Hawaii 'will then hope that the consenting Powers will join in a general convention, guaranteeing the independence of all island communities in which, within a reasonable time such governments as may properly be recognized may be established.' He reiterated that Hawaii had no material aims but, citing the 'Primacy' theory again, 'entered upon the matter from a sense of the duty owed by the most privileged section of the Polynesian Race to kindred people not yet so happily placed as are the Hawaiians.'"[17]

In 1886, when Gibson and Kalakaua considered sending a commissioner to Samoa "to conciliate internal differences there," Carter warned against it. Gibson, after action had been taken by the legislature, instructed Carter to inform the United States, Germany, and Great Britain. Germany and Great Britain did not reply, but James C. Porter, first Assistant Secretary of State, replied for the United States that he hoped the commissioner would be successful in "harmonizing the native factions without incurring foreign displeasure." The key words were "without incurring foreign displeasure." They were overlooked by Gibson.

The dissension in Samoa was growing between King Malietoa and Vice-King Tamasese, who was being supported by the Germans. Ostensibly, the commissioner was to "harmonize" these factions. When the legislature passed the appropriation of $30,000 for the mission, the opposition papers vigorously opposed the plan, the "Gibson-dominated legislature," and the "duties of Hawaii as a leading Polynesian state."

At this point Kalakaua made an unfortunate appointment—that of John Edward Bush as commissioner to Samoa. Bush was warned by Gibson not to take any definitive action, but to move with care. Samoa had been declared neutral territory by the Anglo-German agreement of April, 1886. However, Germany was not to be deterred, and she considered Hawaii's efforts to "harmonize" as an act against Germany.

Bush made no conciliatory effort to Tamasese, but concentrated his attention on Malietoa. Malietoa was not a sophisticated king. He fell quickly in with Bush's flair for entertainment and drinking. Against Hawaiian orders, Bush offered him a subsidy of $5,000 to $6,000 to join the Hawaiian-Samoan Confederation.

Although Britain and the United States actually were in opposition to Germany's encroachment, it was evident they would take no direct steps to protect Samoa; so Malietoa accepted Bush's somewhat flamboyant plans.

According to Robert Louis Stevenson, the Samoans also had a high regard for Kalakaua and his contacts and successes, such as the reciprocity treaty with the United States.[18]

On February 17, 1887, a "Treaty of Confederation" was signed by Malietoa with Bush, who had taken a "definitive step" without authorization. Correspondence among Gibson, Carter, and Hoffnung all indicate that a misunderstanding of the word "treaty" was evident; a "treaty" with Samoa was to enable Hawaii to be recognized as a "treaty power," and meant a treaty of commerce and friendship.[19]

Bush, however, proceeded to make conclusive plans for Hawaii's dominance in Samoan affairs.

In the meanwhile, Gibson was becoming more cautious, but agreed with Bush that a "warship" should be sent to Samoa. Thus the ill-fated *Kaimaloa*, Hawaii's entire navy, came into being.

Against enormous pressure excited by the newspapers and some legislators, a British warship, the *Explorer*, was bought by the government and outfitted as the *Kaimaloa*. It was to be a training ship, and Bush was warned against its misuse. "She will have her band and her saluting guns, and will be able to do ample honor to King Malietoa or other Polynesian Sovereigns," Gibson said, but "her instructions will be that she is not permitted to make war."[20]

By this time, Henry Poor, an emissary of the king, had joined Bush and reported with Bush that the Samoans were ready to fight for their independence. Gibson warned them that their mission was peace—peace between the warring Samoan factions.

According to Stevenson, Tamasese was bribed to come to Honolulu; Poor and Bush attempted a *coup*; they were jailed by the German consul—and in general the Germans were becoming more annoyed. In the meantime, Gibson made efforts to convince the United States that Hawaii should have a place at the Washington treaty conference and stated that only peace and commerce were intended by Hawaii in Samoa.

Warnings from Bayard about the *Kaimaloa* raised serious questions for Gibson and Kalakaua. But it had already been outfitted, and it was sent. During the outfitting, much criticism had arisen. One problematical question was whether the boys from the reformatory school could serve as part of the crew. Gibson argued successfully that the boys in their minority were under the Board of Education, of which he was chairman, and experience aboard the *Kaimaloa* would offer them a useful trade.

Heavy criticism continued to rage in the opposition papers after the *Kaimaloa* had departed. In the meantime, Malietoa had begun to resent Bush. A letter from William Coe, Malietoa's assistant secretary of state, quoted in American papers, said: "I beg to inform you that Mr. Bush's conduct during his residence here is of a most disreputable nature and his habits are very intemperate, as he appears to be addicted to an excessive use of ardent spirits. He is the most dissipated man who has held a high position at this place for many years. His associates here are mostly of the lowest kind of half castes and whites. His Majesty King Malietoa desires me to call your attention to this."[21]

After an interview with H. M. Sewall, the United States consul for Samoa in Hawaii, while Sewall was in route to Samoa, Kalakaua realized his mistake and ordered a return of the *Kaimaloa* and the resignation of Bush.[22] A recall of the entire mission followed. Henry Poor protested, "I fear it will be a great disappointment to Malietoa and his chiefs who rely on the Hawaiian Mission for moral support without which they might be forced into hostilities with the rebels who will grow bolder under their German leadership when they think Hawaii has forsaken Malietoa. It certainly is the fact that the presence of the Hawaiian Embassy in Samoa has tended to preserve the peace, and the arrival of the 'Kaimaloa' served as a strong influence to reunite wavering chiefs under Malietoa and to break up the petty rebellion. I would urgently recommend that a Consul General be appointed here to represent us."[23]

When Bush received his recall, he left the Mission Headquarters and took all the records with him, refusing to turn them over to Poor. He then wrote Kalakaua a letter exonerating himself.

The riots and misconduct of the men aboard the *Kaimaloa* were magnified by the Honolulu press and in Poor's report, which somehow reached the United States: "The native officers were utterly incompetent in their duties and . . . conducted themselves in the most scandalous manner ashore entirely neglecting their duties on ship-board. There was a state of continuous insubordination on the ship and utter disregard of all order and discipline. With a few exceptions the marines and white sailors behaved badly, the marines continually breaking liberty by swimming ashore and disturbing the town with their drunken conduct."[24]

Poor, however, claimed that the conduct of the reformatory school boys on the whole was good.[25]

Unfortunately, the recall of the *Kaimaloa* and its mission was not known to the great powers; consequently, united Anglo-German pressure, primarily through Germany, came upon Hawaii. Bismark threatened the United States as well as Hawaii with war if it supported Hawaii.

Later came news that both the English and American residents in Samoa, "fearing German control, strongly favored some sort of autonomy being established with Hawaiian assistance."[26]

Poor later said that under propitious circumstances the mission could have been beneficial economically to both Hawaii and Samoa. He asked whether Hawaii could be called guilty of political wrong when it could have led Samoa forward to a glorious future.[27]

The mission was to go down in the papers and history as a "grandiose scheme of Kalakaua's to conquer the Pacific."

Gibson and the king found nothing but derision.

❊ ❊ ❊

Then a scandal broke over the government that defied Kalakaua's most persistent defender to explain away. By this time Kalakaua's metal must have been tested to its limits. Every day the *Gazette* , the opposition paper, edited by the *haole* elite–Sanford Ballard Dole and Alfred S. Hartwell– mercilessly sneered and maligned Kalakaua's political and personal character. Even from the pulpit of Kawaiahao Church came verbal bursts of attack from Reverend Henry Parker. Liliuokalani wrote that she preferred staying home in her garden to going to the Congregational church to hear her brother "slandered . . . Although brought up differently– too much politics and sarcasm from pulpit . . . I spent the day in the woods in the silence with One we have been taught to fear, I feel [His] presence," she wrote in her diary. Accusa- tions, just and otherwise, were being levied at the govern- ment: corruption was rampant. Lepers could buy their way out of being sent to Molokai, offices were sold, the legislature had been subverted, only sycophants held offices. Nearly ev- ery royal candidate in 1886 was on the government payroll. (They were all natives except Gibson's son-in-law Fred H. Hayselden) Worse, the country was going into bankruptcy.

It was obvious to the white *haole* that drastic measures should be taken against Gibson, the king, and the govern- ment. The Hawaiian was not ready for self rule.

Opposition was organizing; then the final nail in Kalakaua's coffin was pounded in by the opium scandal.

One can only suspect that at this point Kalakaua simply didn't care. Persistent rumors of threatened assassination plagued the entire royal family. There was nowhere Kalakaua could turn–even Gibson had begun to suspect they had gone too far. The king was growing bitter, but a certain naivete also existed, as exemplified by his words to Consul Merrill, in which he asked indirectly what he had done that was so wrong that the people opposed him. These were words he also used to Gibson and his sister, Liliuokalani.

Actually, animosity was out of control. Volney Ashford spoke openly of assassinating the king. Some of the less bloodthirsty, such as Sanford Dole, resigned from the Committee of Safety that had rapidly been formed —and would grow stronger the next year—the fateful year of 1887.

The opium scandal slid in to fuel the fire. In 1886, after the legislature had passed the Opium Bill into law, rumors began that Junius Kaae, a minor clerk, had sold the opium monopoly license to a Chinese rice-planter, T. Aki, for $71,000, which was to be given as a "gift" to the king. The license was then given to another Chinese, because the larger "present" had been given. The king denied having received the money.

On May 17, 1887, the Hawaiian *Gazette* published a story confirming the rumors, based on affidavits from Aki and others. Kalakaua did not deny the story of the money having been paid to Kaae, but he stated that he had not received it. No one believed him. Gibson wrote that he suspected Kaae of having taken the money, but that the king would protect him.[20]

The king's denial of having received the money brought about a search by Paul Neumann, attorney for the king, for direct testimony from Aki, but it was discovered that Aki had died under mysterious circumstances. Later, when the opposition to the reform government wished to reinvestigate the Aki situation, they were immediately muzzled by the Reformers.

In 1887, however, Aki's estate sued Kalakaua for the money, and Kalakaua was directed to pay. Only a percentage, however, was paid by the king, as the king was judged to be bankrupt by the Reform Cabinet.

The country was ripe for revolution.

10 *Fateful Years (1884–1887)*

Perhaps all of Kalakaua's years as king were fateful. Each political misstep laid the foundation for his fall from political grace. Each step in his struggle to preserve the Hawaiian culture and heritage shook the political foundations but was an upward move into the future as he envisioned it.

To review: In 1839, a year before Kalakaua was a pupil at the High Chiefs' School, Kamehameha III proclaimed a bill of rights, fashioned after the United States Bill of Rights. The first constitution in 1840 was also American in character, although it recognized the rights of the king, premier, and nobles. It was published in English, which was the language recognized for judicial proceedings. In 1852, Kamehameha III adopted a new more liberal, less monarchial constitution. It was the constitution Kalakaua warned against in his campaign. In 1864, it was revised by the Kamehameha V constitution. Kamehameha V had declared his constitution valid, because it was the constitution *his people* wanted, and it gave a strong monarchial basis for government.

Kalakaua became king under this constitution. He used it to his advantage at every possible opportunity. He used extensively his prerogative of changing cabinets and premiers to suit his plans of government. Thus Moreno and Gibson had come into power.

The spectrum of reaction to Kalakaua was broad. At one end was the intense hatred typified by Lorrin Thurston, and at the other was the blind love of many of the Hawaiians, who thought of their chief, their king, as a god.

Lorrin Thurston (1858-1931), the son of missionary parents, was the avowed enemy of Kalakaua. Early on, he revealed himself to be a fighter and rebel against authority, being expelled from Punahou School before graduation. He was a newspaperman and an attorney, having studied law at Columbia University. He became active in politics in 1884, was a leader in opposing Kalakaua in 1886, and was again a leader in the overthrow of the Hawaiian government in 1893.

But even Thurston had difficulty in characterizing Kalakaua. He said in one breath that he was immoral or "unmoral" and in the next that "as a matter of fact, it is scarcely possible to exaggerate the truth of the good things said of Kalakaua by the present royal propagandists. What they say of his personality and public conduct is practically true. The only explanation of the paradox is that Kalakaua was a remarkable incarnation of the Dr. Jekyll and Mr. Hyde of Stevenson."[1] The accusation of immorality or "unmorality" lay primarily in Kalakaua's revival of the hula and the *mele*.

Thurston accused Kalakaua of being dull-witted and cowardly, and yet in his political dealings, which Thurston condemned, he said that "his talent . . . is shown with a brilliancy equalled only by his audacity."[2]

Much has been written about Kalakaua's "cowardice" and his "uncanny sense of the time to quit." Yet it is felt by some that it took enormous courage to continue the projects Kalakaua judged valid, right or wrong, with the constant *haole* opposition always dogging his footsteps.

Politically, the final blow was the opium scandal. Socially, it was Kalakaua's fiftieth birthday celebration, November 16, 1886. Kalakaua, aware of the Hawaiian's love for *alii* celebrations, declared a week-long holiday jubilee. He could have done nothing worse to have inflamed the *haole*, who needed no holidays and who had no desire to honor Kalakaua. Yet they came to the royal *luau*, to the ball, to see and condemn the hula dancers, to criticize the Royal Guards and the parades, and to gaze, but not to participate in the *hookupu*, the giving of gifts to the king. But gifts were given in abundance.

The *mele*, often accompanied by a hula, bore the brunt of criticism as immoral, heathenistic, pagan. It was rumored that one *haole* man fainted when he learned that the words of a hula *mele* referred to a woman's vagina. It makes one wonder at the stamina of the *haole* gentleman. Another affront to the *haole* sensibilities was the revival of Kalakaua's "Mele Mai," the *mele* composed at his birth glorifying his genitals.

Fires of criticism were fueled in every direction. The *Hale Naua* was severely condemned as a hotbed of sorcery used to destroy the Kamehamehas and anyone else who stood in Kalakaua's way. Princess Ruth had died in 1883 and Bernice Pauahi Bishop on October 16, 1884, and the cry had gone out that "the last of the Kamehamehas had gone," with the innuendo that Hawaiian greatness had passed. Dowager Queen Emma died the following year, and the papers said "the last of Kalakaua's enemies is gone." Yet the *haole* were left.

Then, early in 1887, Princess Likelike Cleghorn, the king's younger sister, became ill at her home as the result of a fall from a horse and was under the administrations of Doctors McKibben and Trouseau. The rumors immediately began that Kalakaua as *kahuna* was praying his sister to death.

Likelike was particularly aware of natural phenomena, and when the volcano on the Big Island of Hawaii erupted during her illness, she became convinced that her death was a sacrifice of the Kalakaua family to pacify the goddess Pele.

During her illness she was closely attended by Princess Liliuokalani and Queen Kapiolani, as well as having Kalakaua as a frequent visitor. Her husband, Archibald Cleghorn, the king, and Liliuokalani all tried to persuade her that the rumors and the "eruption for her" were nonsense.

According to Lydia Aholo, Liliuokalani's *hanai* daughter, prayer meetings were held nightly at the palace for her recovery, with Kalakaua officiating in Hawaiian prayer. At Likelike's home a *hooponopono* was held. This is a beautiful ceremony Hawaiians use to resolve problems of differences—to bring a family into understanding of each other. It actually was a family council with eleven steps to the solution of a problem: 1) Statement of problem and "gathering of emotional and spiritual forces" to help; 2) prayer—not that God solves the problem—but for the wisdom to solve it; 3) the injurer and the injured are bound together by doing and "blaming;" 4) the "grudge" or "fault" must be released from the one holding it; 5) a period of silence and reflection; a quieting; 6) both injurer and injured must be released, for each feels the pains of the other; 7) the "layers" of the trouble are talked about from all points of view; 8) forgiveness takes place after confession and repentance; 9) *Kalakaua*, "I unbind you from the wrong and thus I may also be unbound from it"— release of all parties; 10) the wrong is separated from the person; 11) a prayer or act of completion.[3]

Nothing seemed able to shake Likelike's belief that Madame Pele was demanding her life as a sacrifice. She died February 2, 1887, at the age of 38, of "heart attack following exhaustion," according to the newspapers.[4]

* * *

Shortly thereafter an invitation came to the palace for the king and queen to Queen Victoria's golden jubilee. Kalakaua considered it unwise for him to accept, because the *haole* were becoming increasingly opposed to his traveling. He therefore made arrangements for Queen Kapiolani and Princess Liliuokalani to represent him. Kapiolani was reticent because of her shyness and deficiency in English, and Colonel Curtis P. Iaukea was chosen as her attendant. He had returned from his trip to Russia and from later visits to Japan. As a courtly gentleman, he was a worthy companion to the queen.

Kalakaua had hoped that the ladies would wear the *holoku*–the costume of Hawaii.

Isobel Strong Field wrote that Kalakaua said he thought an island queen and an island princess should wear the dresses of their nation. He asked her about designs, as she was an artist. She described him as being impressive and making her "little parlor seem to shrink when he came in."

"It was only on official occasions that the King wore a uniform. When he called on me he was dressed in white flannels; his shoes were white, so were the gloves he threw into his hat. It was a beautiful hat made from the quills of peacock feathers that are like strips of white porcelain. These were braided, sewed together and shaped like an ordinary straw hat. It was snowy and glittering, and the band round it was of pearly shells overlapping. I never saw anyone but the king wear that particular kind of hat and I've always remembered it."[5]

Later he told Mrs. Strong that his the ladies of the court seldom listened to him and had chosen Parisian gowns, although Queen Kapiolani wore a Hawaiian dress on one occasion. It was a gown of Parisian style, with the skirt covered with peacock feathers.

* * *

Honolulu was at the time rigid with tension. Plotting against the king had already begun.

In the election of 1884, two tickets were presented: the Independent or opposition candidates, the majority of whom were *haole*; and National or government candidates, of whom all were Hawaiian or part-Hawaiian except for Fred H. Hayselden, Walter Murray Gibson's son-in-law.

Since 1884, Lorrin A. Thurston and Sanford Ballard Dole, missionary sons and leaders of the opposition party, steadfastly continued pointing out shortcomings and errors of Gibson's administration. Dole and Thurston said all public works, such as roads and harbors, had been grossly neglected because of "frivolous expenses." This was not entirely true.[6]

January of 1884, according to Walter Murray Gibson's diaries, began with tension. The election had become bitter and riotous. Although the royalist party seemed to be on top, both the king and Gibson began a period of rigorous electioneering. The king declared he "did not want a man in office who opposed [him]." The dubious right of the king to import liquor duty-free became a voting edge. At the polling places gin was freely offered. Voters were bought. During this time, Gibson and Kalakaua held many conferences at either the palace or the home of Gibson across the street from the palace.[7]

The greatest opposition was Kalakaua's movement out of a democratic sovereignty into a monarchial kingship. Of course, the storm raged against the king's "pagan" ways of rituals and secret societies, of pride in native lore and history.

The opposition was also as great against Gibson, as the catalyst that had plunged Hawaii into a sugar monopoly via Spreckels, an opium den, a fantasy land of myriad schemes of palaces, coronations, and ocean empires.

Despite the raging fire of antagonism toward the king and Gibson, the nationalists won the election. The underlying blaze was not quenched, but fanned to an open fire after the election. The attack shifted somewhat from a direct offensive on the Gibson and the king to one on the legislature. Yet the legislature constantly resisted Gibson's demands upon the treasury for militaristic, expansionistic, and "frivolous" expenditures of the king. Kalakaua seemed oblivious to the resentment of the drain upon the treasury. The king realized the wealth of the country was a result of his efforts for reciprocity, and felt that now the fruits of the successful endeavor could be used for "Hawaii for Hawaiians." The *haole*, however, felt it was Spreckels who had unfairly profited most. At this point, Kalakaua and Gibson became further embroiled with Spreckels' money.

The years moved on to the 1886 legislative bedlam, at which time an appropriation bill, along with a London loan, enabled the government to buy out Spreckels' loan—to no one's satisfaction and everyone's annoyance. The London loan had been expensive—a $75,000 loss had occurred.

In 1885 the newspapers took up the fight. The *Gazette* unmercifully chastised Gibson and the king until April 18, when a disastrous fire broke out in Chinatown. Grudgingly, the newspaper wrote of a former fire fighter and now king on April 20: "He did excellent work urging on the willing men and exerting himself to the utmost to stay the raging flames. Again and again did the men under his command strive to stay the flames, and again and again were they driven back."

But praise for the king was not long-lived. While the natives generally admired and loved their monarchial king and were proud of their palace, their coronation, the bright festivities, parties and balls, Hawaii was still a divided country. Gibson rightly resented the fact that Hawaii extended the privilege of voting in public elections to citizens of another country. Although this dual-citizenship was offered to the British, French, and German nationals, it seemed to Gibson that only the Americans clung steadfastly to their American citizenship, while vilifying the king and attempting to run the country.

The *haole* fumed that their taxes paid for the "fripperies" of the king, and the Hawaiian vote kept his views alive in government. Bitterness was rising, and by the end of May it reached its zenith in the legislature. Lorrin Thurston, leader of the abuse, attacked every member of the king's cabinet—as well as the king's every action. finally, Gibson recorded in his diary: "The King, with many members, at my house this eve. *Thurston must be suspended.*"[8] Thurston saved himself by an ambiguous apology.

By June the king realized a crisis was imminent. On January 21, he addressed the assembly on economy and entrenchment. "Wise, suave, quick of wit, Kalakaua drew approval, applause, and the usual standing ovation."[9] Kalakaua thus exonerated himself and left the problem with the legislative assembly.

Spreckels at this point decided to take over the government. He made appointments to the cabinet that he wanted Kalakaua to support. Gibson refused to accept the appointments and suggested a compromise group. These Kalakaua accepted, peremptorily dismissing the current cabinet and placing in office two of Spreckels' choices—Robert J. Creighton and John T. Dare. The cry immediately went up of "Spreckels' Cabinet."

This cabinet, which was totally unacceptable to the *haole*, plus Kalakaua's "economy program" balancing the 1887 plan of the queen's and Liliuokalani's trip to London, plus the Primacy of the Pacific plan and the opium scandal, and the culmination of the king's extravagant birthday celebration, brought the tempers of the *haole* to the boiling point.

Thurston and Sanford Ballard Dole emerged as leaders of the Hawaiian League or Reform Party. Dole, a second-generation missionary son, was born in Kauai. He studied law at Williams College and practiced in Massachusetts and Honolulu. He was elected to the legislature in 1884 and was active in the 1887 bloodless revolution. He became president of the Provisional Government, president of the Republic, and first governor of the territory. The Reform Party agreed with Dole and Thurston: Spreckels must go. Gibson must go. The king must go.[10]

Revolution was underway. Kalakaua wrote later (1890) in "The Third Warning Voice" to the legislature (signed by Robert H. Baker but generally agreed to have been written by Kalakaua), that three weeks before he had instructed Gibson to prepare and execute a warrant for the reading of the "Riot Act" and a document "Proclaiming Martial Law" to call the military to the defense of the kingdom in case of revolution.[11]

Gibson had failed to do so, and the government remained indefensible, something for which Kalakaua apparently never forgave Gibson.

Meanwhile, the Hawaiian League was being formed by the king's enemies.

* * *

Thurston met on the street Dr. S. G. Tucker, who spoke Thurston's mind: Kalakaua must go. Thus treason began. Thurston, with S. B. Dole, P. C. Jones, W. R. Castle, W. E. Rowell, C. W. Ashford, H. M. Benson, G. H. Martin, A. T. Atkinson, and N. B. Emerson met to draw up a constitution for the League. Each member was sworn to secrecy and the constitution was memorized and then destroyed, it being seen as too dangerous to be left to fall into the king's hands.

A Committee of Thirteen formed the nucleus of the League and met with others at private homes in Honolulu—a different one each night. The committee was to interview persons whom it thought "safe," and thus expand the League. It grew to 405 members out of a population of 70,000.

The most menacing part of the League was that it had taken over the military organization of the Honolulu Rifles. It was believed by the League that Kalakaua had armed the palace guards to resist, and that he would fight. The most frightening man of the group, Volney Ashford, was therefore ordered to build an old-time company of sixty or seventy men into an army of several hundred, to be called the Honolulu Rifles.

Kalakaua knew about the treachery that was going on and ordered Gibson to have persons infiltrate the group and report to him. What is puzzling is that Kalakaua must have known the Honolulu Rifles and Volney Ashford were dangerous enemies. Ashford even planned to have the king review the Rifles and when his back was turned shoot him. Calmer blood among the League prevailed and determined that the king should not be murdered. Kalakaua, however, did review the Rifles at an exhibition drill. He presented Ashford with a flag. Ashford mouthed the words of thanks to "Your Majesty honored Sovereign." Yet as Gavan Daws, the well-known historian wrote, "Kalakaua must have known that Ashford and a good many other members of the Rifles were also members of the Hawaiian League, and Ashford must have known that the king knew."[12]

It is impossible, in the absence of personally written documents from the king, to fathom what was in his mind. It has been hazarded that the genial Kalakaua could not believe he had an enemy—yet he had commissioned Gibson to investigate, and in his "Third Warning Voice" he implies he had suspicions since 1880 of unrest. That, of course, could have been hindsight. The "Third Warning Voice" was written in 1890.

Gibson had ordered a supply of arms for the palace guards and had barricaded the palace, and the new electric lights lit the whole area all night long. The League was unnerved and suspicious of these events. Yet what did Kalakaua write in his diaries and journals that were so ruthlessly destroyed by the later provisional government?[13]

Diplomats were notified of the intentions of the League. As a result, the United States Minister George W. Merrill visited Kalakaua at the Palace.

He reported that the disingenuous Kalakaua appeared surprised and asked what he had done—and what he could now do to rectify the situation. Merrill told him Gibson must go, a new cabinet must be appointed, and the king should no longer "interfere" in politics.

Kalakaua immediately obliged: All cabinet members, including Gibson, were asked to resign, and a new cabinet was to be appointed under W. L. Green. Charles Reed Bishop, banker and husband of the late Bernice Pauahi Bishop, *hanai* sister to Liliuokalani, brought the news to the committee.

* * *

The Javert complex was too strong among the League to
accept a truce.

If Kalakaua was to Thurston the incarnation of
Stevenson's Dr. Jekyll and Mr. Hyde, members of the
League were certainly to Kalakaua the incarnation of Victor
Hugo's Inspector Javert.

Javert was beside himself with anger. He spent his life
pursuing Jean Valjean, whose crime was stealing a loaf of
bread to feed his sister's starving family. The story of *Les
Miserables* was the stuff of magnificent fiction. The League's
obsession was the stuff of despicable fact. The king must be
hunted down and brought to his knees. A mass meeting was
to be called the next day, June 30, 1887. The king called out
military help to protect property and lives—ironically, the
military was the Rifles, who were under the orders of the
League.

Under the threat of the Honolulu Rifles the king was
forced to sign the Bayonet Constitution of 1887. In his letter
of capitulation, Kalakaua wrote of his gratification that his
people had taken the "usual constitutional step in presenting
their grievances." One wonders if sarcasm underlay his
words as it did in the "Third Warning," in which he wrote:
"We were taught to be more enlightened and less barbarian,
to discard the Ma-lo and assume a little more *Parisian* garb,
to discontinue athletic exercise, and games of surf riding and
(boxing) Lua, for a little more devotion and prayer, to ex-
clude honest work and farming for a little more Mammon,
and less greediness, to give up your lands and properties for a
little more Holy Ghost."

* * *

The demands were that a new cabinet be named, Gibson be
dismissed (these two demands had already been met), the
king return the money to Aki, Junius Kaae be removed from

office, and that the king was to reign—not rule or influence the voters or legislators in any way.

The king was stripped of his power.

❋ ❋ ❋

A puzzle remains. Kalakaua was always militarily oriented. He knew the importance of having a strong military, and his first act on becoming king had been to establish regulations for the organization of the military. During his trip around the world, he had been constantly reminded of the danger of not having a standing army or navy. He wrote in "Third Warning" that the military had always been put down as "a useless and a costly appendage." He continued to point out the need for military protection for the future and said he had hoped to promote it for the past several years: "But what have we observed for the last sixteen years? Only riots, bloodshed, lawlessness and murder, and observe the outer world where every civilized and enlighten [sic] nations of the world are all arming and are armed, only too ready and at any moment to 'Let loose the Dogs of war.' We may not expect it, but it will inevitably come, in spite of our expectations and hope it will never come.

"There are always to be found in every well regulated community, men of such stamp as have figured largely in the late event. Unscrupulous, greedy and bigoted, that nothing is mean enough, but to satisfy their lust and ends. Though unsuccessful and down now, will like the hybrid ophidia will raise [sic] again to take another snap at the bird that innocently roams from branch to branch and from flower to flower, for a brief period only to be swallowed by the hydra never to appear again. This is the condition of the country now, and now is the time to take seriously into heart and consideration to ward off in time an inevitable doom were we to remain in passive ease and in silent assurances that no such danger may be expected. The exhibition of a weak and timid policy is the ruination of the nation, and nothing can exonerate the character of men and Legislature to allow the country to drift to this end, but a stamp upon their brows as partizans [sic] to undermine and ruin the country."

He answered the question of why the king's guards did not attack the Rifles.

"Few outside of naval and military circle know the causes why no shot in anger were fired by the King's Guards at the time and riot of June 30th, 1887, or which the *Friend* the *Saturday Press* and the *Hawaiian Gazette* , have lauded the highly laudable success of the bloodless revolution and rebellions scheme of inaugurated by the Reform Party during that period. It was simply owing to discipline and obedience to orders. In absence of a 'Riot Act' being publicly read, nor a 'Martial Law' proclaimed, to warrant an active demonstration on their part, but in strict obedience to the Constitution and to the Laws of the land, to the Commands and Rules and Regulations of Military Law as prescribed in every well regulated military organization of all civilized nations, and community in the world, no blood: Yea! not even one jot or little of blood was shed.

"Verily! Verily! ! This bloodless revolution, has been tenaciously claimed as a grand and glorious victory gained by the 'Honolulu Rifles, the Boys in Blue,' and for the Reform Party in particular.

"Now that the scene has changed, a proper vindication of the character of the officers of the Guards with their men should be at once recognized, that aspersion should not be cast against them for doing their duty."[14]

It was typical of Kalakaua to want to save the honor of his guards—and people.

❉ ❉ ❉

With Gibson's dismissal, the new cabinet, with William L. Green at its head, included Godfrey Brown as minister of foreign affairs; Lorrin Thurston as minister of the interior, and Clarence W. Ashford as attorney general.

The Reform Cabinet, as the new Kalakaua cabinet was called, set about the first important task to which it had committed itself—securing a new constitution. The actual drafting of the new constitution was done by members of the Hawaiian League. Rushed to completion in a matter of days, it was presented to Kalakaua on July 6, 1887. Sanford B. Dole, in writing to his brother on Kauai, expressed the *haole* mood of the times when he wrote "if he the King doesn't accept it, he will be promptly attacked, and a republic probably declared." After several hours of heated discussion and open argument with his cabinet, Kalakaua yielded to the pressures placed against him and signed the new constitution. Thereupon the chief justice of the supreme court was summoned, and the king and his cabinet swore an oath to support the new constitution.

The new constitution, called the "Bayonet Constitution," inasmuch as it had been secured by threatening the king with the use of armed force, came into existence on July 6, 1887. Kalakaua had been given twenty-four hours in which to sign it.

Kalakaua's signing was a disappointment to the League; it would much have preferred a refusal and consequent overthrow of the government and possible murder of the king. It gave rise to Thurston's chagrined comment of Kalakaua's "uncanny ability of knowing when to quit."

The mood of the League was violent. Deprived of its main prey—the king—the League members turned their frenzied hatred on Gibson. Led by Volney Ashford, members of the League stormed the home of Gibson and brutally dragged away both him and his son-in-law, Fred Hayselden, under the horrified eyes of Hayselden's wife and children. They were taken to the wharf where a hasty hangman's structure was erected.

At the last moment, with a rope around his neck, Gibson was rescued by British Consul Wodehouse. He and

Hayselden were accused of crimes of fraud and misappro-
priation of funds. When no basis could be found to condemn
them, Gibson was ordered out of the country with the threat
of death on his head.

He died in San Francisco on January 21, 1888. At his wish,
he was buried in Honolulu. The old story was that embalm-
ing fluid had turned his skin black, to which the *haole* were to
have said he was as black as his soul, and to which the
Hawaiians responded, "He is now truly one of us."

❧ ❧ ❧

The Bayonet Constitution stripped the king of nearly all
his rights and made him a ceremonial figure. Some of the
more important constitutional changes that took place
were as follows:

1) While the king could still appoint cabinet ministers,
he could no longer arbitrarily dismiss them without a want
of confidence vote by the legislature.

2) The king's veto power no longer was absolute; it could
be overridden by a ⅔ vote of the legislature.

3) The House of Nobles became an elective office similar
to the House of Representatives.

4) The king's authority as commander in chief was
modified, giving the legislature the authority to organize
military and naval forces.

5) Future amendments to the constitution were exclusively the prerogative of the legislature; the king's approval
no longer was needed.

6) The voting privilege was extended to all male residents
at least twenty-one years old who had paid their taxes, had
taken an oath to support the constitution and the laws of the
kingdom, and who could read and write Hawaiian, English,
or some other European language.[15]

If taking the oath to support the constitution did not dis-
qualify the Hawaiians, there was a property-voter restriction
for both candidate and voter that would; for the House of

Nobles required property worth $3,000 and an income of $600 a year, for the House of Representatives the qualification was property worth $500 and an income of $250.

The Reform Cabinet was not free of criticism. *The San Francisco Chronicle* declared that the revolutionists simply engaged in "a game of grab ... an oligarchy more domineering than Kalakaua ever was ... the press muzzled," and "one who looks for facts in Honolulu journals will not find them."

The pro-Hawaiian papers, such as the *Elele* cried: "Ho! ye people of the land. Look to your king! Let us stand up straight and oppose this treason. As these people came to this land, let them depart hence, for their treachery is now exposed to the blade of the sun."

Angry responses came from the opposition: A. T. Atkinson, editor of the *Hawaiian Gazette* , wrote:

"The European and American is not here on sufferance, he is here of right and he is here to exercise his right to build up a powerful and prosperous State, not on effete and feudal ideas, but on broad modern principles of popular freedom ... We did not come here to play at free institutions, we came here to enjoy them."

It was followed by a commentary on the constitution, Article 13:

"The King conducts His Government for the common good, and not for the profit, honor, or private interest of any one man, family, or class of men among His subjects ... It is very plain that the government which has taken for its watchword 'Hawaii for the Hawaiian' is ruling for the benefit of a 'class of men'. As things are managed now, for a man to be of American or European parentage, though he be a subject of the realm ... is to have a bar set against him for any employment under the executive. Those white men who hold office know that they hold it merely as stop gaps, till the government can secure competent Hawaiians."

The *Bulletin* supported the Hawaiian point of view: It doubted that votes of aliens under the "reform" constitution would be legal, and scores of letters in agreement poured in rejecting the *Gazette* demand that names of the writers be published, the editor said: "There was never a period . . . when respectable citizens felt less free to express their thoughts than at present. If a man dare utter an opinion adverse to the extreme notions . . . he is at once marked as an 'enemy of reform'."

The 1887 Bayonet Constitution required a new election for nobles and representatives. The Reform won an overwhelming victory, mostly through the foreign vote on Oahu, which included the Portuguese but not the Orientals, who had no vote.

The Reformers were accused of having in brought in thousands of Portuguese from the plantations on election day. Because many of these could not read nor write, they voted by marked ballots that called for straight reform. Reverend Joseph Poepoe was quoted as saying, "The word Reform has just one meaning–drive all Hawaiians from the soil of their birth."[16] The Hawaiians, in sadness, beheld their defeat.

The Reformers, now in full sway, forced Kalakaua to sign the revised tariff treaty with the Pearl Harbor amendment. The Hawaiian government had steadfastly opposed any action that would relinquish control of its territory and threaten its independence. Kalakaua had negotiated the first reciprocity treaty without making concessions regarding Pearl River Harbor, but now the Reformers, afraid of losing the benefits of reciprocity, worked for the amendment that gave to the United States "The exclusive right to enter the harbor of Pearl River in the island of Oahu, and to establish and maintain there a coaling and repair station for the use of vessels of the United States . . ." A reluctant king signed the bill.

※ ※ ※

With great equanimity, the beleaguered king addressed the Legislative Assembly at its opening on November 3, 1887.[17]

"You have been called together in Extraordinary Session at the earliest practicable moment after your election under the New Constitution, in order that you may revise and amend certain Acts which have been found to be inoperative, unconstitutional or conflicting in their terms. Amongst these are the Opium Bill and the Act to organize the Military Forces of the Kingdom; also the law relating to Notaries Public and that relating to Corporations."

He spoke also of amending measures for a loan, a revision of the police department, curtailing of the salaries, and other expenditures. The final galling words were:

"I take great pleasure in informing you that the Treaty of Reciprocity with the United States of America has been definitely extended for seven years upon the same terms as those in the original Treaty, with the addition of a clause granting to national vessels of the United States the exclusive privilege of entering Pearl River Harbor and establishing there a coaling and repair station. This has been done after mature deliberation, and the interchange between My Government and that of the United States of an interpretation of the said clause whereby it is agreed and understood that it does not cede any territory, or part with, or impair any right of sovereignty, or jurisdiction, on the part of the Hawaiian Kingdom, and that such exclusive privilege is co-terminous with the treaty."

Many Hawaiians believed this was the beginning of the end of their sovereignty.[18]

The Reformers now began destroying all of Kalakaua's "pet projects." These included abolishing the Board of Genealogists, which perpetuated the genealogy of the Hawaiian *alii* and was an integral part of the *Hale Naua*. The Native Board of Health was discontinued. The students-abroad program was stopped, and most of the young people had to return to the islands, although a few secured private funds to continue their studies. Acts were passed to further curtail the king's authority by placing the power with the ministers. When Kalakaua vetoed these acts, he came under attack for disregarding the cabinet's advice. When bills were sent back to Kalakaua for reconsideration and again vetoed, they were considered law anyway.

❋ ❋ ❋

In spite of the incredible opposition from the *haole* from the time he became king throughout his reign, Kalakaua never lost sight of his place as the Renaissance man nor of his attempts to revive the Hawaiian culture.

II Development of the Renaissance Man (1874–1886)

Kalakaua was always the Renaissance man, from his youth when he read voluminously, according to Beckwith, to his early, unsuccessful attempts as postmaster, inventor, newspaperman, and then more successfully as an attorney, as his mind responded to legal intricacies, to the time he became king.

One of his first acts as king was to set aside royal land for a public park, naming it Kapiolani Park after his queen. It was one that both *haole* and Hawaiian could enjoy. It was filled with trails for walking, riding, picnicking, and generally enjoying nature at its best. There were popular race tracks and reflecting pools inhabited by ducks and swans. Pleasant benefit ice cream suppers were held there. Honolulu was famous for its ice cream of banana, guava, strawberry, mango, and pineapple flavors. The Royal Hawaiian Band enlivened the night with music while people strolled along the path or the *haole* ladies, as was common, rode in their two-wheeled carriages. The Hawaiian women, garlanded with flowers, were usually on horseback or sitting in groups strumming guitars and singing love songs. The extensive park also housed summer homes of the Hawaiians and *haole*. The owners sat on their *lanai* and enjoyed the warm evenings and passing parades.

The Princesses Liliuokalani and Likelike, as well as the queen with the aid of retainers, oversaw the tending of the beautiful formal gardens and flower beds. Today Kapiolani Park includes the Bandstand, amphitheater, zoo, aquarium,

and World War 1 Memorial. On weekends artists display
their work at the park.

❊ ❊ ❊

Kalakaua's boat house, "Healani," renamed the "Snuggery" by
the royal circle and called "the den of all iniquity" by the *haole*,
especially those who were not invited to the parties held there,
was also the scene of aquatic prowess and experiments.

Kalakaua was all-Hawaiian. In spite of his missionary-
Christian education and *haole* contact and influence, his
thinking, his interests, and his natural urge were strictly native. "He was totally kanaka–a creature of the sea–with vision
outward to the sea. In the older, fatherly Gibson–himself a
declared creature of the sea–he found a soul who understood,
condoned, and encouraged the very things which brought
shudders and outcries from the less visionary *haole*."[1]

Kalakaua loved ships. He designed and built sailing and
racing boats, sleek canoes, and Polynesian outriggers. He
was a master sailor of every type of craft. He was adept and
graceful on a surfboard. He sponsored and conducted yacht
and canoe racing, regattas, and a dozen kinds of competitive
and aquatic sports. Here he could honor and reward the
highest excellence in Hawaiian water prowess.

The sea was the place of sport for the *haole* as well as the
native. Moonlit suppers aboard ships, beach parties, and
swimmers were described by Gina Sobrero, the Italian wife
of Robert Wilcox, as making one think of "engravings by
Gustave Dore that illustrated the Divine Comedy . . . not
too glowing fancy is needed to believe that one is in the
middle of a storybook kingdom."[2]

Nevertheless, the boat house was to go down in history
and legend as a wild place of orgies:

"Here foregathered in a heady, pungent atmosphere of
Havana long-leafs, flower leis and libations were writers,
musicians and dancers, poets, full-blown *wahines*, florid
politicos, shrewd-eyed diplomats, bon vivants and admi-

rals, partaking of such delicacies as squid, pig, lobster, crab on the half shell, eel. It was usually washed down with steam beer, bourbon . . . and, on occasions, Rothschild's bubbling *sec* laced with thinly sliced cucumbers and cracked ice, ladled from a mammoth cut-glass punchbowl by the Merry Monarch himself.

"There was song, music and intrigues. Often the festivities took place behind locked doors where, it was rumored, ancient hulas were performed by bronze-skinned, buff-bare, undulating, beauties. Gossip also insinuated that Kalakaua revived the old aristocratic group-game which was 'like . . . modern "post office" only more serious.'"[3]

It was true that Kalakaua entertained lavishly and generously. It was Hawaiian to do so. Hawaii had always lent itself to a people generous in sharing hospitality. The food was plentiful and the climate unsuited for storing up foodstuffs. The natives shared with their *alii* and among themselves, and the *alii* were known and loved for their *mana* (goods and wisdom) and their *aloha* (love and sharing). Kalakaua was following an ingrained pattern with his open hospitality:

"According to his [a native's] upbringing," wrote Edwin Burrows, "the way for a man to enhance his status through wealth was not to store it up but to give it away with lavish generosity."[4]

Kalakaua was, however, trying to bring generosity into the modern times of the day. And with this he did a brilliant job.

Natives and foreigners were invited to morning and afternoon concerts and evening musicals. At the musicals, besides Hawaiian music were favorite selections of the king: "Emperor Waltz" (Johann Strauss); Piano Concerto no. 21 in C Major, K. 467 (Mozart); Symphony no. 100 in G (Haydn's "The Military"); and "Radetzky March" (J. Strauss). Dancing would often follow, with the king's favorite waltzes, polkas, schottisches, and gallops.

Dinners were held for dignitaries such as Prince Oscar of Sweden, the Earl and Countess of Rosebery, Lord Provost of Glasgow, ex-Lord Mayor of London, U.S. Consul of Samoa, Prince and Princess de Bourbon, and many others. Numerous benefits were held to help support the Queen's Hospital, Kapiolani's Maternity Home, and Liliuokalani's Educational Society.

Magnificent dresses were worn by the guests, and protocol was extended to *haole* and native alike. Nearly all the enemies of the king, as well as his friends, came to the palace balls and parties. It was the late suppers at the palace or boat house that were resented and criticized. Isobel Strong Field wrote:

"In a small place like Honolulu, teeming with gossip, the King's late supper parties were whispered about as *orgies*, not only by the missionaries, but among a number of those who were much offended at not being invited to join them.

"Though we were served sandwiches and champagne frappe, these were not drinking parties but a gathering of congenial spirits, chosen by the King, I realize now, for our ability to entertain him.

"There were never more than ten or twelve of us."[5]

Among these she mentioned a young Philadelphian who wrote "flamboyant 'odes' to the king." This was Paul Neumann, the attorney, who told stories and "whose droll comments and witty asides were an inspiration to the rest of us." There was also Jake Brown, whose "wife was part Hawaiian of a good family who had brought him a fortune;" Jake was clever with verses about local events and people, and an excellent pianist. In the group were also Captain Haley and his beautiful wife, who was a dancer and actress. Maude Haley was "clever as well as beautiful," and sang the gayest music hall songs, and regaled the group with bits of gossip told in a way that brought shrieks of laughter.

Joe Strong, the artist and husband of Isobel, drew thumbnail caricatures. Isobel's contribution was reading poetry and doing imitations of timid visitors to the king with "twitter of nerves and embarrassment." Her best efforts were "taking off the Missionaries."

"Kalakaua," she wrote, "sitting in a big red velvet chair, laughed heartily, applauding our efforts. He would occasionally pick up a ukulele or a guitar and sing his favorite Hawaiian song, *Sweet Lei-lei-hua*, and once he electrified us by bursting into:

> 'Hoky poky winky wum
> How do you like your taters done?
> Boiled or with their jackets on?
> Sang the King of the Sandwich Islands.'

"Through all our gaiety there was always a deep respect for Kalakaua. None of us called him anything but 'Your Majesty,' and never did I see anyone treat him with familiarity."[6]

Isobel recalled an incident when King Kalakaua suggested that they call him "Rex"—and the reply was "Yes, Your Majesty."

Haole writers, in their attacks upon the Merry Monarch, conveniently passed over the fact that he had an educated and brilliant mind. He was probably one of the most skilled anthropologists to come out of the Polynesian people, according to Paul Bailey, a well-known journalist.

He preserved the feather cloaks and stored and stripped bones for anthropological and archaeological study. The *haole* man on the street had no comprehension of his work, and Thurston relates that a deputy sheriff of Kau, Hawaii, sent the king the bones of a mule, saying it was the bones of Kamehameha. He further declares that Kalakaua bestowed a decoration upon him. Knowing what we do now of the king's work, we must assume Kalakaua had no more than an amused smile for the sheriff. No record is found of any decoration bestowed on Edward "Long" Smith. Yet it was a story Thurston felt worth passing on.[7]

To preserve the history, study the people, and learn from the past, Kalakaua set up the *Hale Naua* Society. None was more vilified during his time.

Therefore, no dissertation of the Merry Monarch would be complete without a discussion of the "infamous *Hale Naua*," held by the *haole* to be a den of iniquity, sorcery, sexual orgies, and a travesty on Masonic rituals–a secret organization into which the *haole* (W. L. Green was an exception) could not enter. *Hale Naua* was translated by San Francisco reporters and Kalakaua as a "Temple of Science."

What annoyed the thrifty *haole* most was that a board of genealogy had been established by the government *at government expense* to study the lineage and heritage of the Hawaiians. The members of the board were part of the *Hale Naua*.

Liliuokalani wrote in her *Story*: "On the twenty-fourth day of September, 1886, by request from the king, a charter was granted by the privy council to the *Hale Naua*, or Temple of Science. Probably some of its forms had been taken by my brother from the Masonic ritual, and others may have been taken from the old and harmless ceremonies of the ancient people of the Hawaiian Islands, which were then only known to the priests of the highest orders. Under the work of this organization was embraced matters of science known to historians, and recognized by the priests of our ancient times. The society further held some correspondence with similar scientific associations in foreign lands, to whom it communicated its proceedings. The result was some correspondence with those bodies, who officially accepted the theories propounded by the *Hale Naua*; and in recognition of this acceptance medals were sent from abroad to the members highest in rank in the Hawaiian society. Unworthy and unkind reflections have been made on the purposes of this society by those who knew nothing of it. Persons with mean and little minds can readily assign false motives to actions intended for good, and attribute to lofty ideas a base purpose or unholy intention. That some good has been done by this organization the members themselves could readily certify. It had been the custom before the days of His Majesty Kalakaua (it is the usage even to the present day [1895]) for the chiefs to support the destitute and to bury the dead. This society opened to them an organized method of doing this; it cared for the sick, and it provided for the funerals of the dead. Had the king lived, more good would have been done, and the society would have been in a more flourishing condition; yet the money contributed for its purposes while he lived was invested in stocks, and many purposes have drawn benefits from the dividends. Although it was small, it was a beginning."[8]

She placed the *Hale Naua* in her book under the category of "Benevolent Societies." The *Hale Naua* dated from the time of Kamehameha I, and according to David Malo,[9] it was actually a building (*hale*) in which the king greeted his guests with the question "*Naua*?" It meant "Whence are you? What is your ancestry?" and was a challenge for the person to answer with his relationship to the king or to some other high-chief lineage. It was not a recitation to display one's ancestry, but was to show a shared legacy from one's ancestors, and only in the company of one's peers. Its early purpose was to prevent bloodshed by uniting the chiefs under the bonds of kinship, friendship, and rank. It was a nonpartisan, peaceful organization. "The most perfect decorum must be observed at all meetings." The meeting was attended by skilled genealogists, who, if recognizing the lineage of a candidate that the candidate had omitted, could add to the recitation.

In Kalakaua's time, the society was enlarged beyond genealogical recitation, although this remained important; therefore, persons recognized as *kahuna* who kept family genealogies were invited to attend. Hence, the much-condemned "ball of twine."

Nonmembers (*haole*) have left for history their idea of the "ball of twine:" The men sat in a circle and each rolled the ball of twine toward a woman whom he desired to sleep with that night. Actually, the ball of twine had knots in it that were placed so that they helped the genealogist, in his long recitation, to remember generation after generation. It was no small task to remember hundreds of names of several generations such as the example of a descendant from an ancient king of Oahu:

> "I am not one to give my name to every challenger,
>> A calabash of *aholehole* fish (for the king).
>> Descended from Kahuhihewa, king of
>> this island of Oahu,
>> And from Meehanau,
>> He was the first king of his line,
>> Paired with Ke-a-nui-a-panee.
>> The issue Ka-ua-kahi-a-ka-ola,
>> A god eloquent in speech,
>> To him was born the I,
>> At Kukaniloko . . ."

The *Hale Naua* was under the auspices of both the king *and the queen*, and its membership consisted of the leading Hawaiian citizens (each held an "office of science"). In 1888, the officers were: Her Royal Highness Princess Poomaikelani, President; Hon. Antone Rosa, Geology; Hon. J. L. Kaulukou, Dialect and History (Ancient Hawaiian); His Majesty Kalakaua, Biology; Hon. J. A. Cummins, Conchology; Mrs. G. Kahalewai, Botany; Mrs. C. H. Ulukou, Archaeology; Mr. J. Ena, Seismology; Joseph Liwai, Ornithology; Hon. E. K. Lilikalani, Minerology; Major J. P. Kahalewai, Meteorology; His Majesty Kalakaua, Geography and Diametral Physiography; Major J. P. Kahalewai, Curator and Museum; Mrs. G. Kahalewai, Secretary."[10]

The much hated and misunderstood hula was also attacked by the outsiders. It was again being revived by the society for "lascivious purposes." The missionaries and the *haole* had never understood the hula. It was in its earliest forms a religious dance. The Hawaiians, never ashamed of any part of their body, did not hesitate to bring glory to it in their dances. The Supreme Being, man, and nature were so intertwined in the Hawaiian concept that they could not be separated. A hula tribute to a woman's breasts could be a tribute to the swelling of the ocean waves as well as the acknowledgment of both the motherhood and the fatherhood of the Supreme Being. The dances usually had these three dimensions—the obvious, the tribute to nature, and the sacred (often only interpreted by the *kahuna*). They also told a story of past events and embodied heroic deeds of legendary men and women.[11]

As for sorcery, Kalakaua attempted to bring to light again the old herbal treatment of the *kahuna* physician as well as to preserve the *kahuna*-priest religious teachings. Kalakaua was himself a *kahuna* and knew much of the old lore which Liliha, his grandmother, and others had taught him as a child.

In 1888, a defense of the *Hale Naua* was published in the *Paradise of the Pacific*.

". . . Having heard much about the society we inquired closely into the matter, and upon investigation we are impelled to acknowledge the good aims of the society, and to give all due credit to the members of the society, and we think that their efforts should receive commendation and encouragement and not ridicule and malice, as has been the case. The greatest possible compliment is paid to the society by that eminent scientific journal *Engineering* of London, which, in its issue of February 24th, devoted more than a page to one of the papers read by one of the members, the Hon. Antone Rosa, entitled *Diametral Physiography*:

'Diametral Physiography

'We are indebted for the subjoined diagrams headed 'Diametral Physiography' to His Majesty King Kalakaua of the Hawaiian Kingdom (better known by the name of the

Sandwich Islands), assisted by his scientific adviser, Mr. J. Degraves, C. E. The diagrams shown are some of a series from which it is intended to construct a model of the world, which model is to be brought before the public at one of the great exhibitions as soon as it is completed. The original was the idea of His Majesty when starting his researches on exhibiting the shape of the earth's crust. Looked at from Mr. Green's [a cabinet member] point of view, and the reader must judge for himself whether Mr. Green's theory is borne out, supposing the heights and soundings given here to be accurate. In any case we are much indebted to His Majesty King Kalakaua and Mr. Degraves for their researches, and look forward to the time when the contemplated models will have arrived at completion.'"

Another quote from the *Engineering* explained:

"The original idea of His Majesty when starting his researches on this matter was to confute or perhaps confirm the theory broached by Mr. W. L. Green (late Minister of Foreign Affairs to the King and now Prime Minister to His Majesty) in his work entitled *Vestiges of the Molten Globe*, that the form of the solid crust of the earth is that of a tetrahedron. . . the diagrams present sections of the land and sea at certain parallels of latitude affording a new view of our globe which is extremely interesting. Briefly speaking, the idea of his Majesty in construction of these diagrams was as follows: Here is a theory as to the shape of the molten globe, let us consider the best way of investigating it. The author takes the North Pole as an obtuse solid angle, so that if I take sections along various parallels of latitude normal to the axis of the earth through the poles, the outline of the solid crust thus shown should represent more or less a figure of six sides . . ."

Completing its quotation from the London *Engineering* , the *Paradise of the Pacific* continued:

"Ka Hale Naua will send a collection of curiosities to the Melbourne Exhibition. Among the articles there is a feather cape, the art of the manufacture of which has been regarded as a lost art, but has been restored by the exertions of the Society."[12]

Sentiment among the *haole* was expressed by Thurston after having read a page or two of Kalakaua's manuscript (probably after the overthrow [1893]), saying that the king was "muddle-headed," and a poor writer of useless nonsense. Yet later after W. L. Green's name was attached to the manuscript, it could not be highly enough praised by Thurston.[13]

Other manuscript pages, possibly rough first drafts that were so maligned by Thurston, were the ones as a finished product Robert Louis Stevenson was to praise as "brilliant."

The *Hale Naua* was not the only benevolent organization Kalakaua supported. Early in his reign he founded the *Hooulu A me Hoola Lahui* Society to engage in works that would help his race to increase in number. The society was under the sponsorship and organization of ladies of the court, although the full responsibility and management of the society was under Kalakaua's supervision and influence. Queen Kapiolani was president and was assisted by her two sisters, Kekaulike and Poomaikelani, Princesses Liliuokalani and Likelike. The two outstanding results of the group were The Kapiolani Home For Girls and The Kapiolani Maternity Home, opened on June 14, 1890. The first cared for non-infected girls of leprous parents of Molokai. The second, as the name implies, cared for pregnant women, so that fewer mothers or infants died in childbirth and infancy.

As for the *Hale Naua* being a "travesty upon the Masonic Lodge," nothing speaks more clearly against the accusation than the high esteem in which the Masons held Kalakaua during his entire lifetime.

A Masonic history of Kalakaua is impressive. "On July 28, 1859, he was raised as a Master Mason in Lodge le Progres de L'Oceanie #124 in Honolulu. He was appointed Lodge Junior Deacon in 1861 and 1863, elected Secretary on December 1,

1864, elected Warden January 28, 1867, and became Worshipful Master on November 29, 1875. King Kalakaua was initiated 411° through 32° of the Scottish Rite in 1874. Installed as Wise Master of Rose Croix, September 12, 1874. He was elected Knight Commander of the Court of Honor on May 31, 1876, and was coroneted 33° by Illustrious Albert Pike on July 14, 1878. He was elected to the Grand Cross of the Court of Honor 33° on October 21, 1880. Kalakaua became an exalted Royal Arch Mason, February 5, 1874; was elected High Priest, Royal Arch Mason, January 27, 1883; Knighted Order of the Temple, Commandery, March 11, 1874; Elected Commander, Commandery, 1877 and 1878; installed as Knight of the Red Cross of Constantine, and installed as Knight Grand Cross, Red Cross of Constantine, 1883.

"In the Appendix of the 1892 Imperial Council Proceedings we read: His Majesty was a . . . Noble of the Mystic Shrine, which grade was conferred on him in full form on Wednesday evening, January 14th, and which was the last social institution he visited during his lifetime. King Kalakaua was initiated into Islam Temple in San Francisco, California, on that day in 1891."

It should be noted that after many years of consideration of the Merry Monarch, the Masonic Club held him in the highest esteem, initiating him into the Mystic Shrine just before his death in 1891.

Quotations are often taken from Henry Adams and others to tell of Kalakaua's impression upon them:

"[Henry] Adams, who had an audience with the king in 1890, noted that he 'talked of Hawaiian archaeology and arts as well as though he had been a professor.' C. W. Stoddard wrote: 'Oh, what a king was he! Such a king as one reads of in nursery tales. He was all things to all men, a most companionable person. Possessed a rare refinement, he was as much at ease with a crew of "rollicking rams" as in the throne room.' John Cameron, who as master of a steamer running to Kauai often found his Majesty seated among his retainers on mats on the afterdeck, termed him 'easy to approach and difficult to leave; unfailingly genial; kind to high and low alike, beloved by his subjects . . .'"[14]

A late-twentieth-century writer paid further tribute to Kalakaua: "Although many historians have portrayed King David Kalakaua as a swaggering, licentious, poker playing, hard drinking sybarite, indisputable evidence shows that he was really a scholarly and gifted gentleman who accomplished much for his people during his rather long reign."[15]

* * *

Gossip would have it that Kalakaua could have populated the entire islands with his own illegitimate children. However, had Kalakaua had any illegitimate children, he would have taken them as *hanai*, as his sister did with her husband's child. The palace was filled with children, for both he and Kapiolani loved them, but none at the time claimed to be his own.

First and foremost were the children of Kapiolani's sisters: David Kawananakoa, Kuhio Kalanianaole, and Edward Keliiahonui; the boys were frequently joined by Princess Kaiulani. But there were many others. After Kalakaua's death, numerous persons claimed unofficial *hanai* and spoke of his kindness to children and young people.[16]

"The palace rang with children's laughter," Curtis Iaukea, one of the king's proteges wrote.

Austin Strong, son of Robert Louis Stevenson's step-daughter, showed in his reminiscence about Kalakaua the king's charm that extended to children. In "His Majesty's Oceanic Goldfish," he recalled that as a boy he had stolen a goldfish that had been a gift to Kalakaua from the Emperor of Japan. He had taken the fish in order to "save face" among his schoolmates, all of whom had goldfish in their watering troughs fronting their homes. As he ran home in the darkening day, the gasping fish hidden in his hat, the king saw him and took him home in his carriage. The king's personal charm encouraged the child to tell him the truth, the dying fish was saved, and he was able to "save face." The following day an equerry in a glistening uniform presented the child with a large gift-bordered envelope on which was stamped the crown of Hawaii. It was a royal grant to "Master Austin Strong," giving permission to fish in Kapiolani Park for the rest of his days. It was signed "Kalakaua Rex."[17]

Kalakaua also had an enormous interest in promoting the welfare of young people. Curtis Iaukea, a young member of the court, spoke of Kalakaua's emphasis on physical and mental fitness:

"Physical fitness had always been deemed a part of Hawaiian chieftainship. Feats of physical skill were greatly admired and an absolute necessity for the young man of my day. Although King Kalakaua was an enthusiastic sportsman and a good shot, he was more interested in the old Hawaiian games designed to sharpen the wits and strengthen the body. He set the example for the younger men in the Palace group by engaging in these contests, often beating his opponents.

"The brain-testing game was *konane*, or checkers, which we played the ancient way–on a flat stone in which indentions were made to place the little round black and white stones that were used for checkers. In ancient times, *konane* was substituted for an invitation to war, that is, if one chief wished to declare war on another, he sent a messenger bearing a black *konane* wrapped in the leaf of the *la'i* (ti) plant. If the challenge was accepted, the black *konane* was returned. If peace was preferred, a white *konane* was sent back.

"The popular game was javelin throwing, called *pahe'e*. It required precision and expert balance. A sport that demanded mental skill, physical accuracy, and sharpness of eye was *kaka la'au*, or fencing with sticks. Great strength and endurance were required in *uma* . . . The players knelt down facing one another, right hands grasped firmly and elbows set rigidly on the ground. The objective was to tip the forearm of the opponent over to right or left and touch the back of his hand to the ground. Foot races, which were popular, were made more interesting to both participants and spectators by active betting. Of course, we all took part in water sports—surfing, canoe racing, and swimming—all of which helped to fit me for the duties expected of me."[18] (Iaukea represented Kalakaua at the coronation of Russian Tzar and Tzarina.)

For a wider sweep of understanding not only for the young but for the potential of the country, Kalakaua had, of course, engaged in an extensive educational program abroad for numerous young men and women.

* * *

Two projects Kalakaua started early in his life and which he continued with his sister, Liliuokalani, were the writing of the *Kumulipo*, the epic story of creation, and his book of legends. Both of these were begun under Kamehameha v, who had realized how quickly all culture and heritage were slipping from the Hawaiian natives.

Kalakaua's early charm that had so endeared him to his people gained for him admittance to their memory treasures. The *Kumulipo* told that out of the vast darkness rose the world and from the depths of the ocean came life in an orderly fashion, culminating in man. The greatest hero—the highest man, was the chief, and because of his greatness he had to be a "god." From his "godly greatness" descended other chiefs of such lineage.[19]

Many Hawaiians called Kalakaua "god," and while in Japan, during his trip around the world, he and the emperor recognized the common belief of god-descendence. When Armstrong sneered at the belief, he was asked by a young Japanese if it were not a nobler concept than chasing the origin of man to a mud hole—as with Adam and Eve. Kalakaua asked Armstrong the same question.

Together he and his sister had collected legends. By 1886 the collected legends and myths, and even more important, the recalled tales of Liliha and the history of Hawaii's past, began to find their way into a publishable format through the help of United States Minister Daggett. Terence Barrow wrote in the new introduction to Kalakaua's *The Legends and Myths of Hawaii* :

"It should be noted that *The Legends and Myths of Hawaii* is not all mythology. It is rich in historical narrative. King Kalakaua relates the stories of certain great events with such verve that one can readily imagine he was an eyewitness. No doubt he had heard the same tales from the sons and daughters of those who had been present on occasions such as the death of Captain Cook. Since the momentous Hawaiian rejection of the ancient gods took place only two decades before his birth, many of the people about him as he grew to manhood lived under the old system. His sources of knowledge were direct indeed."

Although Kalakaua was making one more valiant effort to make Hawaii live again, he had a pessimistic view of the future of his beloved land. He wrote in the introduction to *Legends* :

"In the midst of these evidences of prosperity and advancement it is but too apparent that the natives are steadily decreasing in numbers and gradually losing their hold upon the fair land of their fathers. Within a century they have dwindled from four hundred thousand healthy and happy children of nature, without care and without want, to a little more than a tenth of that number of landless, hopeless victims to the greed and vices of civilization. They are slowly sinking under the restraints and burdens of their surroundings, and will in time succumb to social and political conditions foreign to their natures and poisonous to their blood. Year by year their footprints will grow more dim along the sands of their reef-sheltered shores, and fainter and fainter will come their simple songs from the shadows of the palms, until finally their voices will be heard no more forever and then, if not before—and no human effort can shape it otherwise–the Hawaiian Islands, with the echoes of their songs and the sweets of their green fields, will pass into the political, as they are now firmly within the commercial, system of the great American Republic."

In his revival of the past came rediscovery of the *kahuna* and the old religion.

The "freeing" of the *kahuna* to allow them to come forth as practicing physicians was a revival not only of the *kahuna-*physician but the religious *kahuna* mystics.

Religiously, many Hawaiians held to the old *kahuna* beliefs of healing. In 1886, the *kahuna*'s practice of medicine had been legalized. But their medical practice was not restricted to herbs and foods; it involved "mental practice" and mental malpractice. It is worthy to note that with the *kahuna* (good) who opposed the *kahuna-ana-ana* (evil) there was a practical difference. The *kahuna-ana-ana* could be defeated by the *kahuna* because the former believed in the all-power of evil, and the latter believed that good could overcome evil. The *kahuna-ana-ana* had to possess a material (hair, fingernail, piece of clothing) belonging to his victim, but the *kahuna* needed no material possession; he went straight to his God to annul the evil belief and heal the patient. The Christian *kahuna*, of whom there were now many, made an easy transition to one God, multi-formed in office but one in essence, from the many named gods performing various duties. They made, in many instances, a leap over the prosaic doctrinal *haole* religions to a metaphysical and mystical Oneness beyond doctrinal thoughts and words, which fitted well into the fluid Hawaiian language.

This religious attitude adjusted easily to the ideologies of the past, the *mana* within flowing outward to the good of all who were receptive or in need in the *aloha*.

The king and his sister, Liliuokalani, were fully cognizant of what the Hawaiians believed to be true; they partook of its more mystical principles, as her diary so often testified: ". . . in the stillness is the One whose presence I feel." "The better the day the better the deed"–Hawaiian-oriented to the natural beauty surrounding one, a good day could bring forth a good deed. "I am sad . . . yet why–surrounded by beauty and flowers and sunshine." The goodness in nature was to be absorbed into the goodness of man, to be a part of Oneness of God, man, and nature. The Hawaiians had no division between the land, the sea, the sky–all were one and included man, rocks, trees, birds, animals–all fauna and flora.[20]

Many have tried to explain *Kahunaism*, but only those steeped in its mystical lore can do so successfully. As a mystic once said: "If you can define it, it isn't that."

While the political dogs barked threateningly at his door, Kalakaua continued his projects to make him the Renaissance man.

12 Last Years (1888–1890)

By 1888, the conflict became so great between the king and his cabinet—especially with Clarence W. Ashford, that Kalakaua and Kapiolani went to the summer palace in Kailua-Kona on the Big Island of Hawaii.

Kalakaua, according to Lydia Aholo, felt the need to get back to the soil—to the land. Hawaiians never seemed to get far into the *haole* world, although Kalakaua had gone the furthest as a modern monarch, before feeling the tug of *aina* and all its ramifications—land, air, sunlight, winds, waters, and people.

The *Gazette* wrote on March 13, 1888: "King Kalakaua has been diverting himself at his seaside retreat on the island of Hawaii for the past month. It is reported that he is employing himself in the laudable pursuit of coffee cultivation, which, by the way, is anticipated to be one of the future most important industries of the kingdom . . . its cultivation is, however, behind the times in methods, but a company is now projected to go into the business on a large scale and guided by skill and experience, Mr. W. J. Forsyth, an expert in coffee culture, who brings a good record from India, Ceylon and Central America and is engaged by the Government to superintend new enterprises in those and similar lines of tropical agriculture." Thus began Kona coffee.

Although Kalakaua worked in coffee planting with the help of Forsyth, he began fulfilling the prophesy that his ancestors' bones would have life through him. Kalakaua was changing from emphasis on the political man to the

Renaissance man, although one of his greatest political struggles lay ahead of him.

His sister, Liliuokalani, and he were growing closer. Yet it was to be a period in which they were to become estranged. As *hanai* children, they would have grown up in entirely separate households but united by *ohana*, the extended family. As it was, both Liliuokalani and Kalakaua were brought up together in the foreign atmosphere of the High Chiefs' School, of which Liliuokalani said, "We did not know each other as brother and sister." After the school closed, each went his separate way, but their paths crossed socially as they were both close to the royal house.

They did not always share similar ideas, but their *aloha* (understanding love) continued.

Liliuokalani remained in the Missionary (Congregational) Church until Reverend Henry Parker's haranguing from the pulpit against her brother forced her to consider and later join the Episcopal Church, where Kalakaua had been a member since 1860.

Yet they shared a mystical belief from the old *kahuna* religion, more fitting to the Hawaiian sense of unity among all life.

Liliuokalani had said their faith in God was "hearing the inaudible, seeing the unseeable—a razor's edge—as thin and sharp as a blade of pili grass." The mystical statement of Rudolf Bultman applies: "Anyone who is persuaded by arguments to believe in the *reality* of God can be certain that he has no comprehension whatever of the reality of God."[1]

The *kahuna* medical practice had gained legality in 1886, but the religion was still subverted. Kalakaua continued to search at the *Hale Naua* for answers to Hawaiian religion, culture, tradition—all of which he incorporated in manuscripts. His *Legends and Myths* was rich in historical narrative and his "Diametrical Physiography" was an indepth study of religion, the world, and life. It was as was later called a "philosophy worthy of the best scholar."[2]

Kapiolani's motto, Strive for the Highest, and Liliu-okalani's motto, Persevere While Going Upward, merged with Kalakaua's Increase the Race. Their mutual interests turned to things Hawaiian. Kapiolani, who had always been known for her interest in the lower classes, and Liliuokalani, whom Kuykendall said was widely known for her generosity to the poorer classes, forced Kalakaua's attention on economy.

The entire royal family was again keenly aware of how quickly the land was slipping away. During this period, Liliuokalani had to sell between 77 and 100 acres of *kalo* and *kula* land on Oahu that had come to her from her mother, Keohokalole. She was reluctant and sad because her husband and she had sold the land to Hawaiians, but carried the mortgage which now, according to J. M. Monsarrat, the at-torney-son of Victoria's lover, had to be repossessed because no interest had been paid for several years, and the land should be open to sale or lease again. Somehow in the old system of land tenure this would not have been necessary. Of course they needed the money. They always needed money. The *haole* desire for accumulating money, although new to the Hawaiians, was being brought to bear on them. The free flow of goods among the natives, who had once caught only the fish they could use and if they had excess gave the surplus away, was fading. Now "goods" were packaged and sold and moneys accumulated as a mark of prestige.

* * *

The Reform government had declared the king bankrupt and demanded that out of his personal purse he pay numer-ous debts. That was the main reason the king closed the palace and moved to Kailua-Kona. Colonel Curtis Iaukea was put in the position of managing the Crown lands, as these were the king's income. In Iaukea's words, we see a kind of sad naivete in the king's desire to be more frugal:

"The sincerity of the King's efforts to discharge his financial obligations may be discerned from a letter he wrote me in April of 1888 from Kailua. I was Chamberlain of the Royal Household and to me fell the task of budgeting the expenses of the different households maintained in Honolulu. I had forwarded my estimates to the King and his letter constituted his reply.

"'In running over the household expenses, I think a good deal can be reduced. The electric light can be further reduced; we need not pay so much for meat and fish; milk we can get for nothing here, and ice I can go without. I can get my poi for less than one-half of $70.00 a month. For meat from our ranch we can live on $108.00 a month.

"'By living up here we can get matters settled, the household expenses could be further reduced to $302.00 less than what is exhibited in your table of expenses. Further reductions can be made in the stables, electric light and Palace grounds. Your figures are very low for Honolulu life but as we have to economize, I do not see any other alternative than to make further reductions and live entirely in the country here. We won't be obliged to entertain but if we live in Honolulu the expenses can never be kept down.'

"We did finally manage to clear off the obligations and things went smoothly for a time."[3]

Liliuokalani had opposed Kalakaua's spending and wrote in her diary that ". . . he took my sister [Likelike] and my lands, but we said nothing." The last statement was typically Hawaiian *aloha*. Yet at this time she recognized his attempt to bring his expenditures down.

A stronger family unity seemed to be developing: Kapiolani's *mele* were collected by her secretary Lilikalani; Liliuokalani worked with Kalakaua on the *Kumulipo*. Kaiulani was sent to England for a schooling worthy of the princess and future queen. The young princes had been "adopted" by Kalakaua and Kapiolani after the death of

Kapiolani's sister, Kekaulike. They were continuing their education in the United States, except for Edward, who had died in 1887. In a simpler way, emphasis was being placed on speaking Hawaiian and using Hawaiian names.

Hawaiian, of course, was spoken at the palace, and the name *David* was never used for Kalakaua. Lydia Aholo, Liliuokalani's *hanai* daughter reported, "We were told to speak Hawaiian when we were with the queen [Princess Liliuokalani] and had to use our Hawaiian name. Mine was Kaohohiponiponiokalani but the Queen (sic) called me Kaono(hi)poni."[4]

There was a great deal of unrest among the whole Kalakaua family. They were aware that peace had not come with the signing of the Bayonet Constitution, and they were all still under constant threat of assassination. Anonymous letters, phone calls, and not too quiet rumors reached the princess as well as the king and queen.

* * *

At this point, the Reformers seemed to have won an easy victory. Then problems began. The Portuguese demanded a "fair share." The "Mechanics Union," composed mostly of men from Europe and America, complained that contracts for government work were no longer auctioned but given to the new clique. It was then that a stir was begun by the *Bulletin* about the validity of the opium scandal. It said that the truth was being suppressed by the *Gazette*, which urged "the matter be dropped and forgotten" and no further investigation be made. It was never clear whether the king's emissary had kept the money or given it to Kalakaua.

There was an undercurrent of unrest swelling against the reformers that resulted in the 1889 counterrevolution.

* * *

The 1889 counterrevolution against the Reform movement might have had a better chance of success if it had not been for rumors circulated, it was said, by the *haole* in 1887-1888.

Princess Liliuokalani was *kipi*—a traitor. She wanted to dethrone her brother and become queen.

Princess Liliuokalani gave the opposition its opening wedge when she returned from London after Queen Victoria's jubilee to angrily condemn her brother of "having signed away Pearl River Harbor" to the United States.

Liliuokalani wrote in her diary on December 20, 1887, that James Dowsett "came today and told me that they wanted me to be queen—he said they could not do anything since the king vetoes military police bills—told particularly necessary if king abdicated if king was doing wrong—I would but not until then. In evening went and told king."

There is no evidence that Kalakaua took her particularly seriously. There is implicit evidence in her diary entry ". . . went and told the king. . ." that she did not enter into the intrigue. She wrote in her book that she had always helped missionary causes and "because I had gone hand in hand with them in *good* works they thought I would cast my lot with them for evil."[5]

On January 14, 1888, she was again asked to take the throne. Her answer was the same as she "gave the league . . . would take it when he abdicates and not otherwise." The question arose again on January 16th when "W.W." (identified by Kuykendall as Robert Wilcox and Charles B. Wilson) came to consult her "on matter of importance." "I advise them to use only respectful words and no threats but to explain the situation to him [Kalakaua] how everything, the state of the country might be changed should he abdicate if only for a year, then he should take the reigns [sic] and reign peaceably the rest of his life. W. and W. went to the king . . ."

Wilson and Wilcox returned from the king with the reply that "he would think it over." The next day Liliuokalani wrote quoting Kalakaua, "wait a while—I said yes, then wait . . ."

Liliuokalani's *hanai* daughter later said: "We were not like the Europeans jealous and deceitful in the royal family. We did not plot against each other,–or murder–for the throne. We lived by *kala* and *aloha.*"

Before the month was over, Kalakaua had become suspicious that Liliuokalani was *kipi*. Liliuokalani attributed it to her reaction to the king's statement at a *luau* in which Kalakaua remarked that if the dissension continued he would "sell the country." He had no power to do so, but it was certainly a dangerous statement to make in the presence of his enemies, and was seized upon. Liliuokalani wrote, "I looked displeased." Liliuokalani's looking "displeased" could be judged to be more serious than it was.[6]

It may have established further doubt in Kalakaua's mind.

* * *

Then, in 1889, Robert Wilcox came on the scene. He had returned from Italy–having been recalled by the reform government.

Wilcox was born February 15, 1855, to a Hawaiian mother and American father. He was described as "tall, slender, erect, with flashing black eyes." He was known to writers of the time and later as being mentally keen, shrewd, even brilliant, but having such an emotional and rebellious nature that his convictions were blurred.

He had been selected by King Kalakaua for special military training in Italy. For six years he attended the Royal Military Academy in Turin. His enthusiasm for the life and achievements of Giuseppe Garibaldi led him to call himself the "Hawaiian Garibaldi." He dreamed of leading his own country to heights of glory.[7]

When he returned to Hawaii, the Reform Party made an effort to see that he not secure a position in the government, nor in his field of engineering and military science. He had married the beautiful and talented Gina, daughter of Baron Sobrero and Princess Victoria Colonna di Stigliana. His wife, who found Hawaii particularly frustrating and distasteful, was befriended by Liliuokalani, who offered them her home (Muolaulani) in Palama District.

Wilcox is an extremely difficult man to understand. From many points of view it seemed that he was thoroughly Hawaiian-King-Kalakaua supportive. Yet his wife tells a strange story.

She strongly suspected that Liliuokalani was plotting with Wilcox to dispose of the king. She wrote that Wilcox was commissioned, by whom we do not know, by a drawing of lots, to kill Kalakaua. She says he went to the king's bed chamber, found him asleep, but could not bring himself to plunge a dagger in the king's heart. She viewed his actions as lacking in courage and with contempt.[8]

The Baroness disliked nearly everyone in Hawaii and painted a very different picture of her relationship with Liliuokalani from the princess'–hers was again one of contempt. Yet Liliuokalani showed her and her husband every kindness.

When the surreptitious "plotting" of Wilcox–which the *haole* took to be against the Reform Government to restore the king's rights–became more than a rumor, the Reform Government threatened to imprison him. At that time, through moneys from the king and Liliuokalani and the ministration of the Italian Council, Wilcox and his pregnant wife left for San Francisco. When Wilcox returned from San Francisco, where his wife had given birth to a baby girl and divorced Wilcox and then returned to Italy, Liliuokalani again opened her home to him. It was here that Wilcox continued to plan the revolution of 1889 and involved Liliuokalani: guns were later found buried in the garden. In her *Story*, Liliuokalani denied all knowledge of the revolution, saying at the time she had been in Kauai and later had not lived at Palama but at Washington Place. Nevertheless, information had reached Kalakaua, through one J. L. Kaunamano, according to Thurston, that she was not only actively engaged in plans for a revolution but would replace

him on the throne. As a result, the plans for the revolution
went awry.

❊ ❊ ❊

Early in the morning on July 30, 1889, the revolutionists
marched on the palace. The plan was to meet the king there
and force the Reform Cabinet to return the king to his
proper status. The king, however, was not there, and his
guards prevented the rebels from gaining more than the palace grounds. Wilcox sent a message to Kalakaua at Queen
Kapiolani's residence, inviting him to return; instead the
king, with his guards, moved to the boat house. Kalakaua
had acted on the belief that Wilcox planned to depose him
and put Liliuokalani on the throne.

The revolution was a dismal failure. The Reform government immediately placed sharpshooters in buildings
surrounding the palace grounds and encircled the area with
the volunteer forces. Wilcox and his men were soon forced to
take shelter in a bungalow on the palace grounds. The
fighting was short-lived, with seven insurgents killed and a
dozen wounded. Regardless of this subjugation, a squad of
marines from the USS *Adams* had come ashore and furnished the government with 10,000 rounds of ammunition.

The rebels were arrested. Only three stood trial—one
whose sentence was commuted to a year in prison and
deportation. Another was fined $250. Wilcox was never tried
for treason, because it was known that a native jury would
free him. He was in the minds of the Hawaiians a hero, and
when he came to trial on a conspiracy charge, he was acquitted as being "under orders of the king."

Following the insurrection, the Reform government
became even more stringent: the cabinet was given absolute
power over all departments of the government; all military
equipment was confiscated; the king's guard was reduced; a
native volunteer group was disbanded. The high masonry
wall surrounding the palace was reduced to three-and-a-half

feet, and an open iron fence (which still exists) was installed on top.

But Wilcox's revolution had stirred thought, and by 1890 the Reform Party was beginning to split. The Hawaiian Political Organization (*Hui Kalaiaina*) and Mechanics' and Workmen's Political Protective Union joined to form the National Reform Party. The *Hui* was composed mostly of native Hawaiians, and the Union was made up of foreigners who had become disillusioned by the Reform Party. The *Hui* planned to institute a new constitution similar to that of 1864, one that would restore the powers to the king and under which Hawaii had been successfully governed for over a quarter of a century.

Robert Wilcox rose to the fore as a hero and led the National Reform Party. The election on February 5, 1890, showed the Reformers losing to the National Party, with the severest setback coming from Oahu. The infighting in the ministry, called "one of the bitterest feuds in Hawaii's history," by Kuykendall, continued to grow.

Clarence Ashford, attorney general, opposed Lorin Thurston, minister of interior, and Samuel Damon, minister of finance. As a result, feelings ran high in the legislature. It was even suggested that the members of the ministry had planned to overthrow the government and gain annexation to the United States and should therefore be tried for treason.

Yet Kalakaua gave no indication in his speech to the opening of the assembly on May 21, 1890, of his displeasure with them nor of the secret joy he must have felt of the victory of the National Reformers. He was his suave self, congratulating them on the work of the preceding biennial period: prosperity, friendly foreign relations, financial soundness, public improvements, and education, "which has received the commendations of all nations, as expressed in the Paris Exposition, where our education exhibits were rewarded the highest order of prizes." He expressed hope for interoceanic ship communications as well as an electric cable under the Pacific Ocean.

There was little of a defeated king in Kalakaua's demeanor, but the past three years had taken their toll and his health was failing. Marie Gabriel Bosseront d'Anglade, first secretary in the French legation from 1889 to 1892, described the severely restricted role to which Kalakaua had been reduced over these three years by the Bayonet Constitution:

"Despite his precarious mandate and legacy, Kalakaua remains a most outstanding example of the kind of devotion a sovereign can present to his people. He was sincere, he realized the impossibility of restraining the revolutionary process, he comprehended the larger interests at work, and then he submitted with good grace. Identifying immediately with the new political situation, however painful to him, he became the most proficient of constitutional kings. He presided at the opening of the legislature and read his speeches from the throne. In solemn audience he received foreign diplomats and representatives. He officiated at endless ceremonies etc."[9]

* * *

Meanwhile, the legislators calmed down somewhat, and the legislative body merely demanded the ousting of the cabinet and the appointment of a new cabinet *by the king*. For a few moments the sun shown through the ominous clouds on Kalakaua. He wrote his good friend Charles N. Spencer that he was finally in power to appoint him to a position of minister of the interior.

Spencer and he had been long-time friends, and the small collection of letters[10] to Spencer shows Kalakaua's concern for him. He had for some period of time tried to secure a position for Spencer but was always effectively blocked by the members of the cabinet. He must have felt a new freedom when on June 17, 1890, he was finally allowed to choose his own ministry. The new cabinet included, in addition to Spencer (an American), Arthur P. Peterson (also American), attorney general; John A. Cummins (part-Hawaiian), minister of foreign affairs; and Godfrey Brown (British), minister of finance. It was a well-chosen cabinet, a compromise between the National Reform and the Reform parties. Shortly after the appointment of the cabinet, Wilcox and John Bush, now returned from Samoa, organized a constitutional convention to revise the Bayonet Constitution.

Kalakaua insisted that the change be made in an "orderly way." The writers of the Bayonet Constitution had held no constitutional convention, nor had they allowed the people to vote on the constitutional amendments. It had never been the constitution of the people. Now the king, Wilcox, and Bush planned to reverse the decisions made by the few.

The new amendments were minor, but they were considered a start: voting would be restricted to subjects, rather than residents, of the kingdom; property qualifications were reduced from $3,000 to $1,000; the office of governor on each island was reestablished; the military forces were to be exclusively the Royal Guard. This law repealed the Military Act of 1888 that had nearly put Volney Ashford in the position of military dictator. (Volney Ashford, because of clashes with the Reform Party, was banished. He returned to Canada.) A further act was passed to send young Hawaiians abroad, but their studies were to be strictly non-military.

❋ ❋ ❋

Amidst improvements for the Hawaiians, a cloud loomed on the horizon for the planters from the United States—the McKinley Tariff Bill. The law wiped out the differential advantage Hawaiian sugar had enjoyed in the American market over sugar produced in other foreign countries. Under this law, which was to become operative on April 1, 1891, raw sugar from foreign countries was admitted into the United States free of duty and a bounty of two cents a pound was paid on sugar produced in the United States. The editor of the *Pacific Commercial Advertiser* wrote in a private letter:

"We are here plunged into the depths of despair over the McKinley Tariff Bill. There is no doubt that the situation is a very critical one . . . If they succeed in carrying it through, it is doubtful whether there is a plantation on the islands which could make any money. Probably one or two would, but most of them would collapse if such a state of things continued long. Well, we will hope for the best, and try to make money in something else if sugar busts."[11]

Kalakaua, somewhat optimistic by the turn of political events, decided to take a trip to the United States, ostensibly for his health but actually to go to Washington, D.C. and there again plead for the sugar planters. It was part of the change Kalakaua was going through. He had begun to revise his political thinking from the man who once through naivete had refused advice from the opposition and had isolated himself from feedback except from his two advisors, Moreno and Gibson, who "thought as [he] did." His background led him to recklessness and overreaching himself, to putting aside political benefits for promotion of his culture and race. It is well known that brilliance in one area is no guarantee of success in all areas.[12]

He again, as at the beginning of his reign, listened to the needs of the *haole* advisors. Yet he never lost sight of the importance of his destiny to bring to life and understanding the heritage and culture of his ancestors.

After Kalakaua's death, Colonel George W. McFarlane was quoted in an interview with the *Advertiser*:

"'Now, I will tell you something about His Majesty,' said the Colonel, 'that the world does not know. In the first place his whole heart and soul was in having the provisions of the reciprocity treaty between the islands and the United States preserved intact and taken out of the operation of the McKinley Bill. This was the true reason of his visit to this country. In fact, so much was to be wrapped up in the matter that had not sickness overtaken him it was his intention to have gone to Washington on a flying visit in order to personally see the President and Secretary Blaine on the subject.'"[13]

Liliuokalani wrote in her *Story* : ". . .the principal motive of his journey was to have an interview with Mr. H. A. P. Carter, the Hawaiian minister at Washington, in order to give him instructions in view of the McKinley Bill, which had just passed the American Congress, the influence of which was supposed to be dangerous to the interest of the foreign element in Honolulu, and destructive to the profits of the sugar planters. So the king went cheerfully and patiently to work for the cause of those who had been and were his enemies. He sacrificed himself in the interests of the very people who had done him so much wrong, and given him such constant suffering. With an ever-forgiving heart he forgot his own sorrows, set aside all feelings of animosity; and to the last breath of his life he did all that lay in his power for those who had abused and injured him."[14]

Kalakaua's foreign policy had been far-reaching and outshone his domestic policy. By 1887, Hawaii had treaties with Belgium, Bremen, Denmark, France, German Empire, Great Britain, Hamburg, Hong Kong, Italy, Japan, Netherlands, New South Wales, Portugal, Samoa, Spain, Swiss Confederation, Sweden and Norway, Tahiti, and the United States. Hawaii was also a member of the Universal Postal Union. There were approximately 100 diplomatic and consular posts around the world.[15]

Kalakaua felt he had securely established Hawaii as an independent nation throughout the world. He had failed, through no fault of his policies, to increase the Hawaiian population; however, he had increased the prestige of his nation immeasurably. He hoped his efforts to increase the prosperity of the Hawaiian businessman would promote goodwill within his country, as his other efforts had promoted it throughout the world, and thus preserve the independence of Hawaii.

He had as closely as any head of state achieved in his seventeen-year reign most of his campaign promises, which were stated in his first address as king:

1. Increase the population
2. Advance agriculture and commerce
3. Gain world recognition
4. Not cede Pearl Harbor
5. Retain independence of Hawaii.

13 The Beginning of the End

Whatever Kalakaua might have lost in Hawaii in the way of respect and appreciation was brought back to him when he arrived in San Francisco. The city that had always loved the newsworthy King of Hawaii was ready to welcome him home to them. During the period of his humiliation in Hawaii, the San Francisco papers had continued to support him, and for his third visit they were out in full force to welcome him. *San Francisco Examiner* wrote:

"At 9:30 A.M. yesterday [December 5, 1890] the United States cruiser Charleston was reported from Point Lobos, and shortly after 10:30 o'clock she steamed up the harbor at slow speed. The cruiser looked very neat and cleanly, her white sides exhibiting but very little evidence of the rough weather of the past few days. At her mainmast head floated the Hawaiian standard, indicating the presence aboard of King Kalakaua."

A *Chronicle* representative boarded the *Charleston* before she anchored and was received by Colonel G. W. MacFarlane, the king's chamberlain and secretary. He stated that "the King was already very much improved in health, the sea trip having proved beneficial. Beyond a slight film that had grown over one of his eyes, his health was in no way regarded as being affected. Oculists would be consulted to ameliorate the eye trouble. It was the King's intention to make visits to various points of interest in the State . . .

"The King was on the Charleston's after bridge in company with Rear Admiral Brown and staff while the cruiser was passing up the harbor. A salute of twenty-one guns was fired from Alcatraz and from the United States ship Swatara, her yards being manned...

"King Kalakaua wore a loose blue suit, with straw hat, while his Secretary, Colonel MacFarlane, and Colonel Robert Hoapili Baker, A. D. C. were also in plain costume..."

The king and his company were greeted by the Presidio band and two troops of the cavalry. Kalakaua could certainly feel more like a king here than in Hawaii. It had always puzzled the king and the people of Hawaii that the American *haole* hated royalty with such vehemence. Council Wodehouse had written Lord Rosebery of the London office about the core of resentment that many Americans had for royalty. "He [Kalakaua] is hated on the simple basis he is royal. The Americans hate royalty. The Hawaiians have a more British view. Despite his faults he is after all *Their* King."[1] It was true. Kalakaua, to many Hawaiians, in face of rumors of his personal conduct or political maneuvers, was The King. It was a deeply ingrained love and respect the natives had for the high chiefs and especially the king. Liliuokalani said. "It wasn't so much the king could do no wrong, as it was an *aloha* for their leader."[2]

The king and his staff were driven to the Palace Hotel in a four-horse carriage, escorted by the cavalry and accompanied by the Presidio staff officers. A large crowd gathered at Washington Street wharf, and "impeded the passage of the King and the officers in their endeavors to reach their carriage. Some small boys set up a cheer for the King, which was responded to by the crowd. King Kalakaua was dressed in a plain black Prince Albert coat and suit, with a tall black opera hat, which he repeatedly raised in acknowledging the cheers."

On December 18, the Women's Exchange had as their honored guest the king.

The *Chronicle* reported: "This year the society was in its customary good luck, for in the nick of time arrived His

Hawaiian Majesty King Kalakaua. A genuine live King, whether from the regal palaces of Europe or the less pretentious thrones of the South Pacific, must always of necessity be a social lion, no matter how deeply ingrained the republican principles of his guests." Even in Hawaii, Liliuokalani had reported the *haole* never missed a royal celebration. It was an interesting shift in interest.

"The magnetism of friendly royalty had its effect on the charity ball . . . and never before did the society of kindhearted ladies succeed in bringing together a more brilliant throng than that which paid its respects to King Kalakaua last night.

"The first object to attract the attention of a visitor . . . was the regal chair of state for King Kalakaua. The arms of Hawaii decorated the back of the improvised throne, and above it rose a canopy of imperial design, with the appropriate motto 'Aloha.' The regal chair stood midway on the left side and commanded a full view of the ballroom . . . The crowd of dancers formed a scene of delightful gaiety set in a frame of flowers. Everything lovely that the garden or the conservatory could contribute at this season of the year had been culled to grace the occasion.

"The stage to the left of the King's chair was completely hidden under giant ferns and beautiful palms . . .

"The presentation ceremonies were as successful as they were elaborate. Everything passed off as smoothly and with as great eclat as those grand events at Westminster in the court of Queen Victoria."

The days were crowded with activities, all as carefully planned as the ball, designed to honor Kalakaua. At the Mechanics Pavilion local regiments were reviewed by the king. Time and again, attention was drawn to his dress "simply, even plainly, attired in black . . . He wore a black overcoat and carried a black silk hat in his right hand. No decoration or other insignia of his rank was visible." The simple dress of

Kalakaua is often stressed as the general opinion of the times; now the opinion most often expressed is that the king was never without his uniforms and medals.

The rumors of annexation talks followed Kalakaua and were categorically denied. Colonel MacFarlane stated that "It would be impossible for his Majesty to take personal notice of every item of sensational rumor printed in the newspapers. I desire, however, to contradict this latest report officially. Neither his Majesty nor myself have any desire to discuss the subject, other than to deny the fact. The report was evidently started to boom the sugar market and to influence stocks. On the occasion of his Majesty's previous visits to America similar sensational reports were started for the same purpose."

The newspapers' second interest in the king was centered on the new book he had begun and was contemplating finishing upon his return to Hawaii.

"Having had forced upon him the empty title of sovereign," the *Chronicle* reported, "Kalakaua has turned his time and attention to study and reflection. Being possessed of the natural aptness and ability of his race, under the tuition of a number of learned scholars who had sought a home in Honolulu, he soon acquired a knowledge of the classics that was phenomenal. Besides these he readily acquired a proficiency in French, Spanish, German and English. The acquirement of these languages necessarily bred in his mind a desire for extended study, and that desire an ambition to figure among the royal authors of the century. He had read the work of 'Carmen Sylva,' the Queen of Roumania, and, with a desire to emulate her, with the assistance of Roland M. Daggett, the then United States Minister Resident at Honolulu, he composed a volume entitled 'Legends of Hawaii,' wherein was recited with more than ordinary literary ability the mythology of the islands from the time of the Goddess Pele and her son Maui to the advent of the Conqueror King—a book full of romance and interest, vying in imagery with the 'Arabian Nights.'

"This book, which has been published by a Philadelphia house, is stamped on the title page and preface sheet with the royal coat of arms and the private crests of the King and his royal family. It has met with a success that stimulated the kingly author to enter into a greater and more elevated field of work.

"Kalakaua had long given his time to the study of the works of theological authors, from those of Dun Scotus to the later period of Thomas Aquinas and Ignacius of Loyola. Brooding over the literary productions of these doctors and comparing their views with the doctrines of theosophists and the theories of Darwin, Tyndall and Ingersoll, he concluded that the time had ripened for a new, profound and more elevated theory of the creation and its purposes.

"With this view in his mind he collected all the books, pamphlets and charts relating to the peculiar views expressed by these men, and after many months of study and reflection secured the services of a French adventurer, one Captain de Freese, who had been an engineer in the service of France, and a claimant to astronomical knowledge.

"With his aid the work was commenced, and with the assistance of astronomical charts and Biblical chronological trees the royal author set about the compilation of a work that would, when completed, shake to the very foundation the present theory of theology, and show that all, having its beginning with fire, must necessarily be consumed by that element—showing also by a peculiar logical interpretation of the Testaments that the deluge was a myth, and that flames were the beginning and would be the end. This idea, with a complete denial of the present views on the creation, was the groundwork of the book. It is to be termed 'The Temple of Wisdom,' and will claim to be a 'Diametrical Physiography.'

"The work, which was completed in 1889 as far as the third chapter, was shown to Robert Louis Stevenson, now a visitor at the island, who after a thorough reading of the manuscript, grew enthusiastic over its merit, and lent by way of advice considerable aid to the author.

"The principal problem for solution in the new creed that presented itself to the King, and one scarcely yet completely answered was the question of the Trinity—the union of the three persons in one. In order to complete his theory he would have to overcome this belief. Strangely enough for a sovereign he depended upon the frequent use of the royal 'we' in the Testament in relation to the Creator as a refutation of the unity, and drew his conclusions in accordance therewith.

"The work is still undergoing considerable labor and thought on the part of his Majesty, and may not be produced for some months yet."

Kalakaua, then a the guest of the Southern Pacific Railroad, toured southern California in a private railroad car. Newspapers again followed his tour and reported that he was deeply impressed by "the spirit of enterprise in Los Angeles and San Diego." He was particularly impressed with the San Diego Harbor.

Private individuals as well as public officials entertained the king. He wrote James W. Robertson:

"A spontaneous ovation, I never have seen the like before. . . Not one moments rest. Travelling day and night. Receptions, Balls, dinners, Dinners, Masonic initiation . . . Sun shine, rain, storm, etc . . . it's all the same. Wonder that I am not half dead yet. Anyhow everything has its effect . . . and I have learnt and have seen a great deal. Nice country. Good People and all that but awfully damn cold. Whio !"[3]

This letter was written January 1, 1891. On January 9. the *Chronicle* reported his return from southern California and that he had caught a severe cold in Santa Barbara and possibly would have to cancel his many forthcoming engagements.

The San Francisco papers kept a daily account of the king's health, reporting on January 20 that he was dying.

The previous week, the king had against the advice of his physicians attended two affairs. The first was a banquet given in his honor the preceding Tuesday. The following evening, Wednesday, January 14, 1891, King Kalakaua was initiated to the Islam Temple and introduced into the Masonic Order of the Mystic Shrine. His words, famous in Masonic history, were, despite pleadings he remain in bed, "I must go, and nothing shall prevent me from going." He slept most of the day and roused only occasionally to murmur, "I must go, I must go to the shrine."[4] At 8:30 that evening the Masonic committee conducted him to the temple: it was his last public appearance.

Kalakaua died at 2:30, a.m. January 20, 1891, at the age of fifty-four, in the Palace Hotel in his beloved San Francisco, of uremic complications resulting in blood poisoning. He was attended by three doctors, among whom was fleet Surgeon Woods, who rose quickly to deny accusations of Kalakaua's death being alcoholic-related, saying that he had been abstemious for several past months. Cause of death was given as Bright's Disease.

Hour by hour accounts had been issued concerning his condition.

At his deathbed had been his chamberlain, his equerry-in-waiting, government officials, and other Hawaiian attendants and friends, including Claus Spreckels. Reverend Edward B. Church of Episcopal Trinity Church had been at his bedside intermittently for the several days, during which Kalakaua lapsed in and out of consciousness.

For nearly ten days before the king's death, an Edison phonograph had been placed at his bedside. Its use had been neglected until a few days before Kalakaua's death. Then persuaded by Colonel McFarlane, Kalakaua spoke for a short time in Hawaiian, sending greetings and love to his wife, Queen Kapiolani, and his sister, Princess Liliuokalani. He promised to complete his message later, but he became too ill to do so. His last words were "Tell them, I tried."

King Kalakaua's funeral services were held at Episcopal Trinity Church. After his body had been taken from the Palace Hotel and the casket hermetically sealed, it was taken to the church through streets that surged with people. From Union Square to the church, 30,000 people filled the streets, many of them with cameras.

Although it had been announced that the king's body would not be viewed, and only those who had received official invitations from Mayor George H. Sanderson would be allowed admittance to the church, it was variously estimated that between 70,000 and 100,000 people thronged the streets and attempted to force entrance into the church.

The scene in Trinity Church was one of impressive solemnity. It was death in all its pomp and ceremony, surrounded by the glory of civil and ecclesiastic tribute, carrying in its train the sympathy of the people upon whose shores the monarch had passed away. The black-bound casket rested in its central bower of waving royal palms and ferns within the chancel, among fragrant blooms that cast their perfume in the quiet air. The crepe-covered columns of the altar rose in gloomy outline, until they were struck by the gleaming crown of light that threw its rays into the shadowy arches of the church, down on the golden cross below, and to the splendid floral crown that stood at the head of the black coffin, almost hidden in the beautiful symbols of eternal life.

Within the church stood the Knights Templar, distinctive in rich uniforms and snow-white plumes. Near them were the officers of the state and national troupes, attired in all the glittering ornament of military show; the naval officers, called to sorrow for their dead friend no less than to pay respect and honor to the departed king; dignitaries of every church and every creed; a concourse of private citizens distinguished in the city's history; all were assembled "to honor him whose last moments were passed away from home and kindred and from the sunny western isle whose welcome home will be to the dead.

"The regular tolling of the bell which each second rang out its solemn summons and the weird strains of the funeral dirge announced that the procession had begun its sad march from the dim mortuary chapel of the church. As of one movement the great congregation arose. Upon the central aisle and within the chancel passed the white-robed ministers in slow tread, the dusky body-bearers carrying their burden, and the guard of soldiers who had stood on duty through the night at their posts. The deep voice of the minister leading the mourning column sounded the death prayer above the chant of the choir."[5]

The *Chronicle* writer grew lyrical and lengthy in describing floral tributes that had come to the king.

"The death rite was solemn in its simple dignity. The chant of the burial psalm flooded the sacred building with its pathetic harmony. The hymns, now of sadness and distress, again of gladness and glorification, carried their appealing sentiment and emotion to the throng whose voices swelled the refrain."

The rector of the church, Reverend J. Sanders Reed, spoke. "Death, is not a new thing. It is older than man and came not as the result of Adam's sin. It is not an accident, but one of the deep laws of nature, the condition of life upon this earth. Life is rooted in death and nurtured in decay. Death breaks not the thread of existence. It does not even destroy the body. Before us lies the body of an honored King. Do we believe that the ego, the personality, the individuality that knows without sense, is gone? His body will undergo a change. It will disappear, only to rise again in the flowers, in the verdure of his own beloved isle. Death can neither close nor reverse the tendency and law of development under which we move.

"This King, by his own agency, by his own action, won a character that will forever develop and expand to its goal–the perfect. He has been taken away because a longer life on earth would not advance his development. God has taken him to himself, to the influences that broaden to the end. In the wisdom of God he has been called away that others may follow where he so well and nobly led. Other men in other places have fallen as he, that the glory of their own being might be advanced, that the will of the Almighty might be vindicated."

Frank Godfrey, editor of the *Paradise of the Pacific*, arrived the day before the funeral to tell of the planned reception for the return of the king to Hawaii.

"The royal traveler was to land at the Interisland Company's wharf, where he was to be received by Ministers Cummins and C. N. Spencer and Attorney-General Charles Peterson," said Mr. Godfrey.

"The first arch of evergreens at the landing carried a transparency depicting clasped hands, designed by Mr. Stratmeyer, the artist, to exhibit the cordiality existing between Hawaii and the United States. In order also to show the appreciation Admiral Brown is held in at Honolulu, the motto 'Hawaii Greets Her King and Guest' forms a portion of the display. Eight living persons located on the arch were designed to represent the islands of the kingdom. Banners bearing pictures of the King and the royal arms were to be hung across Fort street, while another wide banner hanging with the inscription Aloha Oe."

Godfrey also spoke of the ball that the princess regent had planned–all was in happy expectation for the return of King Kalakaua to Hawaii.[6]

* * *

On January 29, 1891, the beautifully decorated Honolulu fell to a chill of despair as the *Charleston* rounded Diamond Head with its flags at half-mast. The king was dead.

Decorations were hastily dismantled and the city draped in black. The wharf was thronged with people—all quiet. Soldiers were drawn up in readiness to escort the king's body to the palace.

A firsthand account reads:

"Now the barge from the *Charleston* neared the landing. From the crowd emerged a white-haired Hawaiian woman. She was thin and bent and barefoot. She wore a neat black *holoku* (mother hubbard) and an old fashioned hat of Hawaiian *lauhala* braid. Unassisted, she climbed to the top of the largest pile of coal. There she stood, a slender, dark silhouette against the clear sunny sky. Now the coffin was lifted from the barge. With a queenly, graceful motion, she raised her right arm high above her head. Then in the rich resonant voice of the Polynesian, she began to wail. Her chanting was a wail . . . and her wailing was a chant. No one who has ever heard Hawaiian wailing for the dead can, I think, fail to experience a half-shuddering thrill at the memory of it. Syllables gushed over syllables in the soft Hawaiian language, as she eulogized Kalakaua and recounted the deeds of his ancestors, with poetic reference, now and then to the grandeur and beauty of Nature. Then the wailing would come to a great crescendo, gradually growing softer until the notes wavered and died away, sometimes broken by a sob . . ."[7]

The march to the palace then began where Queen Kapiolani, near collapse, awaited with the Princess Regent, and other members of the family and the court.

The day had been cloudy and overcast. However, as the procession approached the palace, a triple rainbow spanned the entire structure, "embracing the palace." It extended from the Royal Mausoleum to the plain beyond the palace—

the palace in its exact center, reported the *Pacific Commercial Advertiser*. "It was a beautiful omen."

There followed a three-week period of lying in state for the king.

"The coffin containing the remains of the late King was placed on a table in the center of the Throne room. The table is covered by a large feather cloak, formerly the property of Nahelenaina a sister of Kamehameha I. All except the glass front at the head of the casket is covered by another feather cloak.

"All day till 2 P.M. files of people wended their way through the Palace into the throne room, making a pitiful sight to see. A band of girls from Kawaiahao Seminary marched in file from the Seminary to view the remains of their late monarch ... Among others who called were: The Diplomatic and Consular corps, Admiral Brown and staff, the Captain and officers of H. B. M. S. Nymphe and many others. Noticeable among the callers and mourners were the retainers and retinue of Her late Majesty Queen Dowager Emma, also students from St. Andrew's Priory and Iolani College."[8]

Guards were detailed for duty both day and night. Liliuokalani wrote in her *Story* : "For this service twenty men were always selected, whose office it is to bear aloft the royal *Kahilis*, which are never lowered during the course of the whole twenty-four hours. The attendants are divided into four watches of three hours each. Those relieving form a line, and take their positions as the stations are vacated by their predecessors, who, on resigning the plumes of state, return to their homes. The watchers are generally selected from men who can claim ancestry from the chiefs; of these there are quite a number still living, of well-known families, although now generally poor in worldly possessions. While in attendance at the side of the royal casket, some sang the death-wail or old-time *meles* or chants belonging solely to the family of the deceased chieftain; and in the meantime attendants of a younger race composed dirges which were more in accord with the lyrics of the present day. There was also detailed for my brother a guard of honor from the Masonic fraternity; two Masons always remained with the other watchers, and were relieved in a similar manner."

The last morning of lying in state began with the ceremonies of the *Hale Naua* of which Liliuokalani wrote "was one of the most interesting and impressive . . .[she] had ever witnessed." The society honored its head and founder by prayer customs of the organization "similar [to] the Masonic and other fraternal organizations." The high priest who officiated was William Auld, who was assisted by two other lay priests.

"Then entered twelve women with lighted candles in their hands; each one of these bearing aloft her taper, offered a short prayer, the first words at the head, next at the shoulders, then the elbows, then the hands, and so on to the thighs, the knees, the ankles, and the feet. There were six of the torch bearers on each side, and after these formed they surrounded the remains and all repeated in unison prayers appropriate to the burial of the dead. They then withdrew in the most solemn manner. This service, so far from being, as had been alleged, idolatrous, had no more suggestion of paganism than can be found in the Masonic or other worship."[9]

Later the state funeral services took place. An Anglican ritual service was conducted by the Bishop of Honolulu, presiding. The bier was carried in slow marching step through the Nuuanu Valley to the Royal Mausoleum. *Kahili* bearers bore the plumes of various colors above the heads of moving throngs that followed the procession.

At the mausoleum, the casket was placed in the center of the tomb, and the final prayers were offered by the Bishop and Reverend Beckwith of Kawaiahao Church.

The Masonic brethren then filed in slow procession about the bier; surrounding it, they stood in silence of regard and prayer. Then each member placed a sprig of green pine on the casket as a final token of grief and farewell.

The members of the royal family were left alone for fifteen minutes behind closed doors in the recesses of the tomb. Kapiolani's sobbing verged on hysteria, and she had to be raised by her lady-in-waiting and Liliuokalani from the casket on which she had thrown herself, reluctant to leave "my chief . . . my king . . . my love . . . I am yours and you are mine."

The royal family emerged, and the guns of the military escort fired the final salute of three volleys fired above the grave. The funeral procession began its return.

14 Legacy

Legacy: "From this child, the bones of our Ancestors will have life." (Liliha)

The *Pacific Commercial Advertiser* wrote on January 30, 1891, "The biography of the late King, when honestly written, will show that he lived and ruled in one of the most eventful periods of Hawaii, a period in which the nation has prospered and progressed more rapidly than during any similar period, and whatever good name and glory Hawaii possesses now, her late King must share with her. Wherever Hawaii is known, the name of Kalakaua is almost as well known as it is here in his own Kingdom, and it will remain on the page of history as indelible as that of any of Hawaii's sovereigns."

Kalakaua left a rich legacy.

A man of moral courage, he carried out policies to further his own beliefs for what would be good for the Hawaiians and his Hawaii in the face of enormous opposition. He allowed himself to be publicly humiliated by the *haole*, yet retained his dignity and calm as king. His charm and personality carried his name—and the name of Hawaii—throughout the world. Many foreign countries still remember King Kalakaua. In China today, the schools have a celebration commemorating the visit of Kalakaua as the first foreign king in modern times to visit their country. The pantomime show includes gift-giving and presentation of *lei*.[1] He is still remembered in Vienna, as evidenced by a book written by Karl R. Wernhart in 1987: "The resplendent *Schellenbaum*, originally a gift from the German Empire recalling the sovereign's visit to Berlin and recently restored to the Royal Hawaiian Band in the form of an exact replica."[2]

The much negated "fiasco" of Kalakaua's plan of uniting the Polynesian islands was revived in 1989 by King Taufa'ahau Tupou IV of Tonga in a modified form of culture and economics. Kalakaua was ahead of his time.

In 1988, one hundred years after the Bayonet Constitution was in force, Professor Niklaus R. Schweizer wrote: "If one takes a wider view of Kalakaua's endeavors and achievements, it becomes increasingly clear that this Hawaiian king deserves more credit than is usually granted. Notwithstanding the difficult fundamentals prevailing in the last quarter of the nineteenth century, Hawai'i under his leadership enjoyed a measure of good-will around the globe that was without precedent. Kalakaua and his people possessed the friendship of Queen Victoria, Tsar Alexander III, the Emperor of Germany, and even the sympathy of Japan, that mysterious nation in the Far East . . ."[3]

Masons the world over know and acknowledge Kalakaua as a brother. In the Souvenir Program of the Centennial Year of the Hawaiian Lodge No. 21 F. & A. M. (1952), a quotation from J. M. Kapena's speech at the laying of the cornerstone of the Iolani Palace (December 31, 1879) was reprinted: "In our brotherhood of Masonry each member is taught the symbolical meaning of the three rounds of the ladder, which the Patriarch Jacob saw in his dream. They are: Faith, Hope and Charity.

". . . Kamehameha IV as Faith, Kamehameha V as Hope and his present Majesty as Charity. For Liholiho, Kamehameha IV believed the people might be saved by curing the diseases . . .

"His Majesty Kamehameha V hoped for the perpetuity of Hawaiian independence . . .

"To his present Majesty we apply the title of Charity. It is the noblest virtue. Charity, springing from an earnest desire for the prosperity of his people, induced him to leave his Kingdom and to brave the wintry cold of the Rocky Mountains and to face the icy precincts of the world renowned cataract of Niagara with the only object in view of securing for his people the boom of Reciprocity and we have all observed how he and his queen have labored in all weathers throughout the Islands for the welfare of his people. In the words of Paul to the Corinthians I may say 'and now abideth these three, Faith, Hope and Charity, but the greatest of these is Charity.' In the words of our order:

"'For our faith may be lost in sight; Hope ends in fruition; but Charity extends beyond the grave through the boundless realm of eternity.'"

* * *

In 1979 George S. Kanahele wrote in *Hawaiian Music and Musicians—An Illustrated History* :

"Among Hawai'i's modern *ali'i* (nobility) King David Kalakaua epitomized the Renaissance Man—gifted and accomplished in many fields ranging from politics to music and from literature to sports. He catalyzed the Hawaiian cultural renaissance of the last quarter of the 19th century, the monarchy's last great flowering of intellectual and artistic attainment. His impact is still felt today, for the inspiration for Hawaii's present-day cultural resurgence can be traced to his reign.

"Kalakaua's intellectual curiosity cut a wide swath through the arts and he served as patron to all of them, but his primary patronage he reserved for music—from the ancient *mele* to the waltz. Students of his life all seem to agree that he was a lover of music . . . A product of a bicultural upbringing, he was trained as a young boy in both chants and modern music. From his grandmother and court chanters he learned the ancient music; from his mentors at the Royal School he learned the modern."[4]

As in his political life so in his musical; he preserved not only the Hawaiian past but promoted new forms, such as the 'ukulele.

Besides composing, he also encouraged singing and musical performances, theatrical performances—from Shakespeare and Moliere to the most modern plays of the time—from professional production to amateur.[5]

Through his friendship with Henry Berger, he composed "Hawaii Pono'i." He wrote approximately a dozen songs, including "Ninipo," "Koni Au I Ka Wai," and "Ne Lei Na Kealoha". His best known chants or *mele* are "Ka Momi" ("The Pearl") and "Ke All'i Milimili" ("The Cherished One").

Kanahele continues to pay homage to him:

"His active pursuit of the ancient chants was perhaps the most important factor in the revival and perpetuation of the *oli* and hula, for he did this in the face of active opposition and denigration by *haole* missionary-oriented groups of the day. He was accused, for example, of falling back into 'paganism' when he allowed the *oli* and especially the hula to be performed in public. He believed strongly that the political survival of his kingdom depended upon the cultural and spiritual revitalization of the Hawaiian people. Perhaps the most powerful demonstration of this conviction with respect to the chant and dance was the inclusion of the *mele oli* and hula in the ceremonies and programs of the king's coronation in 1883 and jubilee in 1886."[6]

Hawaiian music would certainly have been lost had it not been for Kalakaua's patronage. Even Thurston acknowledged, when speaking of the Kalakaua family, beginning with Leleiohoku: "Hawaii owes them a debt of gratitude for having placed its name high on the music roster of the world."[7]

* * *

Besides music was, of course, his first introduction with his sister Liliuokalani of the *Kumulipo* in 1889, the magnificent "Tradition of Creation." With it came *Legends and Myths*, which came into prominence again in 1988 when Professor Joseph Campbell, a writer, university and television lecturer, referred in his works with legend and myths to those of Hawaii as part of the "Spirituality of Mythology." Whereas many people think of "myth" as something false and imaginary, Campbell and Kalakaua saw the myth as a guidepost to profound psychological and spiritual truth.

Kalakaua, on returning from his world tour, remarked that nations of the world were turning away from organized religion and seeking truths elsewhere. Campbell, according to the *San Francisco Chronicle* (August 15, 1988) found his main audience among those "disaffected with their own religion . . ." He brought the spiritual dimension back by showing the connections between all world religion.

The little information we have of Kalakaua's projected book *Diametrical Physiography* suggests a theme similar to Campbell's, which describes the functions of the myth to: 1) open the world to dimension of mystery; 2) provide cosmological foundation, which "shows us the shape of the universe;" 3) support and validate a certain social order; 4) provide a basis for all education of "how to live a human life under any circumstances."

Those who have written about Kalakaua's projected book believed it to be an offspring of the *Hale Naua* "Temple of Wisdom," which, among many other activities, resurrected the old *kahuna* religion.

❋ ❋ ❋

In 1917, Max Freedom Long,[8] then a teacher in Hawaii, became interested in the *kahuna* religion. Hoping to justify or debunk the *kahuna* religion, Long approached Dr. William Tufts Brigham of the Bishop Museum, who had over a period of many years collected many things Hawaiian. Brigham verified healings and other "magical" phenomena of the *kahuna* and gave Long much of his research material. Although Long, as a *haole*, found little help directly from the *kahuna*, he discovered in prayers and chants recorded by Dr. Brigham a code that was built into the meanings of root words in the Hawaiian language.

Convinced he had found the basis of the old Hawaiian *kahuna* religion, he brought it to the United States as the Huna system. In 1959, Douglas Low, through the work and words of David M. Bray, Sr., an initiated *kahuna*, placed partial affirmation on Long's work. Differences dealt largely with semantics and linear versus Polynesian thinking.[9] Long found the basis of his religion, as did Bray, to be love–*aloha*.

Today Huna seminars are held worldwide. The Huna Research headquarters are at Cape Girardeau, Missouri, under the directorship of Dr. E. Otha Wingo, and contacts exist in seventeen foreign countries: Australia, Austria, Brazil, Canada, Egypt, England, Germany, Holland, Hong Kong, Israel, Japan, New Zealand, Nigeria, South Africa, Switzerland, and Venezuela. Everywhere, Hawaii and Kalakaua's name are known.[10]

* * *

It is hardly necessary to mention that without King Kalakaua there would be no Iolani Palace, no Kamehameha I statue, no coronation to remember, no revival of music or sports, few other remnants of Hawaiian culture and heritage, perhaps even no nationalistic spirit.

In the introduction to her book, *Hawaii: The Sugar Coated Fortress*, Francine du Plessix Gray in 1972 used a quotation from Huey P. Newton, which today speaks directly of King Kalakaua: "The dignity and beauty of man rests in the human spirit which makes him more than simply a physical being. The spirit must never be suppressed for the exploitation of others. As long as the people recognize the beauty of their human spirits and move against suppression and exploitation, they will be carrying out one of the most beautiful ideas of all time. Because the human whole is much greater than the sum of its parts."

Of Kalakaua she wrote, "David Kalakaua, most intelligent and determined ruler to come to the throne since Kamehameha I, was a man profoundly devoted to Hawaiian culture. He collected and stored the stripped bones and magnificent feather cloaks of ancient Hawaiian chiefs, and laid the foundation for the study of Hawaiian archaeology. He commissioned the first translation of the Kumulipo, the beautiful creation chant, that is a basic text of Hawaiian mythology. He sponsored great festivals of Hawaiian singing and dancing and created a secret society restricted to men of Hawaiian blood, [women were later included,] the *Hale Naua*, one of whose objects was 'the revival of the ancient sciences of Hawaii.' He was a gifted writer and musician, and his best-known poem is still heard today in the words of 'Hawaii Pono'i,' the islands' anthem."[11]

In the introduction to Kalakaua's *Legends*, Dr. Terence Barrow wrote: "King Kalakaua ruled his subjects with sympathy and understanding and had a deep respect for their traditional knowledge. He was the initiator of a general renaissance of Hawaiian culture that has continued to this day, regardless of loss of political power and the dethronement of Hawaiian Royalty."[12]

After the king's death, W. O. Smith, his avowed enemy, in an assembly of the Supreme Court and members of the Hawaiian bar said, "In the death of his late Majesty King Kalakaua we recognize that the country has lost a great friend: one whose aim was to place Hawaii high among the nations; whose endeavor was constantly directed toward maintaining and increasing prosperity. He took a personal interest in the development of the industries of the country and saw during the seventeen years of his reign the Kingdom steadily advance in productive resources, in education, in sanitary conditions, and in the principles of constitutional government."[13]

* * *

The Friends of Iolani Palace, on February 12, 1983, commemorated the 100th anniversary of the coronation—an event Kalakaua said should be "commemorated forever."

Present to keep alive the heritage Kalakaua so strongly fought to maintain were the grandchildren of David Kawananakoa: Abigail Kinoiki, Kekaulike Kawananakoa (daughter of Lydia Liliuokalani), Edward Keli'iahonui Kawananakoa, Virginia Poomaikelani Kawananakoa, and Esther Kapio'lani Kawananakoa, the Marchesa de Marignoli of Italy, all children of Helen Kapio'lani. David Kalakaua died without issue in 1954.

Present also were the great-grandchildren of David Kawananakoa, Edward's children: Regina Mary Keopuolani Wahiikaahuula Abigail Kawananakoa Bartels, David Claren Kaumuali'i Kawananakoa, and Andrew Pi'ikoi Kawananakoa (Edward Junior and Quentin Kuhio Kawananakoa were not present). Two daughters of Marchesa Marignoli (Esther Kapio'lani) were present: Emmeralda Kapi'olani and Elelule Theresa Marignoli; her son, Duccio Kaumuali'i Marignoli, was not there.

The Master of Ceremonies, Dr. Niklaus Schweizer, described the events of the first coronation, and emphasis was placed by Speaker Abigail K. Kawananakoa, president of the Friends of Iolani Palace, on the importance of the coronation. The Royal Hawaiian Band played the "Kalakaua March."

In 1986, The Friends of the Iolani Palace celebrated Kalakaua's 150th birthday anniversary—a jubilee celebration similar to that of his fiftieth birthday.

The 1986 reenactment of Kalakaua's 1886 celebration of his birthday included a morning regatta, afternoon processions of members of the consular corps and representatives of Hawaiian Societies, and music by the Royal Hawaiian Band. The evening culminated with a torchlight parade by members of the Honolulu Fire Department, some of them wearing uniforms of a 100 years ago and carrying bamboo torches. Exhibits and entertainments continued throughout the week, including a *hookupu* (presentation of gifts) to the palace. The festivities were highlighted by a Royal Ball on Friday, followed on Saturday by an afternoon of chants and hula. Jubilee celebrations were held at various churches—Kawaiahao, Kaumakapili, St. Andrew's, and Our Lady of Peace, followed by a parade of the Royal Guard, and culminating in a Grand *Luau*.

Through the efforts of the Friends of Iolani Palace, the palace itself is being returned to its original beauty, having been the capital building after the overthrow of the government until statehood. The exterior of the palace has been kept in excellent condition and the interior restored with painstaking work to its original wood-finishing. The world over has been searched for paintings and furnishings. Much has been returned to be restored and placed in its proper settings. Iolani Palace now stands not only as the "only palace in the United States" but as a great memorial to Hawaiian heritage and culture and the memory of King Kalakaua.

Long live the memory of Kalakaua, the Renaissance man!

Epilogue: Succession

Kalakaua left no problems with the interregnums of which he had struggled, but spelled out carefully in his Will the successions to the throne.[1]

It was set forth in his Will that his sister, Princess Liliuokalani, should succeed him to the throne, failing heirs of his body. There being no heirs of Queen Liliuokalani, their niece, Princess Victoria Kaiulani, the daughter of Princess Likelike, sister to Kalakaua and Liliuokalani, was next to succeed to the throne. If she were to succeed before her majority, Queen Kapiolani, if surviving, should be Regent. If neither Liliuokalani nor Kaiulani survived nor had children, Queen Kapiolani was to be proclaimed ruling queen.

Kalakaua further instructed in his will that if his immediate family failed to provide heirs and Kapiolani was no longer alive, the throne should descend to his sister-in-law Poomaikelani, and if she failed to have heirs, the throne should descend to the sons of "our cousin" Kekaulike: Prince David Kawanankoa. If he failed to have heirs, it would descend to Prince Cupid (Kuhio) Kalanianaole and the heirs of his body. Kalakaua desired also that his name and title should be taken by these successors, with himself as Kalakaua 1.

His sister, Princess Liliuokalani, did succeed him in 1891 and was Queen for a brief two years before she was deposed and the Hawaiian government overthrown in 1893. Before her death in 1917, both Queen Kapiolani and Princess Kaiulani had died (1899).

❀ ❀ ❀

Liliuokalani became Queen on January 29, 1891, and by her own words, before she had the opportunity to grieve her brother, she was forced to sign the hated Bayonet Constitution. Attempting to carry out the wishes of her brother and those of the Hawaiian people, she responded to 3,000 petitions for a new constitution. This act was used as a basis to dethrone her for "treason."

The Committee of Safety, of whom not a single member was Hawaiian, in collusion with American Minister John L. Stevens, declared the queen "in Revolution against the government and the Throne vacant." A new provisional government took the place of the monarchy.

John L. Stevens ordered the U.S. Marines to be landed. Queen Liliuokalani, with only a handful of military personnel, saw the impossibility of opposing a 162-man marine force. She wanted no bloodbath for her people.

Not a vote had been taken. Not a shot fired. A new government by the decree of thirteen men was established.

Sanford Ballard Dole was elected president of the new provisional government and immediately demanded written abdication from the queen. Queen Liliuokalani did not, however, abdicate. She was told she could "protest" to the Provisional Government, but she did not protest *to* the new government but "protested and surrendered to the superior forces of the United States." Dole endorsed the document, and the problem of dethronement or reinstatement of the queen became the problem of the United States.

As a result, James H. Blount was appointed by President Cleveland to investigate the justice of the overthrow. Blount's 2,000-page report replied unequivocally to the three points he had been sent to investigate: 1) The causes of the revolution stemmed from the dissatisfaction of the Hawaiian businessmen; 2) Without Stevens' interference there could not have been a revolution; 3) Only a small minority of the people of Hawaii approved the "oligarchy" of the Provisional Government; 4) A majority of natives and whites favored a monarchy.

The queen should be reinstated.

❊ ❊ ❊

"The restoration of the Queen would be 'a very delicate task,' according to *Harper's* writer Carl Schurz. General Olney warned Gresham that 'it is *our* government; set up by *our* minister by the aid of *our* naval and military forces ... (protected) by *our* flag,' and finally that President Harrison had 'practically sanctioned everything Minister Stevens took it upon himself to do.'

"In the final analysis it was decided that in order to restore the queen she must agree to all conditions of the United States including giving full amnesty to all those who had opposed her and her government. It was believed that these suggestions would be acceptable to both sides, and therefore force would be unnecessary, although a tacit promise was present that the United States forces this time stood behind the queen.

"But it was not known that Dole signed the queen's protest without having read it; that none of the supporters of the Provisional Government *now* cared what the United States government decided, unless, of course, if it were in their favor. No one seemed to recall that although the queen had immediately acceded to Blount's request to await the decision of the United States, Dole had been non-committal."[2]

Albert S. Willis was the new minister sent to Hawaii to reinstate the queen if she agreed to the terms of giving amnesty of life and property to everyone who had taken part in opposition to her government, plus paying expenses incurred. The queen agreed to all the terms, and the decision was made that the queen would be reinstated.

At this point, Dole refused to reinstate the queen. Cleveland and Gresham, recognizing that only "unprovoked" war with the United States would restore the monarchy, turned the matter over to Congress.

The Hawaiian question in Congress was one of annexation and continued in infighting. On July 4, 1894, the Provisional Government declared itself a republic, with Dole as president.[3]

The Hawaiians were still not quiet, and Robert Wilcox headed an abortive counterrevolution. Queen Liliuokalani was arrested for treason. At a military trial she was found guilty of misprision of treason. She signed what was termed a "worthless" abdication as, it was said, she had not been queen since January 16, 1893.

She was tried, found guilty, and imprisoned in small quarters on the second floor of Iolani Palace. She described the quarters as "a large, airy, uncarpeted room with a single bed in one corner . . . one small sofa, a small square table, one single common chair, a bureau, a chiffonnier and a cupboard, intended for eatables, made of wood with wire screening to allow the circulation of air through the food . . . There was, adjoining the principal apartment, a bath-room, and also a corner room and a little boudoir, the windows of which were large, and gave access to the veranda."[4]

Here she spent eight months. During that time, she completed the work begun by Kalakaua on the *Kumulipo*, the "Tradition of Creation," and composed "The Queen's Prayer."

THE QUEEN'S PRAYER

Your love
Is in heaven,
And your truth
So perfect.
I live in sorrow
Imprisoned,
You are my light,
Your glory my support.

> Behold not with malevolence
> The sins of man
> But forgive
> And cleanse.
> And so, O Lord,
> Beneath your wings
> Be our peace
> Forever more.

She rewrote the beautiful, haunting "Aloha Oe" which is as widely sung and known as Kalakaua's "Pono'i."

> ALOHA OE
>
> Proudly the rain on the cliffs,
> Creeps into the forest
> Seeking the buds
> And miniature lehua flowers
> of the uplands.
>
> *Chorus*
> Farewell to you, farewell to you,
> O fragrance in the blue depths
> One fond embrace and I leave
> To meet again.
>
> Sweet memories come
> Sound softly in my heart.
> You are my beloved sweetheart
> Felt within.
> I understand the beauty
> Of rose blossoms at Mauna-willi.
> There the birds delight,
> Alert the beauty of this flower.

The ex-queen was released from the Iolani Palace to enter Washington Place under house arrest for five months, then to remain under island arrest for eight months—a total of twenty-one months of restriction. Once released, she made ten futile visits to the United States in an effort to regain some of the Crown and *alii* lands the Republic had taken as its own and later gave to the United States at the time of annexation. The United States was reluctant to annex Hawaii; therefore, annexation was delayed until June 14, 1900, when Hawaii's Organic Act became law.

Queen Liliuokalani died on November 11, 1917, but not before the uniting of all Hawaiians.

Unheralded, and in what had never have been seen by the *haole* nor tourist, was one of the most picturesque parades ever held in Honolulu. It was the final uniting of all Hawaiians.

The newspaper banners announced:

PARADE MARKS ENDING OF CENTURY OLD CLAN FEUD

REPRESENTATIVES OF VICTORS AND VANQUISHED IN KAMEHAMEHA'S WARS

QUEEN'S INITIATION INTO A HAWAIIAN SOCIETY THE CAUSE

The *Advertiser* of December 17, 1916, carried the story: "final testimony to the healing of the sores of a hundred years ago when the island nobility was swept into defeat by the clans under the Great Kamehameha was witnessed yesterday in a unique and pretty parade of the Sons & Daughters of Hawaiian Warriors. The parade was from the Armory to Washington Place, the residence of Queen Liliuokalani. The object was the initiation into the order, the former Queen, hereditary high chiefess of the 'victorious clans,' of I, Mahi, Palena, Kuahine, Paia.

"Queen Liliuokalani, whose own wish it was that she be received as a member into the order, was initiated with simple ceremonies, and the venerable procession went back to the armory where its rites were completed.

"It was a Public Display of Friendship."

The queen was not feeling well enough to attend the meetings of the order, therefore it was necessary that the parade go from the meeting place to her residence. The ceremonial procession thus became what it was, the first appearance together in public, and on the streets, of the representatives of the victorious and defeated clans since the beginning of the past century. "Amity has long privately existed between the two factions, and in fact, one of the objects of the order is to reestablish it, but the new bonds were never before publicly displayed."

The clans of the "eight islands of the rising sun to the setting sun," that is, the seven inhabited islands of the group, were all represented in their proper order of importance. The so-called defeated clans represented were Ihilani, Laoce-Kona, Lo-Alii, Loa, Vili, Hiwauli, Poo Uahi, and Paelekulani. The victorious clans were the I, Mahi, Salena, Lauhine, and Paia.

"It was NOT A STAGED AFFAIR. Each of the representatives were dressed according to the order of their rank. Proud kahilis arose from the little ranks and a bit of the glamour of Old Hawaii, the proud Hawaii shone for a moment. It was not deliberately staged, nor was it intended for public show nor for the credit of tourists. It was strictly of the Hawaiians concerned with their own matters, sacred to themselves, and only the Queen's indisposition, making it necessary to go to her residence gave the public an opportunity of witnessing it all.

"Mrs. Walter Kukailimoku MacFarlane is the premier or kuhina nui, of the society, whose purpose is to preserve the ancient traditions or kapus of the inner circle of Hawaii's ancient royalty.

"The grandfather of Queen Liliuokalani was a warrior with the first Kamehameha."

Liliuokalani had not been able to save her physical country from invaders of thought, destroyers of tradition, and seizers of land, but as Kamehameha the Great had united Hawaii, not only physically but in spirit, so Liliuokalani, the last queen of Hawaii, had united in love and spirit all of Hawaii.

Hawaii became a state August 21, 1959.

* * *

"From this child, the bones of our ancestors will have life," was Liliha's prophecy at Kalakaua's birth.

He remains a controversial king and person 100 years after the overthrow of the Hawaiian monarchy. Yet his motto Hawaii for Hawaiians has been taken up by numerous organizations.

Under the direction of the Friends of Iolani Palace, the palace continues to be restored to its original beauty, as people worldwide return pictures, furnishings, and objects of art to the palace.

Kalakaua is remembered as the "King of Hawaii" in foreign countries. Archives across Europe, Asia, and the United States contain records of his travels, life, and short histories of early Hawaii. He is recorded as "The King of Hawaii"–the Sandwich Islands no longer appear.

If a man's worth can be judged by what those who follow him carry on of his wishes and initial attempts, we must look at present-day Hawaii and Hawaiians.

Recognized by Kamehameha v and the young Kalakaua was tragedy to a people of a nation losing its culture and tradition. Today it is seen that such deprivation results in a loss of identity, self-worthiness, and for many, the loss of willingness to live in a no longer meaningful society.

Statistics since 1893 have shown the native Hawaiians have the worst health profile in the islands, with the shortest life expectancy, highest mortality rates, and greatest prevalence for the most chronic diseases.

The name *E Ola Mau* (Live On) was chosen by a group of Hawaiian health professionals to express the commitment of native Hawaiians themselves to alleviating the health plight of their people.[5] Thus the Hawaiians carry on Kalakaua's and Walter Murray Gibson's cry, "Increase the Race."

Struggle for land, the life blood of Hawaiians, goes on as from earliest times.

"Growing resentment in Hawaiian communities in 1922 led the U. S. Congress to set aside 200,000 acres of government land for social and economic 'rehabilitation' of homesteaders with at least 50 per cent Hawaiian ancestry. The program failed because mostly third-class raw lands were assigned without suitable infrastructure, and financing for housing was inadequate. Most of the usable lands were commercially leased to non-Hawaiian firms for income because no government funds were provided for administration of the program. In addition many of the most suitable lands were transferred for other government purposes without payment of rent.[6]

"In the mid-1960's and thereafter, the boom in the visitor and related industries, created by multinational corporations in alliance with the government, demanded more land.

"Land prices shot upward while the purchasing value of the dollar declined. Rural Hawaiians, living close to the land and the sea, were besieged. Refusing to give up remnants of a traditional lifestyle dependent on reverence for, and nurturing from, nature, our people began to resist.

"As lands for taro and other crops made way for resorts and airports, as fishing grounds were destroyed by harbors, runways and marinas, as access to hunting and mountain-gathering was fenced-off or interrupted by freeways, and as Hawaiians were evicted to make way for condominiums and shopping centers, protests erupted.

"In the 1970s, Native Hawaiian political organizations began to proliferate—The Hawaiians, Kokua Kalama, Congress of the Hawaiian People, ALOHA, Hui Malama 'Aina, Hui Ala Loa, Ho-ala Kanawai and Protect Kaho'olawe 'Ohana.

"From these struggles emerged a new source of strength: there was revitalization of our culture with traditional concepts such as *lokahi*—oneness of our people with our land and our livelihood. This brought widely dispersed Hawaiian communities to realize that our goal was a common one: control of our land to survive as a people.[7]

Kalakaua's revitalization of Hawaiian culture has received a new impetus in the recent years. Halau hula (training schools and repositories of Hawaiian dance) has flourished. Native artists and poets have found audiences. Native song and drama have begun to flourish not only in Hawaii but on the mainland and in Europe. Canoe clubs have become more popular, interest in the Hawaiian language has taken hold, as well as practice in natural medicines of Hawaii. Hawaiian history is being studied and Hawaiian names are being used prominently and with greater insistence in the public.[8]

"Contacts with other peoples, such as the American Indians, Alaskan natives, Tahitians, Maori and Micronesians, accelerated the Native Hawaiian sovereignty movement. 'Ohana O Hawai'i drafted a monarchial constitution and sought U.S., U.N., and World Court recognition.

"Ka Lahui Hawai'i adopted a constitution for a Hawaiian nation within the American nation, and a representative government which enrolled over 7,000 citizens.

"Conservative Native Hawaiian organizations, such as the Association of Hawaiian Civic Clubs, Alu Like, Kamehameha Schools/Bishop Estate, Lili'uokalani Trust, and OHA, while supporting mild degrees of self-determination, remained officially silent on the Hawaiian sovereignty issue. Most Hawaiian churches have remained quiet until June 20, 1990, when the Hawaiian United Church of Christ, in a statewide convention, adopted a resolution supporting the push for Native Hawaiian sovereignty. While not endorsing any group that is seeking to establish a Hawaiian Nation, it recognized the Native Hawaiians to have an inherent right to self-determined governance."· The United Church of Christ is descended from the American churches that began sending missionaries to Hawaii in the 1820's.

Ka Mana O Ka 'Aina (the Power of the Land), a newsletter, defines sovereignty as "the right possessed by a culturally distinct people, inhabiting and controlling a definable territory, to make all decisions regarding itself and its territory free from outside interference."

It asserts that "We native Hawaiians have never voluntarily surrendered our sovereignty. We were never allowed to vote on the Republic or Annexation, and we had no opportunity to vote separately on statehood...

"Politically, we can achieve recognition of our sovereignty by: 1) occupying lands that rightfully and historically belong to us. 2) rejecting bills in the legislature and congress which we do not initiate or are not approved by our own government; and 3) opposing the destruction of our [land and sea and] forests and the desecration of Pele, Kaho'olawe, and the bones of our ancestors.

"Legally, we can achieve acknowledgment of our sovereignty by gaining international recognition of our right to decolonization under the U. N. and/or our right as an indigenous people to have a land base and sufficient resources to maintain our culture, language, and religion. This will bring pressure to bear upon the U. S. government to recognize our sovereignty.

"Economically, taxes by local, state, and U.S. governments would not apply to us. Nonpayment of taxes to a foreign government is not a free ride, but something owed to the Native Hawaiian people as partial compensation for the billions of dollars appropriated by the federal and state governments and general public from their use of Hawaiian lands for the past 97 years." [10]

In January, 1993, Hawaiian groups gathered to protest the illegal overthrow of their government 100 years before. Hawaiian governor John Waihee flew the Hawaiian flag without the American flag. In August 1993, the groups met in a tribunal to declare and promote their rights as a self-determining—or ever independent—nation.

Liliuokalani wrote, echoing Kalakaua's cry "Hawaii for Hawaiians," "The cause of Hawai'i and independence is larger and dearer than the life of any man connected with it. Love of country is deep-seated in the breast of every Hawaiian, whatever his station."[11]

It has been said Kalakaua plowed the fields for the overthrow; can it not be said now that he planted the seeds of sovereignty?

Appendix A: Dates

1. Captain Cook arrived 1778
2. Missionaries arrived 1820
3. Hawaiian Monarchy, 1782-1893
   Kamehameha I, born, 1737; reigned, 1782-1795
   Kamehameha II, born, 1797, reigned, 1819-1824
       (Regency of Kaahumanu)
   Kamehameha III, born, 1813; reigned, 1833-1854
   Kamehameha IV, born, 1834; reigned, 1854-1863
   Kamehameha V, born, 1830; reigned 1863-1872
   Lunalilo, born, 1835; reigned, 1872-1874
   Kalakaua, born, 1836; reigned, 1874-1891
   Liliuokalani, born, 1838; reigned, 1891-1893; deposed
       January 17, 1893; died, 1917

Appendix B: A Geniology of King Kalakaua

courtesy of Hui Hanai

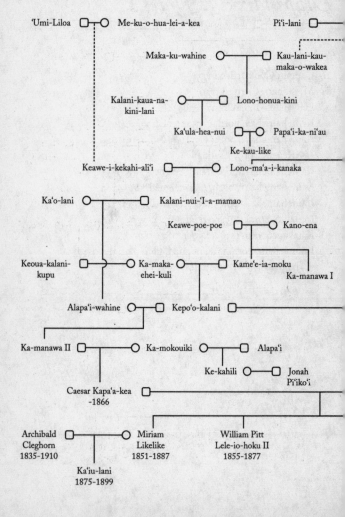

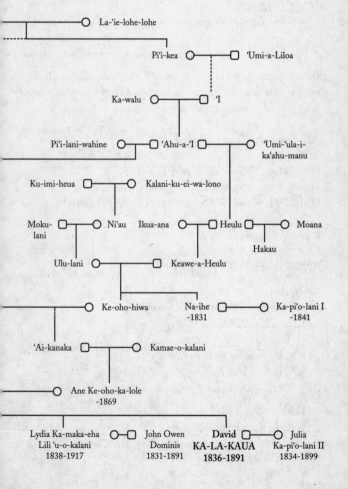

Footnotes

Book titles not cited in full are found in the bibliography. Throughout the notes, the author has chosen to use numerous abbreviations for oft-cited references. The abbreviations are as follows:

AH–Public Archives of Hawaii
BPBM–Bernice P. Bishop Museum Library
HHS–Hawaii Historical Society Library
HS–*Hawaii's Story by Hawaii's Queen*, Liliuokalani
HMCS–Hawaiian Mission Children's Society (Library)
L.C.–Library of Congress
L.Diary–Liliuokalani's diary
LKA–Lydia K. Aholo tapes
BPRO–British Public Records Office

Newspapers:
 P.C.A.–*Pacific Commercial Advertiser*
 D.B.–*Daily Bulletin*
 H. Gaz.– *Hawaiian Gazette*
 P. of P.- *Paradise of the Pacific*
 KNH–*Ka Nuhou Hawaii*

Private Collections:
 D.M.B.–David M. Bray
 R.P.M.–Ruth Prosser McLain
 H.H.–Hui Hanai (Liliuokalani Children's Center)
 L.T.–Liliuokalani Trust

1 *Formative Years*

1 Keohokalole had ten children, four of whom reached adulthood: Kalakaua, Liliuokalani, Leleiohoku, Likelike. (HS).

2 The missionaries continued to call Hawaii "The Sandwich Islands;" another name was Owhyee.

3 John Young was an adviser to Kamehameha i and as such was given vast lands.

4 Judd, *Informal History*, p. 83.

5 Richards, *School*, pp. 43, 89.

6 *Ibid.*, pp. 43 and 89; Minton, "Everything Good," Ms. pp. 10, 11 (HMCS).

7 LKA tape No. 3:68.

8 See Kuykendall, Vol. iii, for complete account of La Place, Paulet, and Thomas.

9 *Op cit.* Richards, *School*

10 Judd, *Informal History*.

2 *Young Kalakaua*

1 "Notes," Mills College archives.

2 Zambucka, *Kalakaua*, p. 9.

3 LKA tape No. 4:23.

4 Twain, *Letters*, p. 34. ff.

5 Harris, 440 2d 76 50/Haw 413: 452: Legal documentation of C. C. Harris (Honolulu Federal Courts).

6 Allen, *Betrayal*, p. 82; for full account.

7 The "rumor" was picked up and popularized by Eugene Burns who wrote *The Last King of Paradise* (Pellegrine and Audahy 1952). Burns has little documented material but based his book on "interviews," letters, and documents.

8 Yardley and Rogers, *Queen Kapiolani*. This biography gives the complete story of Kapiolani's life.

9 Kalakaua letters to Lot, Kalakaua Collection (AH).

10 Kalakaua to Lydia, Kalakaua Collection (AH).

11 Korn, *Victorian Visitors*, pp. 32, 51, 170. Original letters found in Sinclair Library, University of Hawaii.

12 Kalakaua to Kamehameha v, Kalakaua Collection (AH).

13 Allen, *Betrayal*, pp. 122-123 for full account.

14 *PCA*, June 30, 1866.

15 Emma to Peter Kaeo, Queen Emma Collection (AH).

16 Chapin, Helen Geracinos, Hawaiian Newspapers, H & H *Hawaiian Journal of History*, Vol. 18, 1984, p. 67.

17 Kalakaua Collection (BPBM).

3 Interregnums

1   Richards, *School*; Newspaper accounts, 1871.

2   Schofield and Alexander to Belknap, May 8, 1873, SESS. EX. DOC. 52 Cong., 2nd Sess. #77, pp. 150-154.

3   Emma, Collections, AH; Kuykendall, Vol. iii p.256.

4   Bishop to Pierce, November 14, 1873, FO.

5   See Kuykendall, Leprosy, Vols. 1 and 2.

6   *PCA*, February 20, 1891.

7   Thrum's *Annual*: A Completed Resume of Events from the Death to the Burial of His Late Majesty Lunalilo. Second Interregnum. (Thos. G. Thrum, March 3, 1874) pp.1-24.

8   Speeches and Comments compiled from *Gazette, Advertiser* and *Ka Nuhou Hawaii* (*KNH*) and privately printed pamphlets.

9   LKA tape No. 8:2.

4 The Good Years (1874-1880)

1   For speeches quoted here and elsewhere, acknowledgment is made to the Ladies of Assistance League of Honolulu, Iolani Palace; and a master's thesis: "A Rhetorical Analysis of the Speaking of King Kalakaua, 1874-1891" by Elizabeth Nakaeda Kunimoto, University of Hawaii, Honolulu, 1953.

2   Kunimoto, "Speaking of Kalakaua," p. 10 ff.

3   *KNH*, April 14, 1874

4   *PCA*, after Kalakaua's death: "Kalakaua Dead," p. 29, microfilm at the University of Hawaii, February, 1891

5   Complete text: "The principal object which I have had in view in making this journey among my people, is that we may all be in-

cited to renewed exertions for the advancement and prosperity of our nation, the extinction of which has been prophesied. figures of the census have been published to show that we are a dying race. But shall we sit still, and indolently see the structure created by our fathers fall to pieces without lifting a hand to stay the work of destruction? If the house is dilapidated, let us repair it. Let us thoroughly renovate our own selves, to the end that causes of decay being removed, the nation may grow again with new life and vigor, and our Government may be firmly established—that structure which our fathers erected." *PCA*, March 18, 1874.

6   *PCA*, April 18, 1874.

7   Roster: Legislature of Hawaii, pp. 129-131 (AH).

8   Description of Honolulu and Hawaii in the 1870's compiled from Isabella L. Bird, *Six Months in the Sandwich Islands*, (Charles E. Tuttle Co., Rutland, Vermont, 1974); Grant, *Scenes in Hawaii*; E.S. Craighill Handy, *Cultural Revolution in Hawaii*, (American Council Institute of Pacific Relations, 1931); King David Kalakaua, *The Legends and Myths of Hawaii*, edited by R.M. Daggett, (Charles E. Tuttle Co., Rutland, Vermont, 1974); *KNH*; and Thrum's Hawaiian *Almanac* and *Annual*, 1877. Ms. of Glen Grant, used with permission.

9   Coan, Titus, *Life in Hawaii, An Autobiographic Sketch of Mission Life and Labors*, (Anson D.F. Randolph and Co., N.Y., 1882) pp. 256-68.

10 *PCA*, February 15, 1868.

11 Handy, *Cultural Revolution*, p. 31; also Glen Grant ms.

12 *Gazette*, November 18, 1874.

13 *San Francisco Chronicle*, November 30, 1874.

14 Allen, *Dole*, pp. 105-06.

15 *PCA*, February 27, 1875.

16 Liliuokalani, *Story*, pp. 52-53.

17 Emma to Flora Jones, Queen Emma Collection (AH).

5   *The Divided Man*

1   L. Diaries 1886-87 (AH, BPBM).

2   Welch, untitled Ms., pp. 10-15 (DMB).

3   Thrum's *Annual* 1881-1882.

4   The land problem deserves a many-page critique. However, see Kuykendall (3 vols.) and the Great *Mahele* book for high chiefs' divisions.

5   Daws, *Shoal of Time*, pp. 227-229.

6   Kuykendall, *Hawaiian Kingdom*, Vol. iii p. 219.

7   In her *Story*, Liliuokalani wrote that McGrew called himself "The Father of Annexation."

8   Quigg, Agnes, *Hawaiian Journal of History*, Vol. 22, 1988, p. 1171.

9   *Ibid.*

10 Yardley and Rogers, *Kapiolani*, p. 48.

11 Souvenir Program of Centennial Year of the Hawaiian Lodge No. 21, F & AM (1952).

12 *Advertiser*, March 20, 1875 (Iolani Palace files).

13 Kuykendall, Vol. iii, p. 174.

6   *The King Around the World*

The itinerary for the trip has been taken from Wm. N. Armstrong's *Around the World with a King*, Private Collection (F.J. McD). Quotations from foreign news came from three sources: foreign newspapers at the Library of Congress, Washington, D.C.; British Public Records Office, London; and Bibliotheque historique of service de travaux historiques de la Ville de Paris, Paris. Many were translated and quoted in the *Advertiser*.

1   *PCA*, Nov. 2, 1880.

2   Jones, Louise C., "My Journey with a King," *Lippincott's Magazine*, October, 1881.

3   Barrow, Terence, *Around the World*, Armstrong, Intro. p. xix.

4   Iaukea, *By Royal Command*, pp. 28, 61.

5   Armstrong, *Around the World*, p. 16.

6   *Adv.*, April 20, 1881 (Iolani Palace: Junior League Collection).

7   Kerr, "The King and the Emperor's Men," *East-West*, Autumn, 1983, p. 20.

8   *Ibid.*, Winter, p. 30.

9   Kalakaua to Liliuokalani, Kalakaua Collection (HHS).

10 Kalakaua Collection, (BPBM).

11 *St. James Gazette*, February 26, 1881 (BPRO).

12 Armstrong, *Around the World*, p. 114.

13 Abraham Fornander, born in Sweden in 1812, had studied at the University of Uppsala–theology, classical languages, and history. Forced to leave the university by his father's untimely death, he took to the sea, arriving in Hawaii shortly after the missionaries. Almost at once he realized the missionaries were replacing the Hawaiian culture with their own. By marrying an *alii* of Molokai, he first became acquainted with the beauty of the rapidly dying culture. He assiduously collected legends, chants, and mele, and by being extremely careful in using the original wording, he began to find comparisons of words in forty different languages. He added to his body of information, available to him in Hawaii, by a voluminous correspondence carried on with scholars in the United States and Europe.

14 Bibliotheque historique of service de travaux historiques de la Ville de Paris, *Straits–Times*.

15 *Egyptian Unity* (BPRO).

16 Armstrong, *Around the World*, pp. 208, 209.

17 Mellen, *Island Kingdom*, p. 103. (Mellen took much of her information from Hawaiian papers that quoted the foreign press).

18 Allen, *Betrayal*, pp. 122, 123.

19 *The Highlander*, Vol. 31, No. 2, March/April 1993, Burlington, Illinois.

7 *The King Returns and a New Palace*

1 Field, *This Life*, p. 216.

2 Greer, *Royal Tourist*, p. 90.

3 *Ibid.*, p. 105.

4 Yardley and Rogers, *Kapiolani*, p. 59.

5 Castle, "Reminiscences" from *New York Herald*, p. 67 (HMCS).

6 Keep, *Four Score*, p. 71.

7 Thurston, *Memoirs*, pp. 21-22.

8 Ida Pope letter (RP McCol.) January 5, 1890.

9 Daws, *Shoal*, p. 234.
10 Brochures from Iolani Palace.

8 Coronation

1 Liliuokalani, *Hawaii's Story*, pp. 104-5
2 The coronation description is taken from newspapers of the time: *Pac. Com.*, *Adv.*; *Hawn. Gaz.*; *Paradise of the Pacific* and ms. "Coronation of Their Majesties King and Queen of Hawaiian Islands, at Honolulu, Monday, Feb. 12, 1883" (AH)
3 Field, *This Life*, pp. 159; 161-167
4 Liliuokalani, *Story*, p. 104

9 Political Downfall of Kalakaua

1 Newspapers: *Ko Hawaii Pac'aina*; *Ku'oku'a* (May 15-November 10, 1883); *Elele*; *Po'a'kula* (Translated by Dorothy Barrere).
2 Liliuokalani, "Bits of History" (AH)

"As one of the highest chiefesses in the land, Keohokalole was privileged to the ceremony of Puna, and she was so honored by Liliuokalani in a mele, written to commemorate the passing of a tradition, for Keohokalole was the last high chiefess to receive the ceremony.

"At Puna were clear sparkling pools, which represented the miracle of water, a gift from the gods, to the Hawaiians. When a high chiefess planned to visit the pools, the message of her coming was sent to the people of Puna. Then the waters were decorated with lehua blossoms. Each blossom was stuck on a spear of pili grass, so that when the *alii* knelt to drink, the lehua blossom would brush her eyelashes. Thus nature, the gods, who were never separated from nature, blessed the *alii*. In return, the *alii* gave *mana* to the pools of water—so the circle was completed once again; nature, gods, man (or woman) gave and received in *aloha*, and thus gave, and received the blessings of *mana*."

3 Ii, John, *Fragments*.
4 Kapukauinamoku (Hawaii Historian), (*P.C.A.*), December 11, 1955: "Song of Eternity" series. Other sources from pvt. coll.

5 Field, *This Life*, pp. 183-184.

6 Shakespeare, *MacBeth*, Act i, Sc. vii, Line 25.

7 Thrum, *Annual*, 1883.

8 C. R. Bishop to E. H. Allen, Feb. 14, 1880 (LC).

9 Kuykendall, Vol. iii, p. 80; a full account is given in Kuykendall, Vol. iii, pp. 79-115.

10 Adler and Kamins, *Gibson*, pp. 144 ff. (Full account).

11 Kuykendall, *Hawaiian Kingdom*, Vol. iii, p. 305.

12 Horn, "Primacy of the Pacific," p. 74.

13 Bayard to Carter, November 11, 1885, copy enclosed in Carter to Gibson, Nov. 10, Nov. 13, 1885, FO & Ex. AH).

14 Carter to Gibson, No. 12, Dec. 4, 1885, FO & Ex. (AH). The Anglo-German negotiations continued until April 1886, when final agreement on delimitation of spheres of influence was reached. Great Britain's decision to enter into such negotiations in 1885 was due to its desire to maintain friendly relations with Germany because of British fears of Russian intentions against India. The Russians on March 30, 1885, had defeated an Afghan force at Panjedh on the Afghan frontier, thereby raising British fears for India. (Horn, "Primacy of the Pacific", p. 98).

15 *Ibid.*, p.86.

16 Carter to Gibson, No. 20, Jan. 16, 1886, FO & Ex. (AH).

17 Horn, "Primacy of the Pacific," pp. 89-90.

18 Stevenson, *Samoa*, New Zealand, p. 59.

19 Horn, "Primacy", p. 128.

20 Gibson to Bush No. 12, March 19, 1887, FO & Ex. (AH).

21 *San Francisco Chronicle*, March 10, 1883.

22 Gibson & Bush, June 10, 1887, Copy, FO & Ex. (AH).

23 Poor to Brown No. 24, July 19, 1887, FO & Ex. (AH).

24 Poor to Brown, August 23, 1887; Webb to Brown, Aug. 27, 1887, FO & Ex. (AH).

25 Horn, "Primacy," p. 166.

26 *Ibid.*, p. 186.

27 Poor to Brown, August 23, 1887, FO & Ex. (AH).

28 Mellen, *Kingdom*, p. 184.

10 *Fateful Years (1884-1887)*

1 Thurston, *Memoirs*, p. 22.
2 *Ibid.*, p. 51.
3 LKA tape No. 35:III.
4 Allen, *Betrayal*, p. 144.
5 Field, *This Life*, p. 168.
6 See Kuykendall, pp. 79-115 (Vol. iii).
7 Gibson, *Diaries* (1884).
8 Bailey, *Royal Minister*: See Notes 1, 8, p. 297.
9 *Ibid.*, p. 228.
10 Allen, *Dole* (biography).
11 Thurston, *Memoirs*, p. 37.
12 Daws, *Shoal*, p. 246.
13 After the overthrow of the government the provisional government destroyed Kalakaua's personal, private, and government papers. See *Hawaii's Story* by Liliuokalani.
14 Thurston, *Memoirs*. Thurston quoted these excerpts from the "Third Warning Voice" to point out Kalakaua's "muddle-headedness" and inability to write clearly. Although not of Kalakaua's usual smoothness in speaking and writing, it must be remembered the copy Thurston had was a rough draft.
15 Wisnieawaki, Richard A., *Rise and Fall*.
16 Mellen, *Island Kingdom*, p. 207.
17 Roster, Legislature of Hawaii, 1841-1918, p. 171 (AH).
18 Liliuokalani, Diary, September 26, 1887.

11 *Development of the Renaissance Man (1874-1886)*

1 Bailey, *Royal Minister*, p. 193.
2 Sobrero, *Diary*, pp. 93-94.
3 Scott, *Saga*, p. 109.
4 Burrows, *Hawaiian Americans*, p. 147.
5 Field, *This Life*, p. 173.
6 *Ibid.*, p. 175.
7 Thurston, *Memoirs*, p. 42.
8 Liliuokalani, *Story*, pp. 114-115.

9 Malo, *Antiquities*, pp. 191-192; 199-200.

10 Zambucka, *Kalakaua*, p. 91.

11 For further explanation, see books by Nora Beamer and Allen, *Betrayal*, p. 27

12 Quoted from Zambucka, *Kalakaua*. This book also contains excerpts from the Constitution of the *Hale Naua, showing* nothing of adverse character.

13 Thurston, *Memoirs*, p. 29-31; 158.

14 Day, *Hawaii . . . People*, p. 202.

15 Rodman, *Kahuna Sorcerers*, p. 12.

16 LKA tape No. 5:2.

17 Austin Strong, "The Oceanic Majesty's Goldfish," reprinted in Day, *A Hawaiian Reader*, pp. 158-166.

18 Iaukea, *Command*, p. 9.

19 Malo, Kamakau, and John I'i.

20 Allen, *Betrayal*, pp. 242-243.

12 *Last Years (1888-1890)*

1 Bultman, *Faith and Understanding*. Translated by Louise Pettibone Smith, Fortress Press, Philadelphia, 1987, p. 53.

2 *Chronicle*, February 13, 1891.

3 Wilson–Iaukea, *Command*, p. 141.

4 LKA tape No. 12:18.

5 Liliuokalani, *Story*, p. 188.

6 See Allen, *Betrayal*, pp.218-219.

7 Mellen, *Kingdom*, p. 226.

8 *An Italian Baroness in Hawaii: The Travel Diary*, Gina Sobrero, Bride of Robert Wilcox, 1887. Translated by Edgar C. Knowlton; Introduction by Nancy J. Morris, Afterword by Christina Bacchilega, Hawaiian Historical Society, 1991.

9 Marie Gabriel Dosseront d'Anglade, *A Tree in Bud: The Hawaiian Kingdom 1889-1893*. Translated by Alfons Korn (Honolulu: University of Hawaii Press, 1987) 68-9, originally published under the pseudonym G. Savin, *Un Royaume Polynesian, Iles Hawai* (Paris, 1893). Reprinted *Hawaiian Journal of History*, Vol. 25, 1991:

Niklaus R. Schweizer, "King Kalakaua; An International Perspective."

10 Private collection, Julius S. Rodman.

11 Kuykendall, *Kingdom*, Vol. iii, p. 467.

12 "Why Smart People Do Dumb Things," Mortimer R. Feinberg, *Reader's Digest*. Adapted from *The Wall Street Journal*, June, 1993, p. 87.

13 *PCA*, Feb. 6, 1891.

14 Liliuokalani, *Story*, p. 206.

15 F. M. Hustat, *Directory and Handbook of the Kingdom of Hawaii*, 1892.

13 *The Beginning of the End*

1 Wodehouse to Rosebery (BPRO) Dispatch No. 30.

2 LKA tape No. 25:38.

3 Kalakaua to Robertson: F.O. & Ex 1890 (King) (AH).

4 Kent, "...go to the shrine."

5 *Chronicle*, January 25, 1891.

6 Allen, *Betrayal*, pp. 227-229.

7 Zambucka, *Kalakaua*, p. 140.

8 *PCA*, January 31, 1891.

9 Liliuokalani, *Story*, p. 215.

13 *Legacy*

1 Told to author by Chinese guide in 1983 while visiting cities of China.

2 Schweizer, "Revisited," p. 3.

3 Schweizer, Ibid., p. 4.

4 Kanahele, *Music*, pp. 200-201.

5 Frowe, "Theater."

6 *Op. cit.*, p. 203.

7 Thurston, *Memoirs*, p. 19.

8 *Huna Work International*, Publication No. 26, 1987 /4, 290 Cape Girardeau, Mo.

9 Bray, *Kahuna Religion*.

10 *The Abca Cord*, autumn, 1988 (Huna publication).

11 Gray, *Fortress*, pp. 51-52.
12 Kalakaua, *Legends*, Introduction.
13 *PCA*, Feb. 13, 1891.

Epilogue

1 Historically, Kalakaua in his will designated his heirs. However, controversy exists as to the validity of his actions. It has been set forth that Article 22 of the constitutions of 1864 and 1887 barred him from dictating the succession. It has been stated that succession rights of Queen Emma, Princess Bernice Pauahi (Bishop), Princess Elizabeth Kekaaniau (Pratt) *et al*, duly recognized by Order-in-Council of Kamehameha III and by the National Assembly at Lahaina, Maui, June 29, 1844, made these individuals eligible to succeed to an elective throne whenever the reigning line failed.

2 Allen, *Betrayal*, p. 305.

3 Allen, *Dole*.

4 Liliuokalani, *Story*, p. 268.

5 Taken from Blaisdell, Kekuni, M.D., "Historical and Cultural Aspects of Native Hawaii." Special issue of Health of Native Hawaiians, University of Hawaii Press, 32:1, 1989.

6 Trask, M. B., "Federal State Task Force on Hawaiian Home Commission Act." Report to U.S. Secretary of Interior and Governor of State of Hawaii, Honolulu, 1982.

7 Taken from Kekuni Blaisdell, "Hawaiians the State's Landless," special to *Star-Bulletin*, February 21, 1989.

8 Hayden F. Burgess, Mss.

9 *Star-Bulletin* , June 20, 1990

10 Taken from *Ka Mana O Ka Aina (The Power of the Land)* publication, 1989.

11 Liliuokalani, *Story*, p. 302.

Bibliography

Adler, Jacob, and Kamins, Robert. *The Fantastic Life of Walter Murray Gibson, Hawaii's Minister of Everything.* Honolulu: 1986.

Alexander, Dr. William D. *History of Later Years of the Hawaiian Monarchy and the Revolution of 1983.* Honolulu: 1896.

Allen, Guinfread. *Hawaii's Iolani Palace and Its Kings and Queens.* Honolulu: 1978.

Allen, Helena G. *Betrayal of Liliuokalani: Last Queen of Hawaii, 1838-1917.* Glendale, CA: 1982.

—. *Sanford Ballard Dole, Hawaii's Only President, 1844-1926.* Glendale, CA: 1988.

Anderson, Mary. *Scenes of Hawaiian Islands.* Boston: 1865.

Armstrong, W.N. *Around the World with a King.* New York: 1904.

Bailey, Paul. *A Mele For Those Kings and Queens of Old Hawaii.* Los Angeles: 1975.

—. *Hawaii's Royal Prime Minister.* New York City: 1980.

Bingham, Hiram. *A Residence of Twenty-one Years in the Sandwich Islands.* New York City: 1848.

Bird, Isobel L. *Six Months in the Sandwich Islands.* Rutland, Vermont: 1974.

Bray, David K. *The Kahuna Religion of Hawaii.* Kailua-Kona, Hi: 1967.

Bultman, W. A. *Faith and Understanding.* trans. Laurie Pettibone Smith. Philadelphia: 1987.

Burns, Eugene. *The Last King of Paradise.* New York City: 1952.

Burrows, Edwin Grant. *Hawaiian Americans.* New Haven, CT: 1947.

Castle, William R. *Reminiscences of William Richard Castle.* Honolulu: 1960.

Coan, Titus. *Life in Hawaii, An Autobiographical Sketch of Mission Life and Labors*. New York City: 1882.

Davis, Eleanor Harmon, *Abraham Fornander: A Biography*. Honolulu: 1979.

Daws, Gavan. *Shoal of Time*. Honolulu: 1968.

—. and Edward Sheehan. *The Hawaiians*. Honolulu: 1970.

Day, A. Grove. *Hawaii and Its People*.

—. Edited by Carl Stroven. *A Hawaiian Reader*. New York City: 1961.

Dole, Sanford Ballard. *Memoirs of the Hawaiian Revolution*. Honolulu: 1936.

Ellis, William. *Journal of Hawaiian Islands*. Boston: 1842.

Feher, Joseph. *Hawaii: A Pictorial History*. Honolulu: 1969.

Field, Isobel. *This Life I've Loved*. New York and Toronto: 1937.

Fornander, Abraham. *Collection of Hawaiian Antiquities and Folklore.1887, Memoirs of the Bernice P. Bishop Museum*, Vol. 6 , 1919. (BPBM)

Frowe, Margaret Mary. "The History of the Theater During the Reign of King Kalakaua 1875-1891." Unpublished master's thesis. Honolulu: 1937.

Gray, Francine du Plessix. Hawaii: *The Sugar Coated Fortress*. New York City: 1972.

Grant, Glen. Unpublished manuscript regarding Kalakaua.

Greer, Robert E. "The Royal Tourist: Kalakaua's Letters Home from Tokio to London." *Hawaiian Journal of History*. Vol. 5. 1971. pp. 75-109. *Hawaiian Journal of History*, Vols. I-xx.

Handy, E. S. Craighill. *Cultural Revolution in Hawaii*. Honolulu: 1931.

Hopkins, Manley. *Hawaii, Past, Present and Future*. London: 1862.

Horn, Jason. "Primacy of the Pacific Under the Hawaiian Kingdom." Unpublished master's thesis. Honolulu: 1951. Univ. of Hawaii.

Hustat, F. M. *Directory and Handbook of the Kingdom of Hawaii*. Honolulu: 1892.

Ii, John Papa, *Fragments of Hawaiian History*. Edited by Dorothy Barrere, translated by Mary Kawena Pukui. Honolulu: 1963, 1973.

Iaukea, Curtis Pi'ehu and Watson, and Lorna Kahilipuaokalani. *By Royal Command*. Edited by Niklaus Schweizer. Honolulu: 1988.

James, Elias Olan. *The Story of Cyrus and Susan Mills*. Stanford, CA: 1953.

Jarves, J. J. *History of the Hawaiian Islands*. Boston: 1843.

Judd, Gerrit P., IV. *Hawaii: An Informal History*. New York City: 1961.

Kalakaua, David. *The Legends and Myths of Hawaii*. New York City: 1888. (Reprint by Tuttle, 1972.)

Kamakau, S. M. *Ruling Chiefs of Hawaii*. Honolulu: 1964.

Kanahele, George S. *Hawaiian Music and Musicians—An Illustrated History*. Honolulu: 1979.

Keep, Rosalind A. *Four Score and Ten Years*. Oakland, CA: 1946.

Kent, Harold. "Must Go to the Shrine." Unpublished Manuscript. 1966. (HMCS).

Korn, Alfons. *The Victorian Visitors*. Honolulu: 1958.

—. *News from Molokai*. Honolulu: 1976.

—. *A Tree in Bud: The Hawaiian Kingdom 1889-1893*. Translated by Korn, Honolulu: 1971.

Kunimoto, Elizabeth Nakaeda. "A Historical Analysis of the Speaking of King Kalakaua 1874-1891." Honolulu: 1953. Ms. Univ. of Hawaii.

Kuykendall, Ralph S. *The Hawaiian Kingdom*. 3 vols. Honolulu: 1938, 1953, 1967.

Liliuokalani, *Hawaii's Story by Hawaii's Queen*. Boston: 1898.

Long, Max Freedom. *Recovering the Ancient Magic*. Huna Press. Cape Girardeau, Mo. 1989.

Malo, David. *Hawaiian Antiquities*. Translated by Dr. Nathaniel B. Emerson. Honolulu: 1951, 1971.

Mellen, Kathleen Dickenson. *Hawaiian Heritage*. New York City: 1963.

—. *An Island Kingdom Passes*. New York: 1958.

Minton, Linda. "Everything Good and Lovely." Unpublished paper. (HMCS).

Pukui, Mary K., and Samuel Elbert. *Hawaiian Dictionary*. Honolulu: 1977.

—, and E. S. Craighill Handy. *The Polynesian Family System in Ka'u, Hawaii*. Rutland, VT: 1972.

—Pukui, Mary K., and E. W. Haertig, M. D., and Catherine Lee. *Nana IKe Kuma.* 2 Vols. Honolulu: 1972.

Richards, Mary Atherton. *The Chief's Children's School.* Honolulu: 1937.

Rodman, Julius S. *The Kahuna Sorcerers of Hawaii Past and Present.* New York City: 1979.

Schweizer, Niklaus R. "Kalakaua Revisited." Unpublished paper

Scott, Edward B. *Saga of the Sandwich Islands.* Provo, Nevada: 1968.

Sobrero, Gina. *An Italian Baroness in Hawaii: The Travel Diary of Gina Sobrero, Bride of Robert Wilcox 1887.* Translated by Edgar C. Knowlton, Introduction by Nancy J. Morris, Afterward by Christina Bacchilega. Honolulu: 1991.

Stevenson, Robert Louis. *A Footnote to History: Eight Years of Trouble in Samoa.* New Zealand: 1892.

Stewart, Charles. *A Residence in the Sandwich Islands.* Boston: 1839.

Thrum, Thomas G. *Hawaiian Almanac and Annual.* Honolulu: 1874-1917.

Thurston, Lucy. *The Missionary's Daughter.* Boston: 1842.

Tregaskis, Richard. *The Warrior King.* New York City: 1973.

Twain, Mark. *Mark Twain's Letters from Hawaii.* New York City: 1966.

Welch, Charles. Untitled paper read before Young Hawaiian Institute. Honolulu: 1895.

Wirth, Fremont P. *The Development of America.* American BookCo. East Meadow, N.Y. 1973.

Wisnieawski, Richard A. *Rise and Fall of the Hawaiian Kingdom.* Honolulu: (ND).

Yardley, Maili, and Miriam Rogers. *Queen Kapiolani.* Honolulu: 1985.

Zambucka, Kristin. *Kalakaua; Hawaii's Last King.* Honolulu: 1983.

Index